The 2013 PRAIRIE GARDEN

WESTERN CANADA'S ONLY GARDENING ANNUAL SINCE 1937

WRITTEN BY & FOR
WESTERN GARDENERS

A non-profit publication dedicated to the
advancement of horticulture in the Prairie Provinces

74th Annual Edition

2013 Theme

Perennials

Includes General Gardening Information

ISBN 978-0-9736849-8-8

Published by:
The Prairie Garden Committee
P.O. Box 517
WINNIPEG, MB R3C 2J3

Co-Chairs. . . . . Ed Czarnecki & Colleen Zacharias
Editor. . . . . Richard Denesiuk
Treasurer. . . . . Jean Pomo
Secretary. . . . . Linda Pearn
Committee Members . . . . Roger Brown, Reg Curle, Jeannie Gilbert, Susanne Olver, Warren Otto, Andy Tekauz, Kevin Twomey, Sandy Venton, Frances Wershler, Carla Zelmer

Price: $13.95 per copy
Special quantity prices available to horticultural societies, garden clubs, commercial outlets, etc.
For inquiries and order form, see page 184.

Printed in Canada by:
Prolific Graphics
Forest Stewardship Council certified printer
Prepress – all material and chemicals are 100% recycled/replenished/reused.
Press – all inks are vegetable based

Acknowledgements

The Prairie Garden is a non-profit publication. We appreciate support from a number of companies who share our interest in prairie horticulture. The following companies provided financial assistance toward this edition of *The Prairie Garden*. Their help is crucial in bringing this book to you at minimum cost as production and distribution costs rise annually. We welcome and thank the companies who provided sponsorship this year. Readers may contact them at the addresses below and can recognize their products by their logos, found on the back cover and on our Web site:

WWW.THEPRAIRIEGARDEN.CA

FRIENDS OF GARDENS MANITOBA - Box 103, Station L, Winnipeg, MB R3H 0Z4 Ph: 895-4560 website: gardensmanitoba.com, email: info@gardensmanitoba. com (formerly Friends of the Assiniboine Park Conservatory)

JEFFRIES NURSERIES LTD. - P.O. Box 402, Portage la Prairie, MB R1N 3B7 Ph: 204-857-5288 website: jeffriesnurseries.com, e-mail: jeffnurs@mts.net

KACKENHOFF NURSERIES LTD. - P.O. Box 2000, St. Norbert, MB R3V 1L4 Ph: 204-269-1377 website: kackenhoff.com, e-mail: kackenhoff@ kackenhoff.com

THE LILY NOOK - P.O. Box 846, Neepawa, MB R0J 1H0 Ph. 204-476-3225 website: lilynook.mb.ca, e-mail: info@lilynook.mb.ca

LINDENBERG SEEDS LIMITED - 803 Princess Ave., Brandon, MB R7A 0P5 Ph: 204-727-0575 website: lindenbergseeds.mb.ca, e-mail: lindenbergr@ lindenbergseeds.mb.ca

PRAIRIE HORTICULTURE CERTIFICATE PROGRAM, EXTENDED EDUCATION, University of Manitoba, Winnipeg, MB R3T 2N2. Ph: 204-474-6685; toll-free 1-888-216-7011 ext 6685; website: umanitoba.ca/extended/ coned/phc, e-mail: sandra_stechisen@umanitoba.ca

SHELMERDINE GARDEN CENTER LTD. - 7800 Roblin Boulevard, Winnipeg, MB R4H 1B6 Ph: 204-895-7203, website: shelmerdine.com, email: info@ shelmerdine.com

ST. MARY'S NURSERY & GARDEN CENTRE LTD. - 2901 St. Mary's Rd., Winnipeg, MB R2N 4A6 Ph: 204-255-7353 website: stmarysnurseryandgardencentre. ca, e-mail: stmgardn@mts.net

T&T SEEDS - P.O. Box 1710, Winnipeg, MB R3C 3P6 Ph: 204-895-9962 website: ttseeds.com, e-mail: garden@ttseeds.com

The 2013 Prairie Garden
Table of Contents

Front cover photo by Gail Penner <www.throughglassimages.com>

The Guest Editorial
by Jane Reksten, The Prairie Garden Guest Editor

When I was approached to be the guest editor for this issue of The Prairie Garden, I was flattered and excited. I have always loved print media - books, magazines, newsletters or any other type of publication. They provide such a wonderful way for gardeners to share information, knowledge and experience. This publication in particular, with its long history and reputation, plays a valuable role for prairie gardeners. I was even more pleased to learn that the issue I would be involved with had perennials as its theme, as they are my gardening passion.

As I started to think about what topics might be covered and what articles this issue might include I found myself wondering what we were using for our definition of perennials. I come from a science background and am a linear thinker, so when I am teaching or writing I aim to present topics in as clear and precise a manner as possible. It seems important to clarify what we mean when we talk, or write, about perennials. The first feature article you will find in these pages should explain in detail what we considered to be a 'perennial' and therefore fair game for inclusion in this year's edition of The Prairie Garden.

For myself on a personal level, perennials are my raison d'etre for gardening. There are those who put the emphasis on the design of the landscape – shaping the land – the purview of landscape architects in particular. For me, I design a space in order to make a good home for perennials – a place for me to experiment with growing and combining plants. Hard landscaping elements and woody plant material certainly are essential in creating the skeleton and framework of a successful garden design, but once that structure is established I am eager to focus on the 'décor' of the site. Perennials are like the furniture in a room – more easily moved than walls, and less financial investment. (In this analogy, annuals could be considered the artwork and the throw cushions, changed up seasonally to allow the space to be continually refreshed and for the gardener to flex their design muscles.) Perennials are endlessly versatile. They can be used to dress up a fence or wall with vines, to cover the soil surface with ground covers, to attracting pollinators to our yards.

I am fascinated by everything about perennials, including their history and the personalities with which they are intertwined. From plant hunters past (Frank Kingdon-Ward) and present (Dan Hinkley), to the people that have made perennials famous through their gardens and their writing (Vita Sackville West, Gertrude Jeckyll, Beth Chatto), the plants in our gardens connect us to a rich world of people whose passion matches our own. Following the work of today's innovative designers who place the emphasis on the use of plants (Piet Oudolf, Noel Kingsbury) allows us to stay current. Closer to home we populate our gardens with plants introduced by breeders such as Frank Skinner, and follow the writings of gardeners such as June Flanagan and Sara Williams when we seek to add to our gardening knowledge base. All contribute to our collective gardening experiences.

Gardeners love a challenge, and experimenting with zone denial and perennials assumed beyond our reach (hellebores, Itoh peonies) fits the bill. Sharing our gardens and plants with fellow gardeners connects us our local gardening communities. This publication allows us to connect with each other – our fellow prairie gardeners. We hope that this year's edition of The Prairie Garden adds to your knowledge of perennials, and inspires you to learn much more – we have only scratched the surface. 🦔

An Editorial Note
by Richard Denesiuk, The Prairie Garden Editor

Welcome to our second full colour edition! The Prairie Garden has certainly evolved over the years from its earliest beginnings in 1937 as the annual publication of the Winnipeg Horticultural Society.

Gardening continues to evolve, too. The use of perennials is a long-standing tradition on the Prairies, but the range of choices available today has never been greater.

This edition will share some tried and true practices, and explore new and creative techniques in the care and cultural requirements of perennials, to guide you in your selection of plants for your garden.

It has been great to work with Guest Editor, Jane Reksten. Jane's perspective as an Albertan, combined with her experience as Manager of the Botanic Gardens and Wetland Treatment Facility, Olds College, a living classroom, provides a broader scope of information for our readers.

The next edition will celebrate The Prairie Garden's 75th Anniversary. We look forward to celebrating this milestone with you.

To learn more about The Prairie Garden, visit our website, www.theprairiegarden.ca. I hope you enjoy this exciting edition and invite you to contact me with your suggestions for future articles (editor@prairiegarden.ca). 🦔

A   B

C   D

Match the Flowers
Answers on page 178
___ 1. Gentian
___ 2. Primula
___ 3. Canada violet
___ 4. Pasqueflower
___ 5. Masterwort
___ 6. Sundrops
___ 7. Swamp milkweed
___ 8. Bloodroot
___ 9. Astilbe

all photos Marilyn Latta

E   F

G   H   I

Ed Czarnecki

Tulipa tarda

Perennials

by Jane Reksten

Jane is the Manager of Botanic Gardens at Olds College. Jane is a regular writer and speaker on a variety of gardening topics and her love of learning and infectious enthusiasm for all aspects of horticulture is evident in all that she does.

If we take the word perennial literally, the Oxford Dictionary defines it as: 1. lasting through a year or several years. 2. (of a plant) lasting several years.

The Prairie Garden website <prairiegarden.ca> explains the word perennial is from the Latin 'per' which means 'through' and 'annus' which means 'year', indicating a plant that lives for more than two years.

When 'perennial' is used amongst gardeners, most will picture flowering plants that return to life each year after surviving a winter. While this is generally accurate it is definitely not the full story.

More accurately, the term describes the life cycle of a plant, identifying how long it takes for the plant to complete its life and how long it will survive.

Other examples of life cycles include annual and biennial. It should be clear that these life cycles are inherent to the plant regardless of where in the world the plant is growing. How it behaves in different locations and different climate conditions is another matter entirely.

An annual by definition is a plant with a life cycle that is completed in one year. It begins as a seed which germinates, developing into a plant which then matures, flowers, sets seed and dies, all within one year. These plants rely on seeds to reproduce – the original plant does not survive, but new plants are produced from the seeds. Familiar true annuals include lettuce (*Lactuca sativa*), sunflowers (*Helianthus annuus*), and signet marigolds (*Tagetes tenuifolia*).

Biennials require two seasons to complete their life cycle – seed to seed – before the plant dies. Examples include hollyhocks (*Alcea rosea*) and some of the mulleins (*Verbascum* spp.).

In particular here on the prairies where the growing season is so distinct, we tend to label any plant that won't survive a prairie winter as an 'annual'. In fact many of the plants that we use as bedding or container plants such as pot geraniums (*Pelargonium* spp.), petunias (*Petunia* spp.), and heliotrope (*Heliotropium arborescens*), are perennials in their native habitats. The confusion arises because they are tender in our climate. Thrifty gardeners often take advantage of their perennial life cycle, bringing them inside to overwinter in more moderate conditions, moving them back outside in the summer.

Woody and Herbaceous Plants

For our perennial theme, if we use the life cycle definition in its simplest form, we should be including trees and shrubs in our topics. They definitely have a life cycle of more than two years, but their growth habits separate them from what we understand perennials

to be. Instead of the above ground portion of the plant dying back each year, trees and shrubs have a structure that persists over the winter, adding length and thickness to their stems. This structure is botanically described as being woody, and trees are more accurately described as woody perennials.

Perennials that die down to the ground each year are classified as herbaceous plants, with the definition of herbaceous being 'any non-woody seed bearing plant'. This is not a term that is used much outside of academic settings, and I was reminded of this when I worked at the Calgary Zoo and Botanical Gardens and advertised a course called 'Herbaceous Plant ID'. Very few people signed up for the course until I renamed it 'Perennial Plant ID'.

Perennial Diversity

Although all perennials have a life cycle that lasts more than one year, the

Bergenia cordifolia

Puschkinia

Aconitum napellus

all photos Jane Reksten

number of years that a given plant can survive varies greatly. Usually 20 years or more is considered long lived. Monkshood (*Aconitus napellus*) and gasplant (*Dictamnus albus*) fall into this category, but are seriously outlived by peonies (*Paeonia* spp.) which can often survive upwards of 50 years. Peonies also dislike being moved, so be sure to carefully consider where you will plant them! Short lived perennials decline within 3 to 10 years and examples include gaillardia (*Gaillardia grandiflora*) and columbine (*Aquilegia* spp.). These plants may perpetuate through self-seeding, allowing us to enjoy seedlings after the parent plant has died.

Perennials also vary in how their leaves behave during the dormant season. On most herbaceous plants the leaves and stems turn brown and die back each winter, typically being removed or cut down by gardeners in the spring to reveal new green growth. There is, however, a group of perennials that remain green all winter (that is if we can see them through the snow!) and that will suffer if this green material is removed. Elephant ears (*Bergenia cordifolia*), vinca (*Vinca minor, V. major*) and blue fescue (*Festuca glauca, F. ovina*) fall into this category and are considered evergreen herbaceous perennials. The resident hare in my back yard has cut back my fescues for me over the winter, leaving them quite stunted the next season.

Further variety is found when considering stem structure. Although most herbaceous perennials have primarily soft tissues above ground, some develop a partially woody stem, such as Russian sage (*Perovskia atriplicifolia*), lavender (*Lavandula* spp.), and blue flax (*Linum perenne*). These plants are classified as 'semi-woody perennials'. Wait until spring before doing any cutting back on these plants, as this permits you to see whether any of the growth has survived over the winter, allowing the plant to add growth onto this base rather than starting from ground level.

Perennial Bulbs

Tulips (*Tulipa* spp.), daffodils (*Narcissus* spp.) and dahlias (*Dahlia* spp.) are certainly perennials in life cycle, but fall into a separate category based on their unique underground structures, specialized to store nutrients. The term 'bulbs' is used broadly to include a wide range of plants which botanically are separated into true bulbs, corms, rhizomes, tubers and tuberous stems. You can read more about this in another article in this publication.

Hopefully this article has helped to set the stage for what you will find within the pages of this issue of The Prairie Garden. Be prepared to read high calibre articles by knowledgeable and passionate gardeners on a range of topics related to herbaceous perennials hardy to the prairie provinces, highlighting the incredible diversity of this group of plants. We hope you enjoy it. 🦋

The Difference Between Bulbs, Corms, Tubers and Rhizomes

by Melanie Mathieson

Melanie is from northwestern Ontario where she publishes gardening advice newspaper columns, and provides garden design and lessons for individual homeowners. She is an Ontario Registered Professional Forester and Ontario Master Gardener.

Flowers that grow and bloom from bulbs are among the most popular and loved plants in the world. Based on the time of year that they produce flowers, bulbs can be divided into two groups: spring-flowering (which are planted in the fall) and summer-flowering (which are planted in the spring).

Bulbs or bulb-like plants are usually considered perennial plants which have a period of growth and flowering, followed by a period of dormancy when they die back to ground level at the end of each growing season. The end of the growing season for spring flowering bulbs occurs in the late spring or early summer when they die back in preparation to grow and flower again the following growing season. Summer flowering bulbs flower in the summer and die back in the fall, then re-emerge and grow the following spring to flower again in the summer months.

Spring-flowering bulbs such as tulips, crocuses, hyacinths, daffodils, and irises are known as the symbols of spring. Their lush and colourful flowers are the first to emerge, bringing back life to a barren winter landscape. Summer-flowering bulbs such as dahlias, begonias and anemones bring variety, texture, colour and long flowering times to summer gardens.

In general terms, spring flowering bulbs are referred to as hardy because they are planted in the fall before the ground freezes. They require a cold period, known as vernalization, before they can emerge and produce flowers. Spring bulbs therefore are planted in the fall, generally before the first frost. Many hardy bulbs, such as daffodils, tulips, etc., can be left in the ground to flower year after year thus becoming reliable perennials.

Summer flowering bulbs, in comparison, are considered tender, as these bulbs cannot survive harsh winter conditions and must be planted in the spring after the last frost. To enjoy these bulbs year after year, they must be dug up in fall and stored indoors over the winter and replanted every spring. One exception to this is the lily. Many summer-flowering lily varieties are quite hardy and can be planted in either fall or spring up to Zone 2b. They can be left in the ground over winter, to produce blooms the following summer.

To many gardeners, the definition of a bulb is any plant that stores its pre-formed primordia (for root, shoot and influorescence) in an underground fleshy storage structure. The generic term "bulb" can refer to any of the four main types of fleshy storage structures known as true bulbs, corms, tubers, and rhizomes, which store all of the nutrients that the plant needs to sprout, grow, flower and produce seeds.

Tunicate bulb

True Bulbs

Only some of the plants commonly called bulbs actually are bulbs. These are considered "true bulbs". Contained inside the bulb is just about everything the plant will need to sprout and flower at the appropriate time. True bulbs are divided into two types: tunicate and imbricate bulbs. Tunicate bulbs (*Allium, Hippeastrum, Narcissus,* and *Tulipa*), have a paper-like covering called a tunic that protects the scales from drying out and from physical injury while imbricate bulbs (*Lilium* and *Fritillaria*) lack the papery covering.

All true bulbs have a basal, central portion of the bulb where the white, thickened storage leaves, known as scales, cradle an

Imbricate bulb

immature flower or spike of flowers. In most species of true bulbs, the tiny bud already has the appearance of a flower and the scales contain all the food the bulb will need to flower and thrive. The basal plate, located at the bottom of the bulb, holds the roots of the plant and anchors the scales and floral stalk which holds the bud.

Corms

The differences between bulbs and corms are slight and the two may look very similar until cut in half. A corm is a swollen stem base that is modified into a mass of storage tissue. A corm does not have visible storage rings which distinguishes it from an imbricate bulb. Another main distinguishing trait is the method of storing food. In corms, most of the food is stored in an enlarged basal plate rather than the succulent scales. Corms generally tend to be flatter in shape than round to pointed true bulbs.

Corms also contain a basal plate at the bottom of the bulb from which roots will develop, a thin tunic and a growing point. Examples of plants that develop from corms include gladiolus, crocus, and autumn crocus.

Older corms develop cormels that are pea sized mini-corms, formed around the top of the old corm. The remains of the old corm will be directly beneath the newly formed corms. When the corm is cleaned up and the old stem removed, the growing point of the corm will be evident. The cormels can be saved and replanted but may take a few years before they reach flowering size.

Corm

Tubers

A tuber differs from the true bulb and the corm by having neither a basal plate from which roots develop nor a protective tunic covering. As a result, tubers and root tubers are easily distinguished from bulbs and corms. A tuber is really just enlarged stem or root tissue found under the ground that is engorged or swollen and is used by the plant to store food and nutrients. Tubers come in a variety of shapes, from cylindrical, to flat, to just about any combination you can imagine. Many plant species have tubers that are clustered. Tubers only last for one growing season, but if left in the ground past the growing season, new tubers will form from shoots growing off the

Tuber

original tuber the following year. Examples of plants that develop from tubers include caladiums, oxalis, anemones, and the potato.

There are two different kinds of tubers, the stem tubers and the root tubers. Root tubers are different from stem tubers because they actually grow on the root itself, not the stem. Root tubers, such as sweet potatoes, grow under the ground, like stem tubers, but can be found at the end of the root or even in the middle. They function the same as the stem tubers in that they also store nutrients and are used to keep the plant alive during the non-growing season. They are different from stem tubers also because they have the structure of roots and will have additional small fibrous roots coming from them that if left alone, will spread out underground and produce more roots and tubers. If you pull up a sweet potato from the ground, you will see the hairy looking new roots growing off the surface. Root tubers are designed to produce new plants when the growing season comes around again.

Rhizomes

Rhizomes are distinguished from other bulbs because they are really underground stem tissue that sends out roots and shoots from its nodes. Rhizomes can also be referred to as creeping rootstalks or rootstocks.

Rhizomes differ from other storage structures by growing horizontally under the surface of the soil, and on some plants, this type of rooting structure can be very invasive. If a rhizome is separated into pieces, each piece may be able to give rise to a new plant. This is a process known as vegetative reproduction and is often used by farmers and gardeners to propagate certain plants. Examples of plants that are propagated this way include hops, asparagus, ginger, irises, lily of the valley, cannas, and sympodial orchids. Some species of ferns and irises have rhizomes that grow above ground or lie at the soil surface.

When a bud forms on the rhizome, a new shoot emerges and grows into a new plant, even though technically it is the same plant. This is why these plants tend to spread quickly and easily, covering a large area of ground. This is how crab grass and trembling aspen regenerates themselves.

Fast spreading plants can be a good thing for landscaping if there is an empty space that needs filling.

Plants with rhizomes, though, can also become invasive, spreading too fast and becoming troublesome such as quack grass (*Agropyron repens*). A rhizome helps to spread the plant over a large area, which actually makes it a very efficient and effective plant. However, rhizome plants may be almost impossible to eradicate in an unwanted situation.

There are some perennials that you may be familiar with that do not fit into any of the bulb categories. Examples of some of these plants are the peony and daylily which have fleshy roots that store the plant's nutrients over the dormancy period. Sometimes these fleshy roots are misidentified as tubers.

It is obvious that depending on the type of bulb, some require more attention from the gardener than others as far as maintenance, reproduction and overwintering methods. Understanding what type of bulb you have can assist you in planning your perennial garden and scheduling the appropriate time to plant your bulbs.

Rhizome

All diagrams by Melanie Mathieson

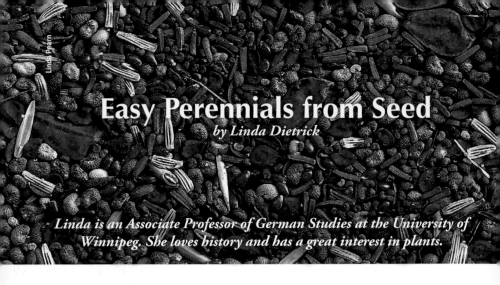

Easy Perennials from Seed
by Linda Dietrick

Linda is an Associate Professor of German Studies at the University of Winnipeg. She loves history and has a great interest in plants.

Even if you start your own annual or vegetable seeds, you may be hesitant to try perennials. Perennial plants — the kind that come back year after year — have a reputation for being tricky to grow yourself. Yes, it's true that some of them have seeds that must be specially coddled and coaxed to germinate, and you might prefer to leave that to the professional growers. Many perennials are just as easy or almost as easy to start as annuals.

I became interested in growing perennials from seed because I desperately wanted certain plants I'd read about, but couldn't find for sale; or I needed a lot of the same plant and knew the cost would be prohibitive to buy them individually. Or I simply found myself with perennial seeds that I'd picked up at exchanges or in my travels, and since my investment was so low, I figured I had nothing to lose by trying to grow them. I have not always been successful, but have managed to acquire quite a few plants in this manner. They are especially dear to my heart because I reared them from infancy.

The key to success is researching each plant's germination requirements. Probably the most important thing to find out is whether it is a warm temperature germinator or requires cold treatment. Exposing seed to cold is equivalent to letting it experience winter. The seeds of some species "know" that they must not try to start growing right after they ripen in late summer, or the young plants will be killed by frost. In almost all species of plants, special chemical blocking mechanisms prevent germination from occurring until those mechanisms have been turned off by certain conditions, in this case, exposure to cold temperatures.

With resources such as the internet, it is not hard to find information for any perennial you are interested in. Of course, seed suppliers (see list at the end of this article)

usually provide excellent germination instructions.

For the most comprehensive
information on germination requirements, the world is indebted to
Norman Deno, a retired chemistry
professor in Pennsyslvania. In the
early 1990's, he conducted carefully controlled experiments on
the seeds of thousands of species to
determine what conditions — cold
or warm temperature, dry storage,
and light exposure — overcome the
inhibitors to their germination. His
book *Seed Germination Theory and
Practice* (1993) is now available on
the internet through Scribd. Using Dr. Deno's work, Tom Clothier
has created a simplified, searchable
database that can be found at http://
tomclothier.hort.net. For whatever
perennial seeds you want to start,
instructions are probably in his list.

You have an excellent chance
of success if you start with the easy,
warm germinators that require no
cold treatment. With these seeds,
you may have to wait several weeks
for the little sprouts to show up,
but it will be under normal room-
temperature (20° C) conditions.
Here is a list of those I've personally
had good luck with. Some I started
under grow lights in the basement,
transplanting them eventually to 3½"
pots and then hardening them off so
they could be planted in the garden.
Others I just sowed directly outdoors
in the spring. The ones marked
"self-seeding" are especially easy to

direct-sow, and they will perpetuate
themselves that way indefinitely.

List 1: Warm germinators

Basket-of-gold (*Aurinia saxatilis* syn.
Alyssum saxatile). 12" plants with
grey-green foliage and lots of gold
flowers over a long period in spring
and early summer. Self-seeding.

False indigo (*Baptisia australis*). Blue
pea-like flowers in early summer;
about 30" tall. Does not like being
moved, so site it carefully (in sun)
and be patient – it can take several
years to bloom.

Chinese delphinium (*Delphinium
grandiflorum*). Sold under cultivar
names like 'Blue Elf,' this delphinium is shorter (18") and bushier than
the familiar spikes. True blue flowers
in summer. Self-seeding.

Yellow foxglove (*Digitalis ambigua*)
and Straw foxglove (*Digitalis lutea*).
Truly hardy foxgloves with creamy
yellow flowers in early summer,
both around 24" tall and tolerant of
partial shade.

Joe Pye (*Eupatorium maculatum*). Up
to 6' tall and a butterfly magnet, with
pink blooms in late summer. May take
a couple of years to reach flowering size.

Blue flax (*Linum perenne*). About
18", with sky-blue flowers in summer. Self-seeding.

Haag's campion (*Lychnis haageana*). About 8-12" tall, with burgundy foliage in spring and true red flowers; much prettier than the more familiar Maltese Cross (*L. chalcedonica*). Tolerates part shade. Self-seeding.

Prairie coneflower (*Ratibida columnifera*). A lovely native plant, about 18" tall, with drooping yellow petals and brown thimble-like centres. Blooms over a long period in summer.

Gloriosa daisy 'Autumn Colors' (*Rudbeckia hirta*). Although the more familiar *Rudbeckia* or Black-eyed Susan 'Goldsturm' is equally easy to grow from seed, I prefer this one for the red- and bronze-marked flowers. About 12-18" tall, it blooms in late summer. Self-seeding.

Rue (*Ruta graveolens*). A finely-textured, fragrant, blue-green foliage plant, about 18-24" tall.

Alaskan burnet (*Sanguisorba menziesii*). Bluish-green foliage and small burgundy bottlebrush flowers in summer. 24-30". Prefers a moist site.

Little bluestem (*Schizachyrium scoparium*). One of the nicest native prairie grasses, about 18-24" tall. Clump-forming, not spreading, it's a warm-season grass that flowers in August.

Wood poppy (*Stylophorum diphyllum*). About 24" tall, it greens up very early and bears small, bright yellow flowers all season. Tolerates deep shade. Self-seeds generously.

Purple mullein (*Verbascum phoenicium*). Not the weedy yellow roadside mullein, but a less common ornamental, forming low mats of foliage and 18" spikes of purple, pink or lavender flowers. Self-seeding.

I have had success growing a number of perennials that require cold treatment to enable germination. If you want to try yourself, seed suppliers or the internet sources cited above will provide instruction. Sow the seeds in damp soilless mix (or place in a folded, moistened paper towel and plastic bag) and put them in the refrigerator between -4 and 4 degrees Celsius (25–39° F) for a specified time. Just storing the seed packets in the fridge will not work – the seeds have to be in a damp medium. When they germinate, transfer them carefully to growing mix. Don't forget to label and date.

My greatest success is simply sowing these seeds outdoors in the fall. They certainly get their cold treatment, just as they would in nature. In addition, I'm reasonably confident that the plants will be adapted to our local climate if they have survived one of our winters in seed form and then germinated in one of our extemely variable springs. Here are some that have grown very well for me from a fall sowing.

List 2: Cold treatment helpful or required

Common hollyhock (*Alcea rosea)* and **Russian hollyhock** (*Alcea rugosa*). The perennial forms of hollyhock have plain single flowers, either in mixed colours (*A. rosea)* or soft yellow (*A. rugosa)*. Flower spikes up to 6' tall appear in the second year. Plants are short-lived, but they are reliable self-seeders.

Western columbine (*Aquilegia formosa*). An attractive 24" species columbine with red and white flowers. Like our local native columbine (*A. canadensis*), not as prone to attack by borers as the fancy cultivars. Shade tolerant.

Carpathian bellflower (*Campanula carpatica*). Widely sold as the cultivar 'Blue Clips.' Violet-blue flowers over a long period. A low plant (up to 12") and tolerant of some shade.

Western blue clematis (*Clematis occidentalis*). A native clematis from the Rockies with lovely nodding blue flowers, climbing up to 6'. Shade tolerant.

Crimson scabious (*Knautia macedonica*). A fairly open plant with 24" stems and small beet-red flower heads all summer. Self-seeding.

Shining penstemon (*Penstemon nitidus*). A Saskatchewan wildflower with grey-green foliage to 8" tall and gorgeous sky-blue and purple flowers in May. Prefers sunny, dry sites.

Rocky Mountain beardtongue (*Penstemon strictus*). Foliage is low-growing, but with 24-30" spikes of violet-purple flowers in May/June. Unlike most commercially sold penstemons, these two have been perfectly hardy in my garden.

Feverfew or matricaria (*Tanacetum parthenium*). 12" mounded plants with white or yellow daisies. The old-fashioned double form resembles a miniature white mum. Self-seeding. Not to be confused with the noxious invasive *Tanacetum vulgare* or common tansy.

When sowing perennials outdoors, it's important to mark the spot, or you may forget the seeds and disturb them when digging and weeding. You can put a miniature corral made of plastic edging or sticks and strings around them. Or you can plant them in a row with a tag at both ends, since a straight line of seedlings will obviously look like something intentional.

Where can you find the seeds for these plants? A good free source is a seed exchange, either through your town's annual Seedy Saturday, a local garden club, or your gardening friends. If you want to purchase seeds, check the on-line listings of the seed companies below. A packet of seeds, with its potential for multiple plants, is usually cheaper than one already-grown perennial from a garden centre, and much more fun.

One caveat: in my experience, perennial seeds do not stay viable for very long. Some, like the seeds of *Helleborus* species, must be sown freshly harvested, while others simply die if you try to store them for more than a year. If you are buying seed, you may want to share any extra with friends or take them to the next available seed exchange. You can test viability by dropping the seeds into water. If they sink, they're probably still okay. 🦋

Sources for Perennial seeds

Prairie Originals, www.prairieoriginals.com. Wildflowers and native grasses of Manitoba.

Heritage Harvest Seed, www.heritageharvestseed.com. Heirloom seeds, including perennials.

Prairie Garden Seeds, www.prseeds.ca. Some heirloom and Saskatchewan native perennials.

Wild about Flowers, www.wildaboutflowers.ca. Alberta wildflowers, including perennials.

Gardens North, www.gardensnorth.com. Most extensive perennial seed listing in Canada.

Lindenberg Seeds Limited, www.lindenbergseeds.mb.ca. Brandon, MB.

Jelitto Perennial Seeds, www.jelitto.com. Respected German firm, shipping worldwide.

Stokes, www.stokesseeds.com. Some perennials in addition to annuals and edibles.

T&T Seeds, www.ttseeds.com. Winnipeg, MB.

McKenzie Seeds, www.mckenzieseeds.com, Brandon, MB.

Favorite (Hardy) Perennial
by Colleen Zacharias
Chelone or Turtlehead (*Chelone*)

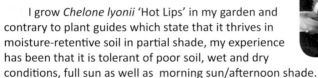

Hugh Conlon

I grow *Chelone lyonii* 'Hot Lips' in my garden and contrary to plant guides which state that it thrives in moisture-retentive soil in partial shade, my experience has been that it is tolerant of poor soil, wet and dry conditions, full sun as well as morning sun/afternoon shade.

Described as a plant that spreads rapidly by underground runners, in my garden it has spread moderately and in short, is an exceptionally well-behaved plant.

I would highly recommend turtlehead for the garden. This herbaceous, pest and disease-resistant perennial which requires no staking and stands up to strong winds is a reliable presence in a flower bed or as a seasonal hedge. Chelone is an underused late-summer blooming plant that never fails to elicit favourable comments from visitors to the garden.

Name and general characteristics	Species and varieties	Growing requirements	Propagation
Chelone Chelone, or Turtlehead	*C. glabra* 'Alba' (White Turtlehead)	Thrives in rich, moist locations. Recommended	Divide every few years in early spring.
Short, stiff spikes of flowers borne in late summer on tall (.6–1.2 m/2–4ft.) branchless stems. Dark green, broad leaves.	*C. lyonii* 'Hot Lips' (rosy pink blooms) *C. oblique* (Pink Turtlehead)	for woodland gardens. Plant in partial shade. Zone 3	Spreads by underground stems or stolons.

Early Bloomers

by Jane Reksten

Nora Bryan

Crocus chrysanthus 'Advance' shows off shades of soft yellow with blush of purple.

Prairie gardeners are a distinctly optimistic, committed, and perhaps slightly deluded group of people. With annual frost free days ranging from 61 in Thompson, Manitoba, to 138 in Edmonton, Alberta, we experience some of the shortest growing seasons in the country. In comparison, Victoria, B.C. typically receives 200 frost free days — no wonder they grow such a wide range of plants virtually year round. Here on the prairies where our gardens are in the deep freeze for six months of the year, we need to explore some methods for extending the season. One is to embrace the fourth gardening season — winter — which you can learn more about by reading Barbara Kam's article on page 112.

Another is to be creative with plant choices, seeking to extend the blooming season as long as possible on either end of the season. In Cal-gary, our first frost free date is typically around the May long-weekend, but depending on the year, you can have colour in your garden as early as mid-April if not sooner. There are some truly reliable, surprisingly impressive early risers.

As a group, these early bloomers are typically small in stature with petite flowers. Individual blooms may be inconspicuous but as the plants spread and naturalize, it is their collective efforts that create high impact, especially on the blank canvas of the early spring garden. Low to the ground, they use their stored energy on blooms instead of upward growth.

Hands down, in my mind, the best choice is hepatica, liverwort and liverleaf (*Hepatica* spp.) and I can't imagine a garden without at least a few specimens. Hepatica displays striking blue petals above semi-evergreen lobed, leathery leaves. One friend described heading out to her garden to pick up a piece of colourful debris that she thought had drifted into her yard, only to discover it was a hepatica bursting out into full bloom! Hepatica continues to perform once the flowers have finished by creating a modest groundcover, and if stunning pure blue flowers are not enough, species and cultivars offer white and even double-pink options. Commonly found species in Alberta include *H. americana, H. nobilis, H. acutiloba.* In my yard I'm starting to find new seedlings arising each year – a lovely surprise.

Blooming around the same time is the native prairie crocus, the provincial floral emblem of Manitoba, but found in all three prairie provinces. So named because its flowers resemble those of the true crocus, *Pulsatilla patens* (synonym *Anemone patens*) is more closely related to buttercups. Pale purplish-blue blooms stand out against the buff-coloured grass of prairie slopes and fields even before their leaves can be seen. Up close a thick layer of woolly hairs are visible. This furry coat, along with saucer-shaped flowers and reflective petals raises the temperature at the centre of the plant. For urban gardeners, this native plant can be a bit tricky to find and to grow, but *Pulsatilla vulgaris*, a close European relative, makes an excellent substitute. The cultivar 'Rubra' offers reddish flowers and was adopted as the city of Calgary's official emblem in 1991.

Many of the other earliest bloomers are those that survive the winter by storing food in an underground storage unit – bulb, corm, tuber or rhizome. This concentrated food source provides fuel that is instantly available, allowing these plants to awaken rapidly with the spring thaw.

Closely associated with spring in gardening circles in Canada and beyond are snowdrops (*Galanthus* spp.). Treasured in England for their ability to create vast swaths of white, drop-shaped flowers, many gardeners are seemingly obsessed with the genus, and are known as 'Galanthophiles'. Here in Calgary snowdrops are somewhat 'hit and miss'. In ideal conditions, with good snow cover they may show their sparkling white blooms, but we will never achieve the results we are truly seeking. One of my fellow Calgary gardeners, originally from England,

Jane Reksten

Hepatica's glowing blue-purple flowers against last year's leaf litter

said in an e-mail, "I did spy THREE snowdrops!! How many drops make a drift?" I love the look of a cluster of snowdrops blooming at the base of a birdbath in my yard, even if I have to replant them each year.

Much more reliable are the hardy *Crocus* species and cultivars, often showing their faces as early as the end of March. Delicate grassy foliage is accented by the silver stripe found down the centre of each leaf. Crocus blooms open only when they feel the warmth of the sun, showing off shades of yellow, white and purple, often with stripes or markings of contrasting colours. Hardy cultivar choices include: *Crocus chrysanthus* cultivars 'Advance' (pale yellow inside, white and purple tepals on the outside), 'Zwanenburg Bronze' (yellow with bronze accents) and Blue Pearl (pale blue), along with cultivars of *C. vernus* and *C. tommasinianus*.

Microbulbs are a group of miniature bulbs that produce tiny plants with blooms that are large relative to their small stature. They are best planted in drifts of at least 15 bulbs in order to get a good effect, and once established, they will multiply or naturalize on their own. In my Calgary garden, *Chionodoxa* usually appears earliest, measuring up to its common name of glory of the snow by emerging even as the snow continues to melt. *Chionodoxa* species are typically light blue-purple in colour but can also be found in white or pink shades. Star shaped

Siberian squill (*Scilla siberica*) shows its blue face to the sun

Carol Huggler

flowers show their faces to the sun, with typically one per stem, but with many stems clustered on each plant. Most commonly found species are *C. forbesii* and *C. luciliae*.

Siberian squill (*Scilla siberica* is the most common species) is valued for its true blue colour - rare in the flower world, and made all the more intense set against the expanse of exposed soil in the spring border. White blooms are available as well (*Scilla siberica alba*). Siberian squill's flowers are similar to those of glory of the snow but face downwards with their petals reflexed. *Puschkinia* are known as striped squill, displaying pale blue flowers with a darker stripe down the centre. *Puschkinia* may look a bit top heavy with clusters of flowers at the top of the stem.

Too large to be considered a microbulb, species tulips such as *Tulipa tarda, T. turkestanica, T. urumiensis* all bloom earlier, multiply easily and return each year more consistently than the more common large and showy hybrid tulips.

Most gardeners are familiar with the tall, dramatic iris found later in the summer, but early in the season it is the miniature species iris that create a show. *Iris reticulata* and *I. danfordiae* can bloom as early as April, rising to a height of 15 centimetres. Their typically iris-shaped flowers are large enough to be almost out of proportion with the rest of the plant, but offer significant appeal even when planted in small groups. *Iris reticulata* cultivars come in shades of white, blues and purples, while *I. danfordiae*'s canary yellow flowers seem to glow in contrast with the rich brown background the soil offers at this time of year.

For success with all the bulbs, look for locations in the garden with well-draining soil, as they typically dislike having wet feet. Resist removing the foliage until it has naturally declined and pulls away cleanly from the bulb – the foliage is feeding the bulb, ensuring blooms for next spring.

This selection of early bloomers all require a healthy dose of sunshine early in the season to assist in bringing them to bloom, but most are happy in shadier conditions once their flowers have faded. Bulbs go dormant for the summer so sunlight is not an issue. Hepatica are woodland plants that are best in dappled shade. With bloom times starting in April, most of the trees and shrubs have not leafed out yet, creating new opportunities where shade usually dominates. These petite early bloomers look wonderful clustered under the branches of woody plant material. Don't think that because these plants are short, they need to cling to the front of the border. With the rest of the perennials still slumbering below the surface, these petite plants hold their own in the middle of the border, fading into the background when their larger counterparts finally emerge.

The show created in the garden by these earliest of spring blooms sets the stage for the perennials that carry the spring display forward such as lungwort (*Pulmonaria* spp.), many types of primulas (*Primula* spp.), elephant ears (*Bergenia cordifolia*), perennial alyssum (*Aurinia saxatilis*) and bloodroot (*Sanguinaria canadensis*).

Winter is a long season, so why not get a jump start on spring by trying some of the early emergers in your garden – you won't be disappointed. 🐌

Drumstick primula
(*Primula denticulata*)

Nora Bryan

Monarda 'Jacob Cline'

Ligularia 'Osiris Fantaisie'

Ann Van de Reep

The Perennial Trial Garden at the Calgary Zoo
by Ann Van de Reep

Paeonia x *'Bartzella'*

*Ann is a former coordinator of the Alberta Perennial Trials and teaches
Perennial Plant Identification at the Calgary Zoo.*

Hardy perennials allow gardeners to extend the season of bloom in short-season prairie gardens from early April until late October. Helen's flowers (*Helenium* sp.) are still blooming long after most annuals have been killed by frost, and many ornamental grasses provide colour and texture throughout our long cold winter season. Many of the old stalwarts, such as *Iris germanica, Paeonia lactiflora* and *Delphinium elatum*, can be grown more successfully here than in many other places in the world. Plant catalogues and garden magazines constantly tempt gardeners with new and exciting perennials; every year there are countless new cultivars, colours and forms on the market. But will they grow in our gardens? Many of the new introductions have never been tested in Northern climates, and the zone rating is just an estimate. In the past, some highly touted new introductions have not performed as well

as was expected. Gardeners want to know if a perennial is truly hardy for our climate before they plant it.

Growing perennials, or plants of any kind, can be especially challenging in Calgary. Our climate is extremely unpredictable; historically Calgary has had frost in every month of the year. With an elevation that ranges from 975–1,295 m (3,200–4,250 ft), low precipitation, a growing season of only 112 days, chinooks in winter and frequent hailstorms in summer, Calgary is not an easy place to garden.

Fortunately for Calgarians, there has been a perennial trial garden in the Dorothy Harvie Gardens at the Calgary Zoo since 1999. From 2002 until 2010 this was one of the sites for the Alberta Perennial Trials, along with two other sites in Alberta, one at Olds College and the other at the Muttart Conservatory in Edmonton. The Alberta Perennial Trials was a research and demonstration project which evaluated new herbaceous perennials on the market. Over 550 varieties of perennials were tested in the perennial trial garden at the Calgary Zoo from 1999 to 2010.

When the Alberta Perennial Trials project ended in 2010, the Calgary Zoo decided to maintain the site at the zoo as a trial garden for perennials. They continue to test new perennials, albeit on a smaller scale, with the help of a wonderful group of Calgary Zoo Master Gardeners and volunteers. All of the data collection and much of the maintenance is carried out by these volunteers.

The perennial trial garden is a hidden gem that, unfortunately, many visitors to the zoo never see. A sign marking the beginning of it can be found near the gazebo in the Dorothy Harvie Gardens. A meandering flagstone pathway leads visitors through the garden filled with some familiar, and some more unusual, perennials. The garden was designed to be both a functional and beautiful demonstration garden. Each group-

ing of perennials are labelled with the common name, botanical name, the year of planting and the source.

Approximately fifteen to eighteen new varieties of perennials are introduced in the trial garden each year. Garden maintenance is meant to replicate home garden conditions. The soil is enriched as required prior to planting, no fertilizers are added for the duration of the trial period and only cultural methods are used to deal with disease and insect problems. Perennials are cut back in the spring and the beds are weeded as necessary. Beds are watered with an automatic irrigation system twice a week. Mulch was not used in the garden until 2010, when the beds were topped with montane mulch, a finely shredded spruce and pine bark mix. The addition of mulch has made a huge difference in the amount of time spent weeding.

Plants are monitored over a period of three years for winter hardiness, plant size and description, bloom period and bloom quality, pests and diseases and overall landscape quality. At the end of three years some of the successful perennials remain in the trial garden, while others are moved to spots throughout the Dorothy Harvie Gardens.

Favourites from the past fourteen years of perennial trials at the Calgary Zoo include:

Anemone 'September Charm', an attractive single form of the fall blooming anemone with soft pink flowers.

Ann Van de Reep

Sedum 'Angelina' and *Iris* 'Clarence'

'September Charm' requires a sheltered location with moist, fertile soil.

Delphinium 'Green Twist' and *D.* 'Pagan Purples', New Millennium hybrid delphiniums from New Zealand which grow about 150 cm (5 feet) tall on bushy and vigorous plants. 'Green Twist' has white flowers while 'Pagan Purples' has vibrant purple blooms. Both were visitor favourites in the garden.

Deschampsia 'Bronze Veil' ('Bronzeschleier'), a beautiful ornamental grass with arching tufts of fine green foliage and tall airy panicles that add late summer, fall and winter interest to the garden.

Euphorbia polychroma 'Bonfire', a new cushion spurge with foliage that emerges green, but quickly changes to a deep maroon red. The bright yellow bracts are particularly showy against the dark leaves in early spring.

Geranium renardii 'Phillipe Vapelle', a compact mound-forming perennial geranium featuring violet-blue flowers with dark purple veins in June to July and large, rounded, blue-gray leaves.

Helenium 'Mardi Gras', a sneezeweed, or Helen's flower, from Blooms of Bressingham which offers a long-blooming display of gorgeous yellow, orange and red petals surrounding a brown cone from summer through fall.

Ligularia 'Osiris Fantaisie', a compact ligularia developed by Serge Farard of Les Jardins Osiris in Quebec with thick, leathery, dark

Ann Van de Reep
Hylotelephium 'Autumn Charm'

green leaves with burgundy undersides and daisy-like, yellow-orange flowers on reddish-purple stems in mid to late summer.

Ligularia dentata 'Britt Marie Crawford', another popular ligularia with huge deep purple, almost black, rounded leaves and orange daisy-like flowers which are a wonderful contrast to the foliage.

Monarda 'Jacob Cline', a spectacular bee balm with beautiful vivid scarlet flowers and a long bloom period from July to September.

Itoh peonies, *Paeonia* x 'Bartzella' and *P.* x 'Cora Louise', are a cross between Japanese tree peonies and the common garden peony, *P. lactiflora*. The new cultivars offer gardeners attractive, bushy peony plants with herbaceous foliage and large flowers in a wide range of colours not found in *P. lactiflora*, most notably golden yellows and coppery oranges. Itoh peonies flower in late June and July in Alberta.

Polemonium 'Stairway to Heaven', a compact Jacob's ladder with dainty green foliage with cream margins. The foliage is tinged with pink in cool weather and the true blue blooms are an attractive complement to the foliage. Deadhead after blooming to highlight the lovely foliage.

Hylotelephium 'Autumn Charm' (syn. *Sedum* 'Autumn Charm'), a variegated sport of *S.* 'Autumn Joy' which forms beautiful sturdy clumps of succulent green and cream foliage. The flower buds turn from white to cream and finally deep pink in the fall.

Sedum rupestre 'Angelina', an attractive sprawling groundcover with lime green to gold needle-like succulent foliage; the leaves tipped with orange in fall. 'Angelina' is great in containers as well as garden beds.

Exciting new perennials added to the trials recently include *Echium* 'Red Feathers', a 2010 Plant Select introduction. 'Red Feathers' is a compact, drought tolerant plant sporting spikes of russet red flowers. *Baptisia* Decadence 'Lemon Meringue' is a new false indigo with yellow flowers from Proven Winners. All five plants in this group emerged strongly after the

Ann Van de Reep

Delphinium 'Green Twist'

first winter. Also from Proven Winners are two new ornamental grasses, *Panicum virgatum* 'Cheyenne Sky' and *Panicum virgatum* 'Dust Devil'.

Following the success of *Paeonia* x 'Bartzella' and *P.* x 'Cora Louise', several more Itoh peonies were planted in the autumn of 2010, including 'Julia Rose', 'Singing in the Rain', 'Sequestered Sunshine', 'Yankee Doodle Dandy' and 'Morning Lilac'.

Several new varieties of clematis developed by clematis breeder Raymond Evison have been included in the trials. Evison clematis are compact plants, some only about one metre tall, and are purported to have greatly improved flowering characteristics. This is the first time that these clematis have been tested in such a cold climate.

If you visit the Calgary Zoo, be sure to take a stroll down the path of the perennial trial garden. Visitors are always amazed at the huge selection of perennials that can be grown in Calgary. There is something for everyone, despite our unpredictable climate. 🐾

The results from the Alberta Perennial Trials from 1999 to 2010 are available online at <albertaperennialtrials.wordpress.com/trial-results>.

The Future of Canadian Rose Breeding

by Rick Durand

Campfire Rose in spring

Rick Durand is the research coordinator for the Canadian Nursery Landscape Association, a national federation of nine provincial green industry associations representing over 3,600 members in the landscape horticulture, retail garden centre, and nursery (primary production) sectors. Rick was guest editor of The 2012 Prairie Garden - Trees.

The best known Canadian shrub roses belong to the Parkland, Explorer and Canadian Artist series. These roses were developed by the Agriculture Canada rose program that first began in the mid-1950's and is still evolving over 50 years later. Dr. Henry Marshall and Dr. Felicitas Svejda are the legendary rose breeders who developed the first of these very cold hardy and popular Parkland and Explorer rose series, respectively. Lynn Collicut, Dr. Claude Richer and Dr. Campbell Davidson carried on the tradition of breeding excellent cold hardy shrub roses and the latest series is called the Canadian Artist series (see the **2008 Prairie Garden featuring Roses** for further details). Larry Dyck's work as breeder, evaluator and propagator was instrumental in keeping the federally-funded rose program vibrant and vital.

Financial support waned over the past few years and on March 31, 2011, the rose programs at the Morden Research Station in Manitoba and at St. Jean-sur-Richelieu, Quebec (formerly at Ottawa and L'Assumption) officially ended. Agriculture and Agri-Food Canada (AAFC), a federal government department, felt that the rose and woody ornamental programs at these research facilities were too expensive to support.

As part of their closure plan they identified a willing and progressive partner to carry on the rose breeding work. After an extensive proposal process, the AAFC selected the Canadian Nursery Landscape Association (CNLA) to maintain and enhance the breeding work developed at the AAFC's research stations. To accomplish this, CNLA acquired access to all the existing genetic plant material developed by the research scientists at the two stations including trees, shrubs, perennials and roses. CNLA was given the right to collect royalties on existing AAFC ornamental introductions. These royalties are collected by the Canadian Ornamental Plant Foundation (COPF), www.copf.org from commercial growers propagating AAFC introductions in Canada and United States. The royalties are the key to providing a sustainable financial base to carry on any further rose and other woody ornamental breeding.

As the CNLA is not in the business of breeding plants, they entered into an agreement with the Vineland Research and Innovation Centre (VRIC) at Vineland, Ontario thus continuing a breeding program for hardy shrub roses. Dr. Rumen Conev is the VRIC's ornamental plant breeder and it is expected he will create many thousands of rose seedlings by 2013. The seedlings will be sent back to Manitoba for cold hardy testing. The CNLA has a 3 acre research plot in the Portage la Prairie, MB area where existing and future rose seedlings undergo testing for cold hardiness, disease and insect resistance, along with being evaluated for many ornamental traits. Each year, rose growers from all over Canada evaluate the thousands of seedlings that are in the Manitoba trial.

The goal of the CNLA is to introduce a new rose to the Canadian market every year for at least the next ten years. In 2012, the first CNLA introduction was commercialized. It is called the Bill Reid rose, named after the renowned Haida artist who introduced the art traditions of the indigenous people of the Northwest Coast of British Columbia to the world. The Bill

Canadian Nursery Landscape Association Rose Evaluation

Rick Durand

Rosa x 'CA29' Campfire   Campfire   *Rosa* x 'CA 33' Bill Reid Rose

Reid rose is the first yellow rose in the Canadian Artist series that began in 2004. Emily Carr and Felix LeClerc are the other two Canadian Artist roses. For more information visit www.canadianartistsroses.com.

The Bill Reid rose is similar to Morden Sunrise but has larger flowers and leaves. In addition, the flower has a more solid golden-colour that persists through the hot, dry summer. The repeating blooms exude a unique citrus fragrance with a hint of vanilla. This shrub rose has a semi-upright habit accompanied with strong vigour. The plant will attain an average ultimate height of 90 cm (3 ft.).

In 2013, the first tri-coloured AAFC bred rose, Campfire, will be introduced as part of the Canadian Artists series. Campfire is the name of one of the paintings of the renowned artist Tom Thompson. The flower colour is truly unique compared to previously introduced AAFC bred roses. The multi-colours of the pink-yellow-white Campfire rose's colour change in intensity and frequency throughout the season. The yellow flower bud opens to the three colours with the pink colour becoming more dominant as the fall season approaches. The Campfire rose has a moderate spreading habit with a mature height of around 60 cm (2 ft.) and a width of 90 cm (3 ft.). The Campfire rose is highly resistant to black spot and powdery mildew.

In 2014, a very fragrant pink rose that looks very much like a tender rose (T-rose) will be introduced. This T-rose has yet to be named and will be the last of the Canadian Artist series. The next rose series will be called CoolRoots. The roses that will be introduced in the CoolRoots series will have the general characteristics of being highly disease resistant, cold hardy and displaying uniquely coloured and shaped flowers.

We must celebrate the past in order to plan for the future. The future of Canadian rose breeding for hardy shrub roses is very bright and promising. The wealth of the rose genetics from the AAFC has been preserved and through government and industry partnerships there will be new and exciting roses to grace our gardens and communities. 🪶

Sprekelia
A Story of Love and Loss

by Dr. Carla D. Zelmer

Carla Zelmer

Sprekelia blooms

---

*Carla Zelmer is a Research Associate in the Department of Plant Science, University of Manitoba and a member of **The Prairie Garden** committee*

I hold in the palm of my hand a small, but exquisite bulb. I suppose in its current state, a lab flask-shaped structure a couple of inches in diameter wrapped by a papery brown skin, some would not consider it a thing of beauty. If, however, you've been fortunate enough to see an Aztec lily in full bloom, you will know what I mean. Inside this humble exterior is the potential for something special.

Aztec lilies (*Sprekelia formosissima*), hail from Mexico and Guatemala. They are perennial plants that recede to dormant underground bulbs to escape inclement weather. When warmth and moisture return, the Aztec lilies respond by producing their elegant, almost orchid-like flowers in eye-catching bright red or orange. The flowers are surprisingly large for the size of the bulb, and emerge before the strappy leaves have fully expanded. Only a single flower is borne by each bulb. A closer look at the flowers reveals the true heritage of this plant. It resembles a small amaryllis (*Hippeastrum* sp.), and indeed it is a member of the family *Amaryllidaceae*.

The bulb in my hand holds the promise of another beautiful display. It was a present for my first Mother's Day. By June, this bulb and its two friends charmed me from a low blue pot on my backyard patio. This was not the first time I had fallen in love with an Aztec lily. While living in

Guelph, Ontario, I had grown a pot of them on the balcony of our small apartment. There was no room to bring them indoors for the winter, so after the glorious show of the summer, I regretfully tucked the pot against the balcony doors, and resigned myself to growing beans or tomatoes in it the following spring. To my amazement, the Aztec lilies survived the winter, perhaps because of the warmth leaking from the poorly insulated balcony doors. You can imagine my joy when these little bulbs that I had abandoned to an icy fate threw up their fiery little flowers once again! Descriptions of the Aztec lily list their hardiness in the range of USDA zone 8 to 11, well outside of Guelph's zone 6. I guess there is a possibility that the parents of my first bulbs were collected from a higher altitude site, and may have been hardier than suspected.

Sadly, this is not the case for the present bulb. Last fall there were other pressing issues that took my attention, and my Aztec lilies stayed out well into the chilly nights of a Winnipeg, MB fall. Eventually I hauled the heavy pot into the garage, and then into the warmth of the house under grow lights. The companion plants sprang into growth from rhizomes in the pot, and I optimistically waited for the Aztec lilies to appear. Gardeners, after all, believe in perenniality! Two months later, my optimism had dimmed, and I dug up the bulbs to check their condition. They didn't look very good. "Grow!", I pleaded,

and I began to promise them many things. I assured them that if they survived, I would be the model Aztec lily owner. I would replant them in good soil with their little pointed noses just showing, in a pot just a little larger than their circumference. I would water them carefully, only when dry, to avoid rotting the bulbs. They would not lack for nutrients, and I would even pull out my favourite organic fertilizers. They would enjoy a sunny but protected location in my yard. Above all, I swore to respect their proper hardiness zone and bring them in long before they could even get chilly. Indoors they would be comfy and dry until spring came once more. Alas, there is no bargaining with dead bulbs, and a horticultural funeral was clearly in order.

Two months have passed, and I am over my bulb grief. Mother's Day will soon be here again, and I am beginning to anticipate finding dormant Aztec lily bulbs among the daylily rhizomes and lily bulbs at my local nursery. To be sure, there is no guarantee I will find them. They are not always stocked, and I have only seen them for sale a couple of times in the last few years. I hope the local nurseries will continue to offer and promote this beautiful, scarcely known little bulb plant. I want you to enjoy its beauty too, but if we are in the same nursery, remember, I am first in line. I have a lot of promises to keep to the Aztec lilies.

Phlox

by Colleen Zacharias

Phlox with hummingbird clearwing moth

Colleen is co-chair of The Prairie Garden, a Master Gardener and Certified Prairie Horticulturalist, co-chair of the Manitoba Master Gardener Association and has a weekly gardening column in the Winnipeg Free Press.

Phlox is an important plant in the landscape, comprising both annual and perennial species ranging from alpine phloxes to border phloxes, allowing for a variety of applications. Phlox can be a highly ornamental presence, attracting butterflies and hummingbirds, and is relatively low maintenance, providing its cultural requirements are met. As a homeowner with a large number of perennial beds, including rockery, I have found many uses in the landscape for phlox, particularly *Phlox paniculata*, one of the longest blooming perennials in the flower garden.

Phlox (pronounced as 'flocks') comes from the family *Polemoniaceae*. It is a genus that comprises over 60 species of North American perennials including a small number of annuals and shrubs. Its origin is overwhelmingly North American (temperate)

although one of the species comes from Siberia (*Phlox sibirica L.* Common name: Siberian phlox).

The genus name, *Phlox*, comes from the Greek word for flame. This can be applied to the showy range of colours of the inflorescence, to the shape of the inflorescence, and to the spiral shaped buds that some claim resembles a torch.

Phlox is hardy from zones 4–8 with some cultivars hardy to zone 3. Overall, phlox is considered to have a moderate lifespan, although this varies: *Phlox paniculata*, or garden phlox, can be a long-lived perennial providing it is divided every few years, whereas *Phlox divaricata* 'Chattahoochee', a dwarf, evergreen variety, zone 4, is a short-lived prostrate hybrid. Phlox has broad appeal for the landscape, as gardeners incorporate species providing bloom from spring through late-summer.

Phlox is considered to be a non-toxic plant for both humans and animals. According to the Education Department of the Lady Bird Johnson Wildflower Center in Austin, Texas, phlox symbolizes sweet dreams and a proposal of love. At one time, phlox leaves were used for medicinal purposes by several American native tribes and were believed to be a cure for upset stomachs, sore eyes, and skin irritations. A laxative was made using an extract from the leaves. Pulverized leaves and flowers were also used by the Cheyenne Indian tribe as a stimulant for body numbness. The Green Pages of the Montreal Botanical Garden lists the edible use of phlox flowers for fruit salad, describing the taste as slightly spicy with a chewable consistency.

Of the many species of phlox, only *Phlox drummondii* is an annual. It was discovered in the 1820's by Thomas Drummond, a Scottish naturalist, who had immigrated to America. Although he never returned to his homeland, he did send seeds back home where European plant breeders quickly embraced it, breeding it into a variety of colours and ultimately sending it back to America some forty years later where it became a popular garden plant.

Three habitats and descriptions

Phlox comes from three habitats: alpine, woodland and waterside.

Alpine species

The alpine or dwarf phloxes are represented by a few species described below. Characteristics include early spring blooming, dense mat forming plants with evergreen leaves. They are most suitable for a low border, mass plantings, rock garden, or ground cover and are commonly described as low creeping alpines. They are relatively long lived (up to ten years) and grow at a medium rate. The following species and hybrids are most suitable to prairie growing conditions:

Phlox borealis (Arctic phlox). Native to Alaska, this perennial is a lovely addition to the spring garden because of its colourful, plentiful bright pink, somewhat lavender flowers and early blooming period. Zone 2a. The foliage is bright green and once the flowers have disappeared, the small, fine, evergreen-like foliage serves as a quick growing, ground hugging mat that is not invasive. Grows to a height of 4 cm (1½ in.).

Jean-Luc

Phlox paniculata

Phlox hoodii (Hood's phlox). A species native to North American prairie grasslands (northern limit is Alaska and southern limit is Arizona). Zone 4. Mainly white species with tiny flowers. Green foliage. Very low in height: 2.5 cm (1 in.) high with a .3 metre to .6 metre (1–2 ft.) spread.

Phlox subulata (moss phlox, moss pink, flowering moss). An evergreen species native to much of North America, occurring naturally in dry, sandy or rocky habitats. One of the best known species. Appreciated for its fine and delicate texture. Zone 4. This species will tolerate poor, dry soils but will not perform as well when growing in unsheltered prairie conditions. This is a creeping species featuring conifer-like leaves and masses of tiny flowers blooming in early to mid-spring with colours ranging from white, pink, lavender blue, or red. A distinguishing characteristic is the bronzy green foliage in fall. As well, the foliage is somewhat prickly. Grows to a height of 15 cm (6 in.). Attracts both butterflies and hummingbirds. Not recommended as a groundcover for large areas as it is not as dense as other species and is prone to thinning out.

Culture and Maintenance

Alpine species perform best in full sun to partial shade. Relatively low maintenance when average moisture levels and a well-drained soil are present. Do not allow plants to sit in standing water. Protect them with a thick layer of mulch in winter to reduce browning and dieback which may occur in exposed, windy areas. The alpine species are susceptible to various fungal infections in regions that have sustained wet winters, hence the necessity for a full sun location. Do not prune off the dead/damaged material until flowering is complete (early June). Shearing after flowering is advised and will encourage compact growth.

Woodland Species

The woodland species are represented by *Phlox divaricata* or woodland phlox. Whereas the alpine phlox thrive in full sun, the woodland phlox – as the name suggests – is more suited to the shady border. As well, its blooming period is mid-spring versus the early spring blooming period of the alpine phlox. It is a medium-sized clump with 4 cm (1.5 in.) flowers that is also suited as a ground cover at the front of the border, being a low, spreading mound, or under trees and shrubs. The following species are perennials and are suited to prairie growing conditions:

Kollar Nursery

Phlox divaricata 'Chattahoochee'

Phlox douglasii

Phlox divaricata 'Chatta-hoochee' (no known common name). Hardy to zone 4. This is a native North American wildflower that can be found growing in woods, fields and along streams. Performs best in partial shade. Attractive and suitable spring-blooming groundcover or rock garden plant that is short-lived. Height is 15–25 cm (6–10 in.). Spread is 30–45 cm (12–18 in.). The bright green lance-shaped leaves have an interesting characteristic: purple becoming mid-green. Fragrant bright-blue tubular flowers sport a red to purple eye. The stems are hairy and sticky. Blooming period is from April to June.

Phlox divaricata '**Louisiana purple**'. An attractive selection with vibrant violet-purple-blue flowers with a darker eye. Hardy to zone 3. The fragrant flowers bloom in mid-spring. Grows to a height of 30–45 cm (12–18 in.) and a width of 30–38 cm (12–15 in.).

Phlox divaricata '**Blue Dreams**' (wild blue phlox). A spreading, hybrid perennial. Zone 4. Performs best in partial shade. Fragrant lavender-blue to pale violet flowers with a dark eye The leaves are hairy and ovate. Grows to a height of 35 cm (1–4 in.) and has a spread of 50 cm (20 in.)

Phlox douglasii (Douglas phlox, creeping phlox). This phlox grows in sun to partial shade. Zone 2. Very similar in appearance to *Phlox subulata*, but is far more dense, forming a low mound or carpet, although it does not get brown or patchy in the way that *Phlox subulata* does.

Culture and Maintenance
The woodland species perform best in mildly acidic to neutral soil. Avoid overwatering as well as overhead watering and do not over-crowd! Powdery mildew can result and become a serious problem, although newer selections exhibit better vigour and disease resistance. It is wise to cut back the stems after flowering as this will help to combat mildew. As well, spider mites are problematic in hot, dry conditions.

When choosing a planting loca-tion, bear in mind that phlox does not respond well to foot traffic. Also, rabbits may be a perennial prob-lem – they find woodland phlox, in particular, very tasty.

Waterside Species
The waterside species is represented by the modern, hybrid border phloxes known as *Phlox paniculata*. The com-mon names are garden phlox, tall phlox and summer phlox. This species

is relatively long-lived and long-blooming, providing that moisture and nutrients are supplied to the roots at all times. The taller varieties may require staking. Best suited to the middle of the perennial border.

Phlox paniculata, or garden phlox, was found growing in the wild in the eastern third of the United States in the early 1700's. European explorers/settlers introduced it to England in 1730 where it became quite popular. Through the ensuing years European breeders (England, Russia, Germany and Holland) created hundreds of varieties until it became commonly available in European nurseries. By 1880, it was reintroduced to Americans in a multitude of colours. American breeders added to the growing number of varieties up until the 1950's. Since those heady times many of the traditional varieties have slowly disappeared. A renewed interest in phlox has resulted in breeding efforts that have produced hardier and more mildew resistant varieties. Colours of flowers range from white to pink, to pale lilac to purple and crimson-red, and are attractive to not only bees and butterflies, but also the occasional hummingbird. Makes a beautiful cut flower.

***Phlox paniculata* 'David'**. Selected as the Perennial Plant of the Year for 2002 (by the Perennial Plant Association), this variety has significant impact in the summer garden. It is hardy to zone 4 but does exceptionally well in my zone 3 garden. The large blooms of pure white flowers are not only richly fragrant but also more mildew-resistant than other varieties. It grows to a height of 90–120 cm (3–4 ft.) with a spread of 45–60 cm (18–24 in.). It is a long-blooming mid-summer perennial: each bloom has an approximate longevity of 7–10 days. As well, cut flowers will last up to 10 days in a vase of water.

***Phlox paniculata* 'Becky Towe'**. This is a recent introduction with variegated leaves. Flowers are rose-pink with a magenta eye. It is a shorter plant than 'David', reaching a height of 50–70 cm (20-28 in.).

***Phlox paniculata* 'Starfire'**. Quite captivating with its unique burgundy stems, cherry-red flowers and foliage that is tinted a dark reddish-green, providing an excellent contrast when planted with 'David'. It is, however, more prone to mildew.

Rizaniño H. Reyes

Phlox paniculata 'Becky Towe'

Culture and Maintenance

Avoid overhead watering as powdery mildew is a significant problem. Instead, water at the roots and maintain a fertile site with medium moisture. Powdery mildew can be worsened if the plants are in a hot, dry situation. Good air circulation is essential.

Phlox are heavy feeders and fertilization is recommended in early spring and again just before flowering. Light shade will prevent fading of bloom colour. Cut back the central portion of the flowerhead as the blooms fade so as to encourage the sideshoots to bloom. This will extend the flowering period. The lower leaves of the plant can be quite unattractive in the summertime as they have a tendency to shrivel and discolour – underplanting with low-growing plants is recommended.

The fine, thin, freely branching roots of *Phlox paniculata* distinguish it from perennials with thick, fleshy roots, such as *Papaver*, requiring a different method of propagation. Root cuttings must be laid flat on the surface of pots or trays of firmed medium and then covered with a moderate layer of additional medium. Division should take place every 3–4 years, which is when the centres generally die out. Lift the plants in the fall and, using a sharp knife, divide the clumps into three small sections, discarding the centre. Because it is essential that *Phlox paniculata* not be crowded, be sure to plant the additional sections in another flower

Phlox paniculata
'Nora Leigh'

Valerie Denesiuk

bed or share with a fellow gardener. Seeding phlox is not recommended as germination is not guaranteed nor will the plant come true from seed. Thinning in the springtime will result in improved flowering. Look for the less vigorous shoots and pinch them out once the plant is about ¼ to ⅓ of its expected height. The resulting larger flowers will be your reward! ❧

References:

Brickell, Christopher (Editor in Chief) and Cole, Trevor. (Editor in Chief for Canada). Canadian Encyclopaedia of Gardening. Toronto: Dorling Kindersley Limited, 2004

Craigmyle, Marshall. An Illustrated Guide to Perennials. Delta, B.C.: Cavendish Books Inc., 2000

Toop, Ed and Williams, Sara. Perennials for the Plains and Prairies. Edmonton: University of Alberta Faculty of Extension, 1997

Valleau, John M. Perennial Gardening Guide. Abbotsford: Valleybrook International Ventures Inc., 2003

Salute To A True Blue Plant
by Barry Greig

Barry is in charge of the perennial collections at the Devonian Botanic Garden and a writer of many garden articles.

Belonging to the poppy family of *Papaveraceae*, the Himalayan blue poppy (*Meconopsis betonicifolia*) was first described in 1886 by a French missionary named Pere Delavay. Delavay was also a keen amateur botanist and collected specimens of this species while exploring an area of Yunnan in China. It was not, however, introduced to the rest of the world, via cultivation, until seeds were gathered from the same location in 1924. Its original geographical distribution included south eastern Tibet, north western Yunnan and Upper Burma at elevations ranging from 3,300–4,300 meters.

For those who are unaware, the Himalayan blue poppy is actually the floral emblem of the University of Alberta's Devonian Botanic Garden. The late Pat Seymour, who had a devout passion for alpine plants, chose it to represent the Garden as it was one of his favourites.

Description

What is so great about this plant you ask? For one thing, as its common name suggests, it has blue flowers – one of the few true blue colours to be found in the plant world, in fact. Many plants with supposed blue flowers in one's garden certainly appear bluish to the eye. In reality though, they are usually tinted with subtle shades of violet or purple. The satiny sky-blue blooms of *Meconopsis betonicifolia*, however, simply stand alone by comparison when talking about purity of colour. Often listed as a short-lived or monocarpic (monocarpic describes a plant which blooms and goes to fruit once then dies) perennial, with loose rosettes of oblong to ovate, toothed, light bluish green leaves, it stands approximately 1.2 m (4 ft.) tall and can grow to be about 45 cm (18 in.) wide. Both the stems and leaves are covered in rust-coloured hairs and the pendent to horizontal saucer-shaped flowers appear in early summer. Conspicuous yellow stamens in the centre of the blooms are borne singly on bristly stalks and are sometimes clustered toward the tops of the stems.

How to grow it

The Himalayan blue poppy can be propagated by either seed or division – although most specimens usually don't live long enough to become a decent dividable size. This is probably the reason why most people just prefer to grow it from seed. Freshly collected seed should be sown immediately in the fall and for older (store-bought) seeds, it helps to treat them first before sowing. Mix the seeds with some moist sand in a small plastic zip-loc bag and place them in a refrigerator for 6 to 8 weeks before sowing. This is called "cold wet stratification" and it helps break down the resistance of the seed's outer coating to the absorption of water. It simulates a natural winter, in effect. Indeed, one of the main activities that trigger a seed to germinate is water penetrating the outer coating to reach the embryo inside. After its time in the fridge is up, sprinkle the sand/seed mixture on top of good quality seed sowing medium and lightly press the mixture flat into the surface. Then lightly cover with some fine gravel grit or coarse sand and press flat once again. Do not use fine silty sand as it may cause a hard

plug to form on top. This final layer prevents the tiny seeds underneath from washing around during subsequent watering and it also provides them with a dark covering and helps with moisture retention. The newly sown pot should then be located somewhere cool with temperatures ranging from about 8° C to 12° C and kept moist but not soaking wet. The light requirements can either be filtered and shady or full and bright. A cooler temperature is essential for good germination, which should take place in about 3-4 weeks. Young *Meconopsis* seedlings are often prone to a disease called damping off. Caused by a fungus, damping off rots the bases of the stems and roots of seedlings and they then fall over flat and wither. It is important to be vigilant for signs of this disease and to treat it promptly with a fungicide product, or try cinnamon – a natural fungicide. Once big enough to be transplanted, continue to grow young plants under cool conditions until the time is right to plant them outside in your garden – once the danger of frost has passed.

Sandy Venton

Himalayan blue poppy

Where to grow it

Originally an inhabitant of damp, protected alpine meadows, *Meconopsis betonicifolia* prefers to grow in an area that has shelter from wind with morning sun and afternoon shade. A neutral to slightly acidic, humus-rich, leafy, moist yet well-drained soil is ideal. Deep, long-term reliable snow coverage throughout the winter and into early spring will prolong the life of any Himalayan blue poppy in your garden. In Alberta, however, that does not always occur, and so it may be wise to mulch your plants well during the fall gardening preparation. In fact, plants can be mulched in the summer to aid with moisture conservation and to facilitate keeping the soil a little cooler during hot periods.

Watering freely during the dry spells in summer is essential to the health of your blue poppies as well. *Meconopsis* are less likely to be monocarpic when growing under moist conditions. It is also recommended that flowering should be prevented until several root crowns have formed, even if it takes a few years. This means sacrificing the first few blooms by plucking them right out at the bottom of the stalk as soon as they appear. It may seem like an unnecessary practice at the time, but it will extend the plant's ultimate life span nonetheless. By exercising a touch of perseverance and patience when growing the Himalayan blue poppy in one's garden, will surely reward one with a truly "blue" feast for the eyes! 🐦

Jane Reksten's Favourite Perennial
Alchemilla mollis (lady's mantle)

Lady's mantle is the perfect supporting cast for the garden's prima donnas. Rounded, scalloped pea-green leaves are covered with fine hairs which causes rain to bead and glisten. The foliage creates soft mounds topped in early summer with airy froths of yellow flowers, which work beautifully as a cut flower. Happiest in morning sun and afternoon shade, lady's mantle

Barefootheart

adapts well to more extreme exposure conditions. Moisture retentive, well-draining loam with additional humus will lead to the best results. Reaching a mature size of 60 x 60cm (24 x 24 in.), lady's mantle is the perfect filler for any part of the garden. Although not aggressive, it will self-seed if permitted.

Mountain bluet
(*Centaurea montana*)

Ed Czarnecki

The Colour of Happiness in the Garden - Blue
by Dorothy Dobbie

*Dorothy Dobbie is the owner and publisher of the **Local Gardener** magazines:*
***Manitoba Gardener, Ontario Gardener** and **Alberta Gardener**.*
She broadcasts a weekly gardening show on CJOB in Winnipeg.

B lue is the colour of my true love's eyes and true love in a gardener's eyes is often associated with blue flowers. Blue in the garden is as luxurious as purple on a queen. It's the ultimate colour of desire in blossoms for everything from petunias to roses, from phlox to daylilies. True blue is elusive in the garden; you'll find it mostly hiding shyly in springtime in shady spots where the sky can't compete in jealousy.

Intensely hued and brilliantly blued is forget-me-not (*Myosotis*) a genus in the borage family. There are both perennial and annual species, but the annuals are such successful self-sowers that they are often mistaken for perennials. Some people think of this tiny blue flower as a weed, but

I love to have its blue carpet cover my garden in springtime. Later, it dies back and the dead foliage can then be removed, but be sure to shake the seed heads over the soil to guarantee a return of the blue carpet next year.

Myosotis sylvaticus, the woodland forget-me-not, is a biennial and is the most common variety found in local gardens. It is considered zone 5 so it may be grown as an annual here. *Myosotis arvensis*, the field forget-me-not, is an annual. *Myosotis alpestris*, the alpine forget-me-not, is the state flower for Alaska, and is a perennial. *Cynoglossum amabile*, the Chinese forget-me-not, while not a real forget-me-not, is a biennial.

Forget-me-not is a many-storied flower associated with the memory of the poor and of war dead. It was the flower of remembrance in Newfoundland until the poppy was adopted, but there are still Newfoundlanders who wear the forget-me-not to remember their lost soldiers.

An annual that blooms blue-ly all summer long is the lovely little *Browallia speciosa*, a shy little plant with five-petalled flowers that grows to eight inches in the shade in my garden, but reaches over a foot in others. The blue is blue enough to call one variety 'Bluebells", but browallia also comes in violet and white. The blue browallia is the prettiest.

Mertensia virginica is a native North American perennial, with clusters of nodding, bell-shaped, sapphire blue flowers. A woodland plant that loves shade, it is also called Virginia cowslip or Virginia bluebells and is generally 12 to 24 inches tall, blooming in springtime and into early summer, dying back and leaving room for hostas or some other shade-lover to take its place.

Lovely blue delphiniums will grow in the sun but they are happy in part shade. The originals, *Delphinium elatum,* were so blue that the dye from their blossoms, mixed with alum, was once used as ink. Larkspur is the common name for delphinium, but *Larkspur consolida,* the closely related genus, is an annual with an open spike, where the flowers are threaded onto the main stem in a much looser way than are delphinium flowers. Some varieties are brilliantly blue.

All parts of the delphinium plant contain an alkaloid, delphinine, similar to the alkaloid of *Aconitum.* This means that they are very poisonous, causing vomiting when eaten and death in larger amounts.

Speaking of deadly plants, what could be bluer than *Aconitum napellus?* The beautiful but lethal monkshood or wolfbane, is a violent midnight blue, reflecting its dangerous properties. In Roman times, it was used to eliminate prisoners and criminals and was so associated with death that it was banned; anyone caught growing it could themselves be put to death. The plant's toxic substance, aconite, has also been used for good, and minute quantities were once prescribed to slow down the heart, reduce fevers and treat pneumonia. Externally, an ointment of aconite soothed the pain of rheumatism, lumbago and neuralgia.

In the sunlight (or even part

Clematis 'Daniel Deronda'

shade), think of the blue *Nemophila insignis,* also called California blue bells or baby blue eyes, with its five cupped petals and white centre. It's a low-growing, clump forming plant that can be found growing wild in parts of Canada. Native to North America, it has been collected, hybridized and adopted all over the world for its perfect sky-blue colour.

This small, low-rise plant grows as an annual and blooms faithfully over several months, dropping its seed in autumn to increase, but it is best in springtime or early summer when it has little competition from taller plants. *Nemophila* grows less than a foot tall, usually to just over eight inches. Give it morning sun and afternoon shade. It will self-sow even in Alaska.

Centaurea cyanus, bachelor buttons or cornflowers love to grow in sunny places and are quite good at regenerating themselves in the right conditions. They are called cornflowers in the United Kingdom because they were considered a weed growing among fields of grain, when all grains there were called "corn". The species plant came in blue as testified to by its specific epithet of *cyanus,* from the Greek *Kyanus,* meaning dark blue. Another of its common names is bluebottle. Bachelor button flowers were used as an eyewash to cool tired eyes. In folklore, a man would wear a bachelor button to show his interest in a girl, but if the flower faded quickly it

Sandy Venton

Delphinium

symbolized her disinterest. Bachelor button was the favourite flower of John F. Kennedy. His son, John F. Kennedy Jr., wore it at his wedding to honour his father.

There is also a perennial variety, *Centaurea montana,* that is not as showy but which is very photogenic and, of course, blue.

Nothing is bluer than a blue morning glory and, even though pushing the colour boundary towards purple, I am now in love with the *Ipomoea nil* 'Picotee Blue' which has a dignified rim of white around its stunning dark blue, star-shaped flowers.

In the bulb section, 'Blue Tango' grape hyacinth is a true, sky-blue. The staunch little *Muscari neglectum*, grape hyacinth, will faithfully reproduce its dark blue flowers in the garden over many years. For a tone-on-tone effect, plant it with *Muscari armeniacum,* which is a paler blue. Don't overlook *Scilla siberica,* which, over time, will carpet a spring garden under a tree. Blue allium is another favourite; only 17 out of 850 allium species are true blue, but they are worth seeking out. Look for *Allium caeruleum,* which is commonly available.

Jane Reksten

Monkshood or wolfbane
(*Aconitum napellus*)

I could go on and on about blue, my favourite colour in the garden; I haven't mentioned everyone's new favourite, 'Endless Summer' hydrangea or all the blue iris or even Himalayan blue poppy or *Linum,* the true-blue flax seed flower. But I cannot leave you without mentioning gentian.

There is a place in Manitoba where the fringed gentian blooms wild, waving innocently in a dusty ditch among the lesser grasses of the prairie. There is nothing as lovely. I will never tell where it is so that it may continue to bloom, unassaulted by certain rapacious gardeners, but oh, my readers, you would die to see it.

Fringed gentian (*Gentianopsis crinita*) opens in the sunshine its dark blue petals wrapping around each other in a spiral pattern when it closes to shut out the clouds. It is a short-lived biennial that begins life as an insignificant rosette of leaves the first year, then bursts into bloom some 12 to 18 inches above the ground the second, spilling its seed lightly on the earth in open spaces. It likes boggy areas and sunlight. Yes, there are garden variety gentians, renowned for their blue and pretty in their own right, but the wildness of the fringed gentian has stolen my heart and made it hard to accept anything less.

For me, blue is the colour of happiness in the garden. I have to think that whoever chose the colour blue to associate with sadness could not have been a gardener. ❧

Hardy Geraniums
by Barbara Jean Jackson

'Tiny Monster'
(*Geranium
sanguineum*)

Barbara Jean Jackson

BJ is a Master Gardener from the University of Saskatchewan and holds a certificate in Horticulture from the University of Guelph. She gardens in Brandon MB. <jacksonb@mts.net>

If ever there was a misunderstood perennial, it would have to be the geranium. Because the *Pelargoniums* are also commonly known as geraniums, most people do not think twice and just assume they know what a geranium is. But I am here to tell you, there is more to the geranium than just the plant that most of us are familiar with.

The true geranium comes from a group of over 400 species, most of which are not hardy on the prairies. Very few species are used to produce the truly hardy plants that deserve a greater presence in prairie gardens. These include fewer than 15 species, the most popular hybrids arising from *Geranium sanguineum, G. pratense*, and a few others.

Hardy geraniums are commonly known as 'cranesbill' geraniums. This name comes from the appearance of the seed capsule of some species that have a unique and quite distinctive mechanism for seed dispersal. This consists of a 'beak-like' column which springs open when ripe and casts the seeds over a wide area. The seed capsule consists of five cells each containing just one seed. This capsule is attached to a column in the centre of the old flower. The common name, therefore, is derived from the shape of the un-sprung column, which is long and to some, looks like the bill of a crane. The most easily identifiable species with this configuration for seed dispersal is *G. pratense*.

This method of dispersal accounts for you finding new babies growing everywhere! If you don't want them to take over your garden, the best bet is to cut the spent bloom stalks after bloom and before the seed is ripe. In fact, cutting the whole plant down severely after bloom will result in a second flush of growth and bloom later in the summer. They do tend to get rather ratty looking after blooming; cutting them back rejuvenates the plant, and lets you look forward to another flush of bloom. Any babies that get away can always be dug out before they get too large and shared with gardening friends or donated to plant sales.

What is the thing that draws me to the hardy geraniums? What makes me want to have almost every new introduction that comes on the market and test just how hardy it is? The first thing that comes to mind is the foliage. There are hardy geraniums with fuzzy and hairy foliage. There are those with tiny and delicate foliage and even those with variegated foliage. The range is incredible. Want a hardy geranium with highly aromatic foliage? Those derived from the species *G. macrorrhizum* will fit the bill. Many hardy geraniums also take on brilliant fall colours in the garden when there is precious little colour available but brown.

Hardy geraniums can be trailing or mounding in habit, and low growing to several feet tall. Basal rosettes of leaves arise from thick rhizomes or taproots depending on the species. The leaves are typically rounded in outline and palmately lobed but exhibit a variety of shapes, sizes, textures and colours. Shapes and sizes vary from the small, deeply dissected stem leaves of bloody cranesbill (*G. sanguineum*) to the broad basal leaves of Armenian geranium (*G. psilostemon*), while textures range from the wrinkled Oxford cranesbill (*G. oxonianum*) to the felty *G. renardii*. Shades of green to gray-green predominate, but plum-purple and golden-green are also found, while some leaves are variegated, blotched or banded with cream or purple. What's not to like?

The variance in flower form and colour is obvious. From the small dark burgundy of several *G. phaeum* species of hybrids to the delicate, shell pink of 'Striatum' to the blues of the old favourite and garden staple 'Johnson's Blue', size and colours are many and varied. There truly is a hardy geranium for everyone's tastes.

What else adds to the allure of the hardy geranium? I would add their versatility to the list. These perennials can grow and thrive in almost any conditions, everything from full sun, to dappled shade, to almost full shade.

all photos Barbara Jean Jackson

'Phillippe Vapelle' foliage

Phaeum foliage

'Tiny Monster' foliag

'Canon Miles'

If grown in full sun they will benefit from supplemental watering in the heat of the summer. That aside, there are few garden plants that require such little care and concern. There are virtually no pests of note. Hardy geraniums make exceptional companion plants to small shrubs, lilies, daylilies, iris, peonies, and the list goes on. They just seem to 'fit' wherever they are planted in the garden.

However, all is not rosy in my hardy geranium garden. There are a few that do not do well no matter how hard I try (and I do try over and over!). Case in point, *G. wallichianum* 'Sweet Heidi/Heidy'. I am unable to get this one to thrive in my garden and I have 'killed' it twice already. I tried again three years ago and though it survives, it is not very happy. Another *G. wallichianum* hybrid I am unlucky with is 'Rozanne'. I do not understand the why of it, since one of its parents, Buxton's Variety, is one of the hardiest geraniums ever. The other parent *G. himalayense* is hardy, and I have come to the conclusion that it must be me or my garden it doesn't like.

I will continue to try, perhaps moving the non-performers to another area of the garden will do the trick. Another that refuses to survive is *G. pratense* 'Midnight Reiter' and a sister introduction 'Dark Reiter'. It is time to try them both again and see what happens.

If it was easy, what would be the challenge? 🦡

Hardy Geraniums BJ's Top Picks

- *G. sanguineum* 'Striatum' - shell pink with darker veins, compact and mat forming

- *G. sanguineum* x *G. psilostemon* hybrid) 'Tiny Monster' - sprawling habit, vibrant bright magenta blooms, very vigorous

- *G. pratense* 'Splish Splash' - tall deeply lobed foliage with white streaked blue blooms

- *G. phaeum* 'Spring Time' - tall with masses of dark burgundy blooms above hairy, light green splotched burgundy foliage

- *G. renardii* 'Philippe Vapelle' - mounding habit with rough textured foliage and bright blue-violet striped darker blooms

- *G. macrorrhizum* (big-root geranium) - instead of a clumping habit, it grows from a ropelike rhizome that seems to barely need to touch the ground to root. It can be a thug but this is compensated by its attractive foliage and its highly aromatic, spicy scent.

Persicaria affinis

Fleece Flowers
by Sara Williams

Sara Williams, retired from the University of Saskatchewan, gardens near Saskatoon, SK. She is the author of many gardening books including the new edition of **Creating the Prairie Xeriscape** *to be published in early 2013.*

H ere's a group of outstanding garden perennials which have the added advantage of being moderately to extremely drought-tolerant. Not too long ago they were mostly included in the genus *Polygonum* but are now considered to be in the genus *Persicaria*. *Polygonum* (the older botanical name) means many-jointed knees, referring to the stems, while *Persicaria* is the medieval name for this plant, derived from *persica*, meaning peach and alluding to the similar shape of the leaves.

Dwarf fleece flower, or Himalayan fleece flower (*Persicaria affinis,* **syn.** *Bistorta affinis)* forms a low mat of leathery leaves covered with rose-red flowers from mid to late summer. The leaves often turn a bronzy-red colour in fall. It makes an excellent ground cover in either full sun or partial shade on well-drained soils and is moderately drought-tolerant once established. (The older name *bistorta* means twisted and describes the roots.)

'Dimity' (also called 'Superbum'), with a height and spread of 20 by 30 cm (8 by 12 in.), is a more vigorous selection. The pink flowers turn crimson as they age, giving the clump an interesting two-tone effect.

Fleece flower, or knotweed (*Persicaria bistorta* 'Superbum', syn. *Polygonum bistorta* 'Superbum', *Bistorta officinalis)* is native to Europe and Asia. Be aware that common names can be misleading. Although fleece flower is a member of the same genus as the knotweed in our lawns, the similarity stops there. Fleece flower is 45–75 cm (18–30 in.) in height, with dense spikes of pink flowers resembling bottlebrushes in mid to late summer, which are held well above the foliage. The distinctive basal leaves are 10–15 cm (4–6 in.) long, with wavy margins and a white midrib. The roots are very thick.

The cultivar 'Superbum,' meaning superior, has larger flowers.

Fleece flower is excellent in perennial borders, massed, used as a ground cover, and as a cut flower. It has been used to skirt a large spruce tree in the Calgary Zoo gardens.

White fleece flower, or giant fleece flower (*Persicaria polymorpha*) is native to China, Korea and Japan and was introduced to North America by the German-American landscape architect Wolfgang Oe-hme. In spite of its enormous size, it is clump-forming and noninvasive. It looks like a large shrub, and the flowers are reminiscent of a Japanese tree lilac. I was introduced to it by a friend and excellent gardener in Dawson Creek, British Columbia, and carried a bit back home in my hand luggage. It has been a part of my landscape every since and always elicits positive comment.

Forming a strong upright clump with a height and spread of 2 m (6 ft.) or more, it has large white flowers that begin blooming in July and continue through the end of August.

Place in full sun. It is adaptable to various soils. Use in borders and as a specimen plant. 🌿

Jean Pomo's Favourite "Non-hardy Winter" Perennial Angelwing

I love these plants because I have been told it is "Not" a perennial. I bought an 'Angelwing Begonia' in the spring of 2006, in a little 3 inch pot. This little plant became so big, it literally filled a 14" pot that summer. I am told the angelwing (*Begonia metallica*) is a member of the large Begoniaceae family, originally from Brazil. It grew so easily, I had to keep moving it into larger pots to provide it room to expand, with lots of watering 'angelwing' became a very healthy compact plant with deep green bronze-tinted foliage. The flowers are medium sized delicate pink flowers that just fill the plant with their beautiful faces. Over the summer this plant grew to a height of nearly 18 inches and a width of 20 inches. I had been told that because they can grow so tall, one should prune it to help it remain compact, healthy and strong. Each fall, I take her inside into the cool basement and place her under the grow lights. By spring time, I have strong healthy 'babies' to be planted in my large planter and around the front garden to show their big green leaves and wonderful pink flowers.

Veronicas – Varied and Valuable!

by Sara Williams

Speedwells form a large group of perennials, some of which are both hardy and drought tolerant. Many have graced prairie gardens for decades. Flower colour ranges from blue through pink and white, and heights from ground-hugging mats to spikes of about 1 m (3 ft.). The genus name, *Veronica,* is associated with St. Veronica for reasons lost to antiquity. The common name, speedwell, is derived from their once presumed medicinal value. Also included here is the closely related Culver's root (*Veronicastrum*).

Hungarian speedwell, Austrian speedwell (*V. austriaca*, syn. *V. teucrium*) is a prostrate species with a height of only 15 cm (6 in.) and double the spread that is native to southern Europe. 'Trehane' is a wonderful selection with yellow foliage and contrasting blue flowers in July, but it may be short-lived.

Gentian speedwell (*V. gentianoides*), from the Middle East, produces loose racemes of small, pale blue flowers in early summer, 15–50 cm (6–20 in.) above a mat of glossy, 5 cm (2 in.) long leaves. In full sun it is only moderately drought tolerant.

Woolly speedwell (*V. incana*) native to Russia, has spikes of violet blue flowers in July, 30–45 cm (12–18 in.) above mat-forming, silver-gray foliage. Woolly speedwell can be rejuvenated after flowering by shearing.

Turkish speedwell (*V. liwanensis*) has tiny evergreen leaves and delicate blue flowers from May to June.

Comb speedwell (*V. pectinata*) produces tiny, deep blue flowers with a white centre in June and July. The small, oval leaves are toothed. With a height of 8–15 cm (3–6 in.), it forms a prostrate, gray mat. Both the common and species name describe the leaf shape, which resembles a comb used to card wool, a reference that is probably lost on most gardeners today.

Russian speedwell (*V. peduncularis*) has bright blue flowers in early summer. Untried through most of the prairies, it is best placed in a sheltered location.

'Aztec Gold' (*V. prostrata*), with a height and spread of 30 by 40 cm (12 by 16 in.), has lime green to gold foliage and blue flowers.

Creeping speedwell (*V. repens*) has light blue or white flowers in late spring above mossy green foliage with a height and spread of 5 by 20 cm (2 by 8 in.).

'Spike speedwell' (*V. spicata),* with a height and spread of 15 by 75 cm (6 by 30 in.), is the tallest of the drought-tolerant veronicas and has the greatest number of cultivars. Native to Europe and Asia, it blooms over a long period from late summer to fall. In shady conditions or with poor air circulation, it sometimes gets powdery mildew.

Among the cultivars are:
- 'Blue Spires' (75 by 30 cm/30 by 12 in.) with blue flowers.
- 'Giles Van Hees' (15 by 30 cm/6 by 12 in.) is a dwarf dark pink.

- 'Red Fox' (40 by 30 cm/16 by 12 in.) has deep pink flowers.
- 'Royal Candles' (40 by 30 cm/16 by 12 in.) is violet blue.
- 'Sunny Border Blue' (50 by 30 cm/20 by 12 in.) is blue.

Whitley's speedwell (*V. whitleyi*) has blue flowers in spring over a gray-green mat of foliage (5 by 20 cm/2 by 8 in.).

Speedwell prefers full sun and well-drained soils. Depending on their height, speedwells are valued as cut flowers, dense ground covers, among paving or patio stones, edging, in rock gardens, and border plants. They are a nectar source for bees.

Van Noort Bulb Co.

Veronica 'Royal Candles'

Culver's root (*Veronicastrum virginicum,* syn. *Veronica virginica*)

Culver's root is closely related to the veronicas. It is native to North America, including a very small (and endangered) population in Manitoba. It was grown and sold by the Shaker community of Massachusetts as a medicinal plant in the early 1820s. Culver was apparently an early pioneer doctor or practitioner who popularized the medicinal use (the roots served as a purgative) of this plant. Widely used by Aboriginal peoples for a variety of ailments, it was included in the first *United States Pharmacopeia* published in 1820.

The flowers, generally white but also pink or pale blue, are formed in dense spikes on long, sturdy, arching stems in late summer. Plants are 1–1.2 m (3–4 ft.) in height forming large, upright clumps. Leaves are dark green, arranged in whorls around the stems.

- 'Alba' has white flowers.
- 'Fascination,' with lilac-purple flowers, was selected for its fasciated flower stems, 90–120 cm (3–4 ft.) in height.
- 'Rosea' is pink.

Plant Culver's root in full sun to partial shade. It is adaptable to various soils and is drought tolerant once established. Use it in borders and as a cut flower. It attracts bees and butterflies. 🐝

Davis Landscape Architecture

Culver's root (*Veronicastrum virginicum*)

Flower arrangers often suggest that a flower arrangement should contain flowers showing a range of flower shapes, such as round, flat and spiked to provide a pleasant contrast. The spiky flowers of any of the veronicas make a good addition to arrangements and hold up well as a cut flower.

See **Floral Artistry for Beginners** a beginners guide to the art of flower arrangement on The Prairie Garden's website <prairiegarden.ca>

Salvias Galore!

by Sara Williams

Common sage (*Salvia officinalis* 'Purpurascens')

M ost prairie gardeners are familiar with hardy perennial salvias such as *Salvia nemorosa,* 'May Night' which are frequently found in our landscapes. There are also many drought-tolerant annual and tender perennial salvias, mostly from the tropics, each capable of adding a different dimension to our beds and borders. *Salvia* is a Latin word meaning to heal and alludes to the plant's reputed medicinal properties. Native to the Americas and Europe, salvias are members of the mint family, with typical square stems and opposite leaves. The two-lipped flowers are arranged in whorls around the stem.

Most require full sun and good drainage and are moderately to extremely drought-tolerant. Many will self-seed in subsequent years.

Depending on their size, salvias can be used in rock gardens, mixed borders and containers. Attractive to hummingbirds, bees and butterflies, many are also excellent for cut flowers.

Silver sage (*Salvia argentea*)

has outstanding foliage. Formed in a rosette, it is thick, woolly, silver and gently lobed, ranging from 20–60 cm (8–24 in.) in height. The pinkish white flowers are also attractive. It is a native perennial to southern Europe, but treated as an annual on the prairies. Place in soil with excellent drainage in a full sun location.

- 'Artemis' is taller (90 cm/36 in.) with pinkish white flowers.

Texas sage (*S. coccinea*)

is native to tropical South America and widely naturalized elsewhere. Two identifying characteristics are its widely spaced flowers along the stem and its almost translucent green, triangular, hairy leaves. The flowers are narrow and in shades of scarlet, red, pink, salmon or white, contrasting well with the nearly black stems. The plants are 30–60 cm (12–24 in.) in height. It will take light shade.

- 'Coral Nymph' ('Cherry Blossom') is 40–60 cm (16–24 in.)

in height and has pale coral-salmon flowers with a deeper salmon lower lip. I was awed by it on a visit to Monet's garden in Giverny, France.

- 'Forest Fire' (60 cm/24 in.) has fiery red flowers with contrasting black calyces.
- 'Lady in Red' (35 cm/14 in.) has uniform red spikes.
- 'Mesa Scarlet' (45–60 cm/18–24 in.) has red flowers and aromatic foliage.
- 'Snow Nymph' (60 cm/24 in.) has pure white flowers.

Mealycup sage (*S. farinacea*)

Farinacea means meal, reflecting the fact that each flower is supported by a floury-looking, cup-like calyx, hence the species and common names. The small (2 cm/1 in.), violet blue to lavender to white

Salvia 'Evolution'
Benary

flowers are produced on long spikes, and the upright plants reach 60 cm (24 in.) in height. The shiny foliage is gray-blue. It is used in both fresh and dried arrangements.

- 'Evolution' has 15 cm (6 in.) spikes of deep, dark purple on well-branched plants of 40–60 cm (16–24 in.).
- 'Strata' (25–30 cm/10–12 in.) has silver spikes with clear blue florets and a white calyx.
- 'Victoria' (40–60 cm/16–24 in.) has spikes of violet-blue or white.

Common sage (*S. officinalis*)

a native to the Mediterranean area, has a long history as a medicinal and culinary herb, but is also valuable as an ornamental. Although variable in size, flower and leaf colour, most have bluish flowers and attractive foliage. It is useful for edging in more formal designs.

- 'Icterina' (60 cm/24 in.) has variegated cream and green foliage.
- 'Purpurascens' (20–40 cm/6–16 in.) has purple-and-green leaves.
- 'Tricolour' (60–80 cm/24–32 in.) is a blend of green, white, and pinky-purple

Gentian sage (*S. patens*)

from the mountains of Mexico, is seldom seen in our gardens. It performs better during hot summers. The flowers are formed in whorls around the stem, on plants 45–60 cm (18–24 in.) in height. The pale to bright blue colour is truly wonderful, and the hooded flowers are large, but to its detriment, it is not very floriferous. The deep green leaves are long (15–20 cm/6–8 in.), triangular and pointed.

- 'Blue Angel' (60–70 cm/24–28 in.) has 5 cm (2 in.) tubular blooms and is long flowering.
- 'Cambridge Blue' (60 cm/24 in.) is a soft, pure blue.

Scarlet sage (*S. splendens*)

a native of Brazil, has two-lipped, tubular flowers formed in spikes of red, burgundy, pink, orange, cream, blue, purple or yellow. Branched and upright to 60 cm (24 in.), its green leaves are oval with serrated edges.

- 'Mojave Red' is early with vivid red spikes on compact, well-branched plants of 23–25 cm (9–10 in.).
- 'St. John's Fire' (25–30 cm/10–12 in.) has early, scarlet red blooms.
- Salsa series flowers prolifically in nine colors on compact plants of 35 cm (14 in.).
- Sizzler series (25–30 cm/10–12 in.) has early, long-blooming, tight, compact spikes in nine colors.

Clary sage (*S. viridis*, syn. *S. horminum*)

is not planted as much as it once was, yet it always invites positive comments when people see it for the first time. Native to southeastern Europe and the Mediterranean. The spe-

Parks Seed

Salvia officinalis 'Icterina'

cies name, *viridis,* means green and describes the green bracts of some forms. Clary means clear-eyed, alluding to its former use in healing eye afflictions. The seeds were leached in water to use as an eye-wash. Interestingly, the gray-green foliage is used in the modern pharmaceutical-cosmetic industry. It will self-seed.

Plants are 30–60 cm (12–24 in.) tall. The showy, petal-like bracts are in pastel shades of blue, pink, purple, cream or white, while the real flowers above the bracts are small and inconspicuous. It is good for naturalizing in dry areas, on slopes, in annual or mixed beds, containers, cottage gardens, or for fresh or dried arrangements. It is excellent in a pastel border.

Marble Arch mix comes in rose, deep blue and white on uniform plants of 30–45 cm (12–18 in.).

Tricolor mix (60 cm/24 in.) is in blue, pink and white.

Peonies - The Perfect Spring Perennial
by Melanie Mathieson

'Bowl of Beauty'

A.K.A. The Gardening Guru. Melanie is an Ontario Registered Professional Forester, certified Ontario Master Gardener, and has over 30 years gardening experience in Fort Frances (zone 4) and Thunder Bay (zone 3), Ontario.

When people hear the word peony, they often think back to their grandmother's or great-grandmother's garden. Peonies have been around for generations because they are reliable, winter hardy, quick growing perennials with one of the most favoured flowers. These deer-resistant, easy-care perennials provide a garden with a sweet scented blast of late spring/early summer colour. The variety of colours available include many shades of pink, and new shades like red, crimson and yellow and the old traditional white and cream coloured flowers.

Originally native to southern Europe and China, peonies are well-adapted to Canada's climate. Two of the varieties that grow in my garden have been established from my grandmother's original plants. As they are drought resistant, peonies can tolerate well-drained soils and can be planted in areas that do not get a lot of moisture, like under the eaves of houses.

Peonies have reddish stems and dark green leaves. Mature plants can mimic the look of a shrub and can develop into 1–2 m (3–6 ft) tall plants in clumps almost as wide. They are appealing in the garden even without their flowers and are often used along property edges.

Peonies are extremely long-lived plants lasting up to 50 to 70 years, and once you get them planted correctly, you will enjoy them for years and years, provided they receive proper nourishment. Peonies need full to part sun (minimum of 6 hours per day), average moisture and well-drained soil that is enriched with compost or other organic material annually. Fertilize lightly with a bulb fertilizer, like a 10-20-20, at plant emergence in the spring, and

again in the summer after blooming. Select a fertilizer with lower
nitrogen as too much causes excess
foliage growth without encouraging blooms. Because they like full
sun, ensure they
receive ample
water, and do
not get too dried
out when flower
buds are develop-
ing. You may
need to supple-
ment moisture
with regular watering in order to
have showy blooms. After flowering
and for the rest of the season they
are quite tolerant of dry conditions.

Peony crowns have buds which
are often called "eyes" and can look
like pinkish roots, sticking straight
up. When planting, be careful not
to touch or bump them as they break
and bruise easily. Set the roots so
that the tips of the eyes are pointing
upwards and about 2.5 cm (1 in.)
below the finished surface of the soil.
Carefully check to see that the crown
(where the 'eyes' of the plant emerge
from) is no more than 2.5–5 cm (1–2
in.) below the surrounding grade. If it
is planted too deeply, pull the soil covering the crown back to that depth.
If you plant peonies too shallow in
cold weather climates, the crown
risks damage by winter weather, and
alternatively, if you plant too deep, the
plant will spend valuable growing time
reaching the right depth rather than
producing flowers.

> **Gardening Guru Tip:** If you are divid-
> ing and replanting or transplanting
> from a pot, ensure you place the plant
> in the soil at the same level it was
> planted before dividing. This helps
> the plant to better re-establish itself.

Plants are unlikely to flower the
first spring after planting, but they
should flower every year thereafter. As
plants mature they become prolific
bloomers. A peony covered in blooms
can become very
heavy, so I recom-
mend a strong
support system.
The options are
endless with
either homemade
or commercial
cages and support
systems. Whatever you use, be sure
to adjust the height and width of the
system every few years as the plants
become larger and more mature.

Why Peony Buds Are Not Opening:

Weather

The most common reason buds fail
to open in our area is due to a frost
or chill at the wrong time for that

Close-up of a classic peony

Fran Wershler

variety. A sudden chill at a later stage of development can damage just the inner flower parts, but not the outer parts. This allows the buds to swell, but cause the interior tissue to fail and not properly develop. Peonies can sometimes be frustrating, some years they are terrific and other years they do nothing. If your peonies are having an off year, continue to water and fertilize, and be patient.

Botrytis

Botrytis is a common problem for peonies in certain climates, especially where a cool damp spring can encourage this fungus. Botrytis is a grey fungal mould and should be treated with copper sulfate or other fungicides such as fungicidal soap. Botrytis causes a fuzzy gray coating on the flowers and often kills the buds. It thrives in humid conditions and can be avoided or minimized by making sure the peony is planted where it receives adequate sun and good air circulation. Once the disease is noticed, it is too late to save the buds for that season. Diseased areas should be removed from the plant and thrown in the garbage. Never compost diseased material. To prevent botrytis, allow for air circulation around the plant and destroy the foliage after it dies back in the fall to reduce the possibility of disease.

Water

Too much or too little water during flower bud development may cause them to wilt and die. Try to keep the soil evenly moist and make sure the peony is planted in well-drained soil.

In my garden, I have an area totally dedicated to peonies where some of the newest varieties are mixed in with some of my grandmother's plants that I have had for over 20 years. When guests visit they are immediately drawn to this flowerbed because it gets more and more spectacular each year.

I encourage you to visit your local nursery to see the varieties of peonies available as this is a perennial plant that will last for years and is worth far more than its initial cost. ❧

Sea of Peonies

Melanie Mathieson

Mixed coloured callas

Sandy Venton

Calla Lilies
The All-Occasion Beauty

by Sandy Venton

Sandy lives in Winnipeg, MB and is Canadian Vice-President of the North American Lily Society as well as secretary of the Manitoba Regional Lily Society and a lily judge.

The calla lily (*Zantedeschia* spp.) has been associated with special occasions because of its purity of colour and shape. Although originally associated with funerals, it is now becoming very popular for use in wedding bouquets. I am never without at least one, and usually have three different giant white calla lilies growing in the house. They are breathtaking in their beauty and simple to grow.

All calla lilies are not created equal. Though they all start off as brownish rhizomes, they have to be planted either in pots for subsequent storage (in a cool place) over the winter, or planted directly into the garden, dug up in the fall and stored in a cool place for the winter. Either way, at the end of the summer they all have to be taken inside

for protection. The coolest temperatures that callas tolerate is 10–13 °C (50–55 °F), so those of us who live on the prairies in zones 2–3b must always dig them up for the winter.

Zantedeschia aethiopica, the species calla commonly called the giant white, has large green arrowhead-shaped leaves. There are two cultivars (named varieties). 'Crowborough' is a giant white and is reputedly somewhat hardier than the species, although that is a moot point when it comes to growing them year round in zones colder than zone 8. 'Green Goddess' is a giant white with green streaks throughout. This calla species and its two cultivars grow in muck and never go dormant. I have a huge pot of each and bring them in for the winter, placing them in front of an east-facing window. I give them a great amount of water in big tubs with no drainage and never, never let them dry out. They grow wild in Los Angeles on the boulevards, so it's a good guess that they like lots of light and heat — 25°C (75 °F) is good enough.

Other species of calla lilies include *Zantedeschia elliottiana*, a large yellow with the arrow-shaped leaves speckled with silver; *Z. rehmannii*, a smaller pink, with all-green lance-shaped leaves; and *Z. maculatum*, a smaller-flowered white with green leaves narrower than arrow-shaped, not quite lance-shaped, but with silver markings. All of these have been hybridized with each other, and there are now all types of hybrid callas in different shades of gold, pink, white, dark purple, dark red, dark pink, bright orange, and pretty

Calla 'Flame'

Sandy Venton

much all colours except blue. Packages of dormant rhizomes may be purchased at big box stores, garden centres, or wherever there is a plant department. All of these rhizomes will rot if they get too much water and therefore perfect drainage is a must — I learned that particular fact the hard way!

I personally choose the mixed shades, which I put into pots, cramming in as many as possible, so that I get a large group of different flowers, although I have been known to plant a whole bag of the same colour, just for effect.

If you put them in pots, fill the pots with a well-draining potting soil mix to within 10 cm (4 in) of the brim. At this point I put a pinch of mycorrhizae, a biological growth supplement, where the rhizome will be placed. It is necessary for the roots of the rhizome to be in direct contact with the mycorrhizae, so putting a bit on top of the soil will have no effect whatsoever. Then take the rhizomes and push them into the soil so that the top parts are barely showing, and then cover them with soil up to 4 cm (1½ in) inches from the brim.

Just out of curiosity, I performed an experiment shortly after the mycorrhizae supplement came on the market. I planted one group of callas with the supplement and one group without, but otherwise provided exactly the same growing conditions. Within several weeks the treated rhizomes had white roots going all through the pot and practically on top of the soil, whereas the untreated group just sat there and took about three times as long to get started.

Calla rhizomes have a top and a bottom. They are not round, but one side will have little nubs sticking up which may or not be green when you purchase them. Plant these facing up. A good time to start them is in late April or early May (don't start them too early as this causes them to send out long, light-seeking leaves – they will elongate properly once they are outdoors with adequate light). Water the pots, place them in a cool dark place in the basement, and keep watch. Once they sprout, move them into a brighter location. Watering once every couple of weeks with a balanced fertilizer doesn't hurt either, as callas are hungry feeders and will deplete the nutrients in the soil fairly quickly.

I grow my hybrids in pots on the east side of the house and monitor their moisture levels very carefully. I had several pots of hybrid callas rot due to excess moisture during a particularly rainy summer. Err on the side of caution when watering, too little water may cause them to wilt, but too much water will actually kill them.

Take the whole pot inside in the fall before freeze-up, withhold water and put the whole container in a cool, dark place, such as the basement. They will go dormant. You can take them out of storage in early May to get them re-started. You will be amazed and delighted with the flowers that will start to appear in early summer and continue up until frost.

Remember, the only callas that do not go dormant are the giant whites. All others will. The final rule – "when in doubt, don't water!"

Susanne Olver's Favourite Perennial
Chrysanthemum

Jeffries Nurseries

Tigertail Chrysanthemum

I love them for not only their beauty but that they flower bravely late into fall almost into winter, even up until snowfall. They brighten up the otherwise drab landscape with bronze, yellow, pink or red blooms.

Beware! Most chrysanthemums sold at garden centres in the spring are not winter hardy in the Prairie Provinces. However, quite a few hardy 'mums' have been developed at the Morden Research Centre at Morden, MB, and these will give the gardener years of joy.

The Amaryllis That Isn't

by Susanne Olver

eStranky

---

*Susanne Olver is a retired greenhouse supervisor from the Dept. of Botany, University of Manitoba and a long time committee member of **The Prairie Garden** committee.*

Scientifically, the plant we commonly know as the amaryllis is called *Hippeastrum* and its ancestors come from South America. The real *Amaryllis*, which is similar, comes from South Africa and is neither hardy here nor suitable as an indoor plant. Both of these 'amaryllis' belong to the family *Amaryllidaceae*. I will use the common name 'amaryllis' when I talk about the beautiful bulb we can grow so easily in our homes.

Amaryllis bulbs are available in the fall in most garden centres, and many retail outlets as well. Usually, they are sold in boxes complete with a pot, peat moss and planting instructions. You can follow the instructions and be reasonably certain of success. However, if you desire to keep your flower bulb over several years, or even propagate more, here are my suggestions:

To begin, use a larger pot – I prefer a 5 cm (12 in.) clay pot which will provide more room for the growing bulb. Use a good potting soil for a better supply of nutrients than just peat can provide. This will also save transplanting the bulb for the next year or two. Amaryllis do not like to be transplanted too often as their fleshy roots are brittle and can be easily injured. When planting, about one third of the bulb should protrude above the soil. Water well, but not again until the soil feels dry to the touch.

Hopefully, by that time, signs of growth such as tips of leaves or a bud will have appeared. If nothing happens, wait a while before watering again. Keeping a resting bulb constantly wet will cause it to rot. Patience! The commercially produced bulbs are very dependable and ready to grow. It is more likely that the owner of an older plant is impatient and does not let his bulb rest long enough. At first, the amaryllis will need very little water (after the initial soaking) but, as it begins to grow, it will need more and more water. When the flower stalk begins to elongate, it needs to be staked – when buds and flowers appear they will be too heavy for the stalk to bear. Sometimes the flower stalk appears before the leaves, sometimes the other way around – both are normal. I feed my amaryllis during flowering and growth, about once every two weeks with a 15-30-15 fertilizer, stopping towards fall.

The amaryllis can spend the summer outside, but not in full sun or its leaves will burn. It should be brought indoors before any danger of frost, and can be rested dry in a cool dark place. Do not remove the leaves until they have dried off – the bulb needs to re-absorb the nutrients from the leaves which in turn, promotes next year's flower development.

When new growth starts to appear, after 3-4 months rest, the plant needs to be moved to a warmer brighter environment and given a good watering. The same regime as the year before should be followed. If a larger pot was used, your amaryllis does not need to be transplanted. After a year or two small bulbs will appear, arising from the side of the mother bulb. I like to leave them until they are big enough to flower. A mature amaryllis with 4-5 flower stalks is a spectacular sight. Eventually, the pot will become too crowded as the amaryllis produces more and more bulbs. The plant needs to be taken out of its pot (carefully) and divided. Some of the young bulbs can be potted up separately and added to your plant collection or given away. Smaller bulbs (not the flowering size) should be grown continuously, without a rest period until they are flowering size. In order to flower, they need to be rested like the older bulbs. Dividing has to be done very carefully so that each bulb retains its basal plate. This is where the roots come from. Not to worry if some break, there will still be enough.

It is not practical to grow and collect seeds from the amaryllis as it is a hybrid and will not come true from seed. For anyone who has the patience and space to grow amaryllis from seed, there are some seed houses who do advertise hybrid amaryllis seeds. These would then grow into the lovely big flowering plants much like the ones commercially available. This process takes several years and lots of space. For the average homeowner, I recommend buying flowering size bulbs. Keep and store for many years to come – they are worth it! ❧

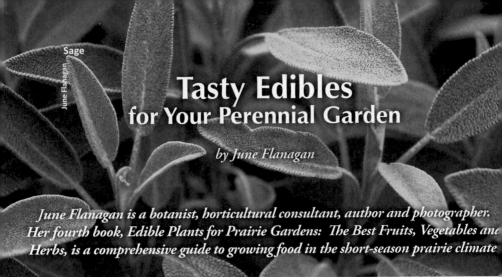

Sage

June Flanagan

Tasty Edibles
for Your Perennial Garden

by June Flanagan

June Flanagan is a botanist, horticultural consultant, author and photographer. Her fourth book, Edible Plants for Prairie Gardens: The Best Fruits, Vegetables and Herbs, *is a comprehensive guide to growing food in the short-season prairie climate*

By choosing perennial plants that are edible, you can transform your outdoor space into a sensory experience that enhances your table as well as your garden, year after year. The perennial herbs and small perennial fruits described here are great food plants for urban dwellers with busy lifestyles; these plants are relatively easy to establish and maintain, and they suit small spaces while looking attractive throughout the season.

Perennial Seasoning Herbs
A collection of prairie-hardy seasoning herbs such as chives (*Allium schoenoprasum*), garlic chives (*Allium tuberosum*), Greek oregano (*Origanum vulgare* ssp. *hirtum*), sage (*Salvia officinalis*) and French tarragon (*Artemisia dracunculus* var. *sativa*) makes a fine perennial border of culinary classics. One plant of each herb is usually plenty, as it takes only a few

fresh sprigs to impart homegrown flavour to a salad, soup or sauce. Some of these herbs are available in an assortment of cultivated varieties, also known as cultivars, that offer a spectrum of fragrance, flavour and foliage or flower colour. It's important to note that winter hardiness varies between cultivars.

The spicy foliage of Greek oregano forms a dark green mound that stands out nicely against linear leaves of chives and garlic chives, and the upright form of French tarragon. Many cooks prefer the white-flowered Greek oregano for seasoning Mediterranean tomato-based dishes over its pink-flowered relative, known as common oregano (*Origanum vulgare* ssp. *vulgare*). Greek oregano grows best in well-drained soil and a sunny, hot location, where it receives at least six hours of direct sun each day.

French tarragon grows in partial shade (four to six hours of direct sun), but the plants are more robust in full sun. French tarragon is a bushy cultivar of Russian tarragon with anise-scented foliage that goes well with fish. It rarely produces seed and is propagated by division. Its seed-grown Russian cousin tastes bland and is considered inferior for culinary purposes.

Like French tarragon, sage, chives and garlic chives also tolerate partial shade, but the growth of these three plants is less leggy and more satisfactory in full sun. Sage adds the nostalgic flavour to poultry stuffing that is a familiar staple of holiday dinners. This plant contributes cool tones to the garden with its pebbly-textured, aromatic silver leaves and violet blossoms. Chives have tubular leaves with delicate onion flavour and lavender pom-pom flowers, while garlic chives hint at the taste their name suggests, and sport white blossom heads. The leaves of both chive species are delicious chopped on potatoes, or sprinkled into salads.

June Flanagan

'Blue Fortune'
anise hyssop

The leafy stems of Greek oregano and sage can be bundled and hung upside down to dry. After drying, the crumbled leaves are useful to season dishes well beyond the growing season. Neither French tarragon nor either type of chives dries well; these herbs are best enjoyed fresh from the garden. It is possible to preserve their delicate flavour by steeping chive blossoms or sprigs of French tarragon in white vinegar, to make fine herbal vinegars that can be used to personalize salad dressings.

Stately lovage (*Levesticum officinale*) is another seasoning herb, which makes an excellent accent plant for the centre or background of a bed, as it grows to a height and spread of over six feet! The tender young leaves taste similar to celery, only the flavour is more intense, and they are delicious chopped in salads. Lovage is prized for seasoning soup and stew. In mid-summer the plant is topped by a profusion of flat, lacy blossom clusters, which produce seeds that can be dried and used similar to celery seed for seasoning. The plant prefers moist soil and grows well in partial shade, and thrives in full sun if it is mulched.

Perennial Herbal Tea Plants

Perennial herbs such as anise hyssop (*Agastache foeniculum*), lemon balm (*Melissa officinalis*), and mints like peppermint (*Mentha piperata*), and spearmint (*Mentha spicata*) pleasantly perfume the air near a patio or walkway with their aromatic leaves. The fresh or dried foliage of these plants can be steeped in hot water to make refreshing herbal teas. The species mentioned here are all relatives in the mint family.

Anise hyssop is a cultivated form of a native prairie wildflower;

> **Herbal tea** can be brewed from dried or fresh stems of mint, lemon balm or anise hyssop. To brew fresh herbs, pour boiling water over a handful of fresh leaves or several stems in a teapot, and steep for about five minutes. For dried herbs, use about 1 teaspoon per cup. Sweeten if desired. Iced herbal teas make especially refreshing summer drinks.

'Blue Fortune' is a favourite with licorice-scented leaves and lavender blue flower spikes that bloom for a long period during summer. Lemon balm foliage is citrus-scented, with insignificant-looking flowers that can self-sow prolifically.

There are many variations on the volatile oils that give mints, like peppermint and spearmint, their flavour and fragrance. Most are aptly described, like ginger, pineapple, orange or chocolate mint, and it is best to purchase named cultivars of known fragrance and hardiness. Many have a habit of creeping across the garden in an invasive manner, so it is a good idea to plant all mints in an area where they are restricted by a barrier such as a sidewalk or a deep, bottomless container, sunk in the ground. Perennial herbs can be grown in containers, but they will not survive the winter outdoors unless the container is sunk up to its rim in the ground, or the plant is transplanted into the ground in September, and repotted the following spring.

Anise hyssop, lemon balm and the mints grow well in full sun to partial shade. Young leaves have the

June Flanagan

'Canada Red' rhubarb

best flavour, and frequent harvesting helps keep the plants neat, compact and full. At the end of the growing season, leave the spent stems in place to trap snow, which insulates the plants during winter and supplies them with moisture when the snow melts. Cut the spent stems back when the plants re-sprout in spring.

June Flanagan

Greek oregano

Perennial Dessert Plants

Rhubarb makes a dramatic addition to the perennial garden and it is also the earliest fresh dessert ingredient. Its striking crimson leaf stalks are delicious baked into fruit crisps and pies, but the leaves contain toxic compounds and should never be eaten. Rhubarb leaves can be added to the compost pile, as the inedible compounds will not affect the compost.

Plant rhubarb from potted nursery stock or a division and set the crown, where the shoot meets the root, about 5 cm (2 in.) beneath the soil surface. Popular cultivars include 'Canada Red', 'MacDonald' and 'Valentine'. 'Honey Red' is a prairie introduction from A.J. (Bert) Porter of Honeywood Nursery in Saskatchewan.

Refrain from harvesting stalks the first year, and pick only a few stems, if any, the second year. From the third year on, harvest rhubarb by grasping the base of the leaf stalk and pulling it straight up and out of the plant. Cut the leaf off the stem immediately to prevent the stalk from wilting, and chop the stalk before baking or stewing it.

Strawberry season usually starts in early July on the prairies, with bumper crops of berries produced

---

**Viola Flanagan's
Strawberry - Rhubarb Crumble**

Fruit base:
3 cups strawberries, rinsed, hulled and sliced
3 cups rhubarb stalks, rinsed, and chopped in 2.5 cm (1 in.) pieces

Topping:
1/3 cup melted butter
1 cup brown sugar
1/3 cup flour
2/3 cup oats
1 tsp cinnamon

Combine strawberries and rhubarb and place in 1.5 l (9-inch) greased pan. Mix topping ingredients and spread across the fruit. Bake at 375 degrees F until fruit is tender and mixture is hot and bubbly, about 30 to 40 minutes.

Recipe can be made with frozen fruit. To freeze strawberries: rinse and hull. Simply rinse and chop rhubarb stalks before freezing.

on so-called "June-bearing" plants that set buds the previous season. The shorter days of late summer cause June-bearing plants to initiate flower buds, but they don't bloom until the following spring, so the first harvest occurs a year after planting. After that, a large crop is produced each year, but the picking season is quite short. If you plant day-neutral strawberries instead of the June-bearing types, you can harvest fresh berries long past the standard strawberry season.

Day-neutral strawberries bloom as soon as the plants become rooted, regardless of the day length, and continue to produce a supply of berries through the season, right up until frost. Fruiting typically begins mid-July, with the heaviest berry production in August and September. 'Tristar', 'Fern' and 'Seascape' are hardy day-neutral cultivars that are recommended for the prairies. Day-neutral strawberries expend a fair amount of energy producing berries, and don't send out many runners.

Strawberries must be planted so that the mid-point of the short stem between the leaves and roots is level with the soil surface. If it is buried too deep, the plant will rot, and if too shallow, the plant will dry out. Because strawberries are shallow-rooted, the plants need evenly moist soil throughout the growing season, and they should be mulched to retain soil moisture and to keep the fruit clean.

Drying Herbs

Perennial herbs such as oregano and sage retain excellent flavour when dried. To dry homegrown leafy herbs, cut stems at least 8 cm (3 in.) long, and rinse them and pat dry or spin them dry in a salad spinner. Bundle about six stems with an elastic band at one end and hang them upside down in a dark, well-ventilated place, or spread leaves or sprigs on a screen or paper towel, and dry them until the leaves feel crisp and brittle, for about two weeks. After drying, strip the leaves from the stems and store them in a tightly sealed glass jar, in a cool, dark place. Finely crumble the dried herbs, just before using. Drying concentrates flavour; when substituting dried herbs in place of fresh ones, use only one-third to one-half the amount.

Growing Perennial Edibles

Perennial edibles have simple growing requirements: provide them with enough sun, space and water, along with well-drained soil and a layer of organic mulch, and you will be rewarded with productive plants. Situate your perennials in a permanent location where they receive the optimum amount of sunshine, allowing enough space for air circulation, with adequate room for each plant to grow to maturity.

During the first three growing seasons, plants require deep irrigations to establish strong root systems. Create a small basin around the plant to hold water, and make sure it drains so that the water percolates through the soil, rather than pooling at the surface. Probe the soil to determine when to water, and allow it to dry moderately between irrigations.

Organic mulch, such as wood chips, around the plants reduces soil moisture loss and weed seed germination. This type of mulch also returns nutrients and organic matter to the soil as it decomposes. The mulch should be applied in a layer that is 8 cm (3 in.) deep, with the depth tapered up to each plant so that it is shallow near the plant crown, where the roots meet the shoots. To avoid rot, do not cover the crown of the plant with mulch. Never use a landscape fabric barrier under mulch as it blocks the recycling of nutrients and organic matter to the soil. Mulch is left in place permanently, and must be topped up every year to maintain its effectiveness as it breaks down. If you maintain an adequate mulch layer, it's unlikely that you will need to supplement perennial plants with fertilizer.

It's best to locate edible perennials in an area that is separate from those that are grown simply for foliage or flowers, to avoid ingesting leaves of a potentially harmful plant, as some perennials are poisonous. However, it is appropriate to combine perennials that are edible with other perennial species that have edible flowers, such as daylilies (*Hemerocallis* spp.), clove pinks (*Dianthus caryophyllus*) or the native prairie wildflower, wild bergamot (*Monarda fistulosa*). Wild berga-

---

Herbal Vinegar

Herbal vinegar is one way to capture the essence of herbs that do not dry well, such as tarragon and chives, to infuse a salad dressing or marinade with flavour. Choose a glass container with an acid-resistant cap (canning jars work well), and rinse and pat dry enough herbs to loosely fill it. Leafy tarragon stems produce a classic anise-flavoured vinegar, while a handful of chive blossoms adds onion overtones with a pale rose colour. Cover the herbs with plain white vinegar. Cap and place the mix in a dark cupboard at room temperature for four weeks. Pour the vinegar through a strainer to remove the herbs and decant the herbal vinegar into a glass container. Store it at room temperature.

Basic Herbal Vinaigrette Dressing: Combine 1 Tablespoon herbal vinegar and 3 Tablespoons canola or olive oil in a lidded jar and shake vigorously. Add salt and pepper to taste and serve over fresh baby greens. Refrigerate up to 3 days, allowing the dressing to come to room temperature before serving.

---

mot also has edible leaves that can be steeped fresh or dried to make an herbal tea reminiscent of the bergamot orange, which imparts its flavour to Earl Grey tea. Edible flowers might be considered an acquired taste, but they are quite useful to decorate desserts or garnish serving plates. Before combining any flower with food, be absolutely sure you have identified it correctly and confirmed that it is edible. 🌺

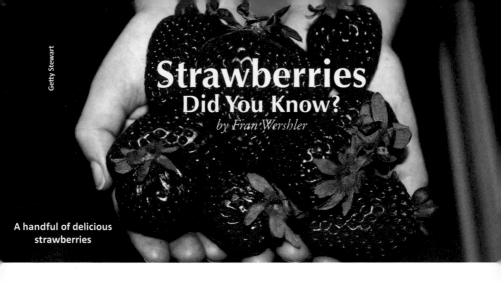

Strawberries
Did You Know?
by Fran Wershler

A handful of delicious strawberries

Fran is a longtime **The Prairie Garden** committee member and former Editor. She gardens in the St. James area of Winnipeg, MB.

For dessert let's have a nice bowl of aggregate fruit with ice cream. Mmmm! Doesn't that sound delicious? To most of us it should sound delicious, because I'm actually referring to a bowl of strawberries.

It is a strange name and the strawberry is a strange form of perennial fruit. The word aggregate means 'collection', since, like a raspberry or a blackberry, a strawberry is a collection of tiny fruits or fruitlets around a centre receptacle. The strawberry and the raspberry, though similar in appearance, are not true berry fruits. Both of these cone-shaped fruits develop from a single flower as a cluster of many little fruits around a single receptacle or 'peduncle', but the raspberry gives us a better picture of how that works.

In botany, a berry is a fleshy kind of *simple fruit* consisting of a single ovary that has multiple seeds. Such *simple fruits* include grapes, bananas, tomatoes and blueberries and they have many seeds within a fleshy pulp. While gardeners don't think of cucumbers and tomatoes as berries, botanists consider them to be berries but say that strawberries and raspberries are not.

Most people think of the strawberry as having seeds on its exterior, but these are actually the true fruits called *achenes,* a seed-like fruit. A strawberry 'fruit' is really unusual because the red, fleshy part is the inflated receptacle, the enlarged tip of the flowering stem to which the flower was attached. The strawberry is said to have an *accessory* fruit because so much tissue, other than the ovary, is part of the 'fruit'. In technical and culinary terms the entire structure is considered a fruit.

The garden strawberry (*Fragaria* x *ananassa*) is grown worldwide for appetizing fruit with bright red colour, succulent texture, attractive aroma and sweet flavour. Eaten fresh or in prepared food like jam, juice, pie, ice cream and smoothies, strawberries are wholesome and delicious. We value strawberries for their nutrients: Vitamin C, folate, potassium and Vitamin A.

Strawberries were known in France and England, but when explorers came to North America they found the berries used by aboriginals to be superior and took samples back to Europe. The woodland strawberry is said to have been hybridized in France (about 1750) from plants originating in Chile and Virginia. The woodland strawberry was later replaced by *Fragaria* x *ananassa* in hundreds of varieties adapted to different areas, growing conditions, and uses.

Different varieties of strawberries may have fruit from early-, to mid-, to late-season, depending on the variety and local growing conditions. On the prairies that would be mainly during June and July. Some varieties are considered 'day-neutral' or ever-bearing and bear fruit from July through October. Soil and weather conditions from one year to the next make a difference. In 2011 strawberries were scarce in some prairie areas because of extremely wet growing conditions and in other areas little fruit was produced without ir-

rigation. Familiar varieties include 'Kent', a June bearing fruit that produces abundant fruit over a short season. 'Ogallala' and 'Fort Laramie' are ever-bearing, the former a firm, large berried dark red fruit that is excellent for eating fresh or for freezing. The latter has a bright scarlet berry and is known for vigour and heavy production of fruit. 'Glooscap' is an older variety, with pale raised seeds, and a calyx that removes easily, making it popular with people who process or freeze the fruit.

Recent hybridizing of strawberry plants has produced some changes in use and the colour of both blossom and fruit. Perhaps the strangest is a cultivar that lacks the flavonoids that turn mature berries of other cultivars red. This fruit is pale yellow, white or golden. The thinking behind this is twofold: the first concerns allergies to strawberries and the second is the hope that berries lacking colour will not attract birds. There are people who experience anaphylactic reactions such as breathing problems, hay fever-like symptoms or skin reactions such

Emmbean

Pineberries

as hives from eating strawberries. Some scientists believe that a protein involved in normal ripening and containing the colour inducing ingredient may be the irritant causing allergic reactions. A colourless fruit may be an option for allergy sufferers. Someone dubbed these pineberries and a variety called 'Sofar' is said to be 'virtually allergen-free'.

There are also ornamental strawberry varieties produced by crossing *Fragaria* with a species like *Potentilla* to produce pink, red or double flowers instead of the familiar white flower. *Fragaria vesca is* advertised in the Dominion Seed catalogue as a perennial having large, rose, abundant, almost semi-double flowers with elongated fruits and trailing runners that make it suitable for planting in hanging baskets and pots. T&T Seeds sell a perennial day-neutral strawberry called 'Rosalyne' that has large, pink blooms and medium size fruit with a wild strawberry flavour.

Garden centres carry ornamental strawberries labelled 'Pink Panda', 'Red Ruby', 'Lipstick' and similar names. These groundcover strawberries spread by runners as do the familiar plant and most have a bright bloom with a tiny fruit similar to the wild strawberry. They are too new to know whether they may be invasive, but they make a bright note at the edge of a flowerbed. The cultivar *Fragaria × ananassa* 'Variegata' is grown mainly for the decorative qualities of its variegated foliage.

Strawberries are easy to grow, and can be grown almost anywhere on the planet as they can survive under most varied conditions. The best time to plant is in early to mid spring. They prefer full sun and a sandy soil, but during flower and fruit formation require adequate water. A strawberry plant sends out shoots in an attempt to propagate a new plant, and, if left alone, it will do so, but this shoot may be cut off and planted where a new plant would be useful.

Strawberries are ready for picking when they are dry and uniformly shaped, firm, but not hard and have

June Flanagan
Strawberry

Ornamental strawberry 'Lipstick'

full red colour. Green or white spots around strawberry crowns do not ripen after picking and the fruit will remain hard and less flavourful than a ripe berry. The strawberry is very perishable and should be picked into a shallow container, carried carefully – unwashed – and stored in a refrigerator. They deteriorate quickly at room temperature.

The amazing strawberry may be eaten many ways and its great virtue is that it is so easy to serve. Fresh strawberries sliced on cereal, yogurt or cottage cheese make a great way to start the day. Spinach salad is at its best when dressed up with toasted pecans, red onion and sliced strawberries for a noon or evening treat. Any one of many strawberry pie recipes is a perfect ending to an evening meal.

Strawberries are good with:

- Herbs – such as anise, tarragon, chervil and sweet Cecily
- The peppery flavour of nasturtium, water cress or black pepper
- Gouda and other semi-hard cheeses
- Peaches, nectarines, rhubarb and other fruits
- Other berries including black berries, blueberries, loganberries, raspberries
- Toasted walnuts, pecans, pine nuts or sunflower seeds
- Desserts using chocolate, creamy toppings, lemon and other citrus fruits
- Balsamic vinegar, rum or maple syrup drizzled over them
- Chicken or mild fish like haddock, tilapia, orange roughy, sole and pickerel
- Sour cream and brown sugar for dipping

Treat strawberries tenderly when preparing them to eat. Wash them gently with calyx attached just before using. Hold them in a sieve under gently running water, but never soak in a sink full of water nor wash with a heavy stream of water. Drain, pat strawberries dry and remove the calyx.

Strawberries freeze well in two ways. Wash, hull, dry and place on flat pans to freeze. When frozen, place into resealable plastic bags and return to the freezer. You may then remove appropriate quantities for use as needed. For dessert, slice the fruit into plastic bags and stir in a small amount of sugar before placing in the freezer. Let the berries thaw a short while prior to eating.

Despite their strange name and form of fruit, strawberries are easy to grow and most delicious to eat! 🐾

Marilyn Latta

Smooth aster and
Jerusalem artichoke

Perennial Vegetables For The Prairie Garden
by Janet Melrose

Janet is a Master Gardener with the Calgary Zoo and Botanical Gardens and has lived i Calgary since 1969. After leaving a career in the corporate world, she now lives her passion for horticulture as **Calgary's Cottage Gardener.**

Many perennial ornamental and edible plants are grown as annuals on the Prairies due to the region's short growing season and severe winters. In common terms, a vegetable (often considered annuals on the prairies) usually refers to an edible plant grown for its savoury roots, bulbs, stems, leaves, flowers, axil buds, fruits and seeds. Edible flowers, sweet fruits and aromatic herbs are generally placed in their own arbitrary categories. As a result, this mixture of botanical terminology blended with cultural and culinary traditions makes for lively discussions, including the 'perennial' one (pun intended!) of whether a tomato is a vegetable or a fruit.

Using this 'precise' definition, here are five perennial vegetables that grow wonderfully on the Prairies: asparagus (*Asparagus officinalis*); Egyptian walking onion (*Allium* x *proliferum*); horseradish (*Armoracia rusticana);* Jerusalem artichoke (*Helianthus tuberosus*); and rhubarb *(Rheum rhabarbarum).*

Asparagus (*Asparagus officinalis*) is a herbaceous monocot in the *Asparagaceae* family. It is an ancient plant, whose edible young sprouts or spears were consumed by Egyptian and other ancient civilizations. Originally native to the Old World, asparagus has been naturalized around the globe. Globalization has made it possible to have asparagus on the grocery shelves year round, but traditionally this seasonal delicacy is available only for about six to eight weeks when the soil is warm enough for these succulent shoots to grow.

Our northern temperate climate is perfect for asparagus to thrive as it needs to have a dormancy period each year where the ground is frozen. Our cool spring and early summer temperatures are perfect for producing very sweet sprouts with high sugar content.

The gardener looking to establish an asparagus bed needs to consider that asparagus is really long living, so look for a spot that will not be disturbed for years, that receives full sun and preferably shelter from prevailing winds. Asparagus can be planted in traditional vegetable beds, but is also suitable for narrow strips beside buildings and fences.

Before planting the area needs to be deeply dug, making sure that all perennial weeds are removed. Dig in copious amounts of organic matter and create a trench about 15 cm (6 in.) deep. Set newly obtained crowns, either one or two year roots that have at least 10 roots in the trench, spaced 30-45 cm (12-18 in.) apart. Cover the crowns with 5 cm (2 in.) of soil and gradually add soil as they grow until the soil mound is at ground level. Mulch the bed with straw or other organic matter to keep the soil cool, reduce weed germination and conserve moisture.

Since asparagus is a perennial, it needs to be firmly established before it can sustain being cropped. Allow the plants, for the first two seasons, to develop full growth and enjoy the lovely feathery fronds that generally reach .6–1.5 m (2–5 ft.). Female plants will develop 'red 'berries' at the end of the season which should be removed before they split open and scatter seed. In the third spring a limited harvest can be sampled, making sure that there are lots of sprouts left to develop full foliage and die back that fall. Once the asparagus bed is mature it can sustain a six week harvest cycle as long as organic matter is added every year to ensure the soil has lots of nutrients to feed the plants.

Asparagus is rarely troubled by pests, with only the asparagus beetle a possibility in late summer. Consider planting tomatoes, interplanted with carrots, parsley, and basil to control pests. Intersperse annual flowers like cosmos and marigold to create a lovely polyculture that will keep all members thriving.

Cultivars worth looking for include: 'Jersey Giant', an all male cultivar that is vigorous and resistant to asparagus rust; 'Martha Washington', an old-fashioned hardy cultivar;

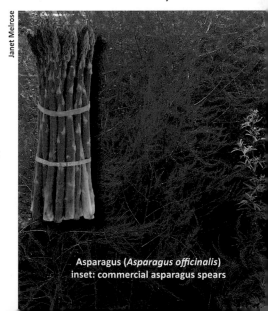

Janet Melrose

Asparagus (*Asparagus officinalis*)
inset: commercial asparagus spears

and a new arrival 'Guelph Millennium' bred out of Guelph, Ontario.

While asparagus is a lot of work to get established, once you have tried the local fare you won't go back to store bought. I guarantee it!

Perhaps as compensation, the next four Prairie hardy perennial vegetables are a breeze to establish.

Egyptian walking onions (*Allium × proliferum*)

are a hybrid of the Welsh onion (*A. fistulosum*) and the common onion (*A.cepa*) that originated in the Mid-East. Also known as tree, perennial or top-setting onions, this species botanical name says it all. They are a very unusual but prolific onion and tough as nails. In early spring frost tolerant slender shoots emerge to become stalks with marble sized bulblets developing at the top, similar to garlic. Under the weight of the maturing bulblets the stalks bend down and where they touch soil, the bulblets will

Janet Melrose

Egyptian walking onions
(*Allium × proliferum*)

take root and naturalize in the garden.

The base of the original plant are pungent, tough skinned elongate bulbs that can be cured and used as regular onions. The early young stalks can be used like scallions and the young bulblets are tender and tasty. It is like having a three in one crop.

To establish in the garden select a sunny site with well draining soil, high in organic matter. Till the soil to a depth of 20 cm (8 in.) and amend with compost. Place bulblets at a depth of 2.5–5 cm (1–2 in.) and cover with soil. The first year the plants will not produce top-sets, as all the energy is devoted to growing the bulbs at the base of the plant. In following years once the top-sets mature, bend down to the soil and take root, the stalk can be cut through to create daughter plants. Every few years the mother plant can be dug up and divided for more plants.

Egyptian walking onions are rarely bothered by pests and are great companion plants for many plant families in the traditional vegetable garden. They are 'at home' in a mixed edible landscape, or planted in containers.

Horseradish (*Armoracia rusticana*)

is believed to be native to Southern Russia, but is now cultivated throughout the world. A member of the large Brassicaceae family, this plant is grown for its pungent root that has many medicinal qualities, in addition to flavouring many cultural dishes besides traditional English-style roast beef.

An extremely long-lived plant that can be propagated from pieces of root, it requires careful cultivation practices to make sure that it is well-behaved in the garden. Choose a sunny location with well-drained, fertile soil, though horseradish can tolerate a wide range of adverse conditions. A good technique for cultivation is to sink, right into the soil, a tub or container that either has drainage holes or the bottom cut out of it. Allow space for the plant to grow up to 60–90 cm (24–36 in.) in height and 60 cm (24 in.) wide. The tapering roots can grow 60 cm (24 in.) or more into the subsoil and bring up valuable nutrients.

Horseradish is a handsome plant with large oblong, dark green crinkly leaves growing from a basal stem. If left alone small white typical Brassica flowers arrive mid-summer. Deadhead before seed sets to avoid self-seeded plants from taking over the area. Rather than relegating it to the 'back-forty' of the garden, horseradish is a good companion plant for potatoes as it helps ward off Colorado potato beetle. Other crops that might bolt in summer heat do well in the shade cast by its large leaves.

To harvest, either dig up the whole plant and replant pieces for the next season or take side roots off the mother plant. The root has the strongest flavour in fall, but it can be equally harvested in spring before new growth resumes.

Janet Melrose

Horseradish (*Armoracia rusticana*) at Olds Botanical Gardens July 2012

Jerusalem artichoke Sunchoke or Girasole (*Helianthus tuberosus*)

is neither an artichoke nor is it native to the Mid-East. A relative of the annual sunflower, the name is thought to be a corruption of its Italian name (Girasole) with the artichoke coming from the similar nutty flavour of the edible tubers. Jerusalem artichoke is actually native to Eastern North America where it was considered an emergency food for settlers. Rather than producing starch, it produces the carbohydrate insulin which is not as readily absorbed by the body, making it valuable for people with diabetes.

A vigorous big tall plant that can grow between 2–3 m (6–9 ft.) and 120 cm (4 ft.) wide, it produces distinctive yellow sunflowers in late summer which should be deadheaded to boost the size of the tubers. Full sun and well-draining, organically rich soil are preferred for tuber production, but the plant is also useful for breaking up heavy clay soils or as windbreaks for crops that need shelter. Jerusalem artichoke can serve as a substitute for corn in the traditional 'Three Sisters' plant guild (corn, beans, and squash), providing support to pole beans. As with horseradish, this plant can be aggressive and should be situated where cultural control methods, such as mowing, are easy to deploy.

The tubers are ready to harvest when the foliage dies back. Plants can either be dug out entirely with some tubers replanted or portions of the root harvested.

Rhubarb or pie plant
(*Rheum rhabarbarum*)

is often used as fruit, yet it is the petiole that is edible and valued for its medicinal as well as culinary attributes. The leaves and roots contain oxalic acid, toxic to mammals, which explains why this plant is deer, raccoon and rodent resistant.

A native of Siberia, rhubarb grows the best in cool, moist summers and cold winters that freeze the soil and induce dormancy in the plants. It prefers a pH of 6.0–6.8 and sandy, well drained soil which is a challenge for our Prairie clay-based alkaline soils, so regular addition of compost and other organic matter is essential. Rhubarb is a heavy feeder and will not produce many stalks if there are not enough nutrients in the soil. Additions of fish emulsion or kelp meal is helpful as is annual mulching with manure or other organic matter.

New plantings of rhubarb are easily obtained by splitting divisions from dormant clumps in early spring with a sharp spade, making sure that there is at least one bud with each section. Plant each division 90–150 cm (3–5 ft.) apart, or plan for 1 m (3 ft.) square for each plant. Set pieces deep in soil so that the crown is 5 cm (2 in.) below the soil level and cover.

Wait until the following year of planting to start harvesting and then only remove a few stalks for a short period. Once well established, rhubarb can be prolific but always leave four to five leaves to sustain the plant. To harvest, twist stalks away, rather than cutting so as to avoid introducing disease into the plant. Stop harvesting before mid-June to allow the plant to set buds and accumulate reserves for next year. Rhubarb leaves are excellent for a tough mulch cover or blended in water to make an effective foliar insecticide.

There are several cultivars available with' Canada Red', 'Valentine' and 'Strawberry' being Prairie favourites.

Consider adding at least one of these perennial vegetables into your garden. The benefits they bring are manifold: reliably productive, important as part of an Integrated Pest Management system, largely trouble free, and beautiful in their own right. They bring a sense of permanence to the edible garden, besides being terrific to eat! 🐾

Blueberries – a Healthy Choice
by Wilhemina Kalt

Dr. Wilhelmina Kalt is a Research Scientist with Agriculture and Agri-Food Canada. Current research concerns the bioactivity and bioavailability of blueberry anthocyanins and factors responsible for the health protective effects of blueberries.

While fruits and vegetables still add the same tasty appeal to our diet, their value to health conscious consumers is soaring as new research increasingly reveals the health benefits of plant-based foods.

While we've known for some time that fruits and vegetables provide essential vitamins and minerals to our diets, we've only recently learned (from population studies) that they also provide health benefits over and above their contribution of those essential nutrients. People that consume more fruits and vegetables enjoy improved health and wellness and reduced risks of degenerative diseases. These observations have stimulated research to determine the ways that a diet rich in fruit and vegetables can provide these benefits.

An excellent example of a Canadian commercial crop that has been transformed by research on its health benefits is the blueberry. Canada is a major commercial producer and exporter of both cultivated blueberries (*Vaccinium corymbosum*) and wild blueberries (*Vaccinium angustifolium*).

Blueberries have been designated as a "Super Fruit" as new research demonstrates the various ways these berries may protect the brain and the heart, promote blood glucose regulation and mitigate the chronic inflammation that underlies physiological stress, diseases and the aging process. While the potent antioxidant power of blueberries was first thought to be important in conferring health benefits, research is showing that the picture is more complex than that.

Blueberries as a Healthy Food

Blueberries were used as a food and medicine by native North Americans based on historical records, which described the consumption of fresh blueberries and the use of sun-dried fruit in breads, cakes and stews. Dried berries were crushed with meats and fish to make pemmican which could be stored for long periods. Blueberry syrup was used to treat coughs and was also used as a diarrhoea remedy.

Related species like the North American cranberry (*Vaccinium macrocarpon*) have a long history of use in the prevention of urinary tract infections. The medicinal use of European bilberry (*Vaccinium myrtillus*) dates to the Middle Ages, and bilberry has been part of traditional European folk medicine since the 16th century.

The health benefits of blueberries are due to their flavonoids. While other fruits and vegetables also contain flavonoids, blueberries and other related species are very rich sources of this interesting group of compounds.

Other berries and foods such as dark chocolate, green tea, red wine and pomegranate contain an abundance of various flavonoids that are being studied for their health benefits.

Flavonoids

Building on a scientific consensus that fruits and vegetables contain compo-nents that promote health and wellness, research activity has blossomed to characterize various phytochemicals ('phyto' = plant) in plant foods and their actions in the human body.

In the case of blueberries where flavonoids appear to confer health benefits, one class of flavonoid called anthocyanins may be especially important. Anthocyanins are the pigments (antho = flower/cyanin = blue) that give blueberries their intense blue colouration. Anthocyanin flavonoids are responsible for the range of pink, red, purple and blue colouration of flowers and fruit.

When in foods, anthocyanins are easily detected by their colour while another group of flavonoids, the proanthocyanidins, can be detected by the astringency (dryness) they cause in the mouth (imagine the sensation of chewing raw cranberries). Some flavonoids from the peel of citrus crops are very bitter.

Plants, including fruits and vegetables, synthesize flavonoids for a variety of reasons. Flavonoids help to protect the plant against insect and disease attack, and protect plant tissues from solar ultraviolet damage. Anthocyanin flavonoids act as a visual attractant to signal fruit ripe-

Basket of blueberries

ness, which is easily seen when fruit turns to red, blue or purple colour and seeds mature and fruit becomes palatable. Some flavonoids found in forages bind nutrients to prevent their absorption by grazing animals.

It is fascinating to consider whether the human health benefits of fruit and vegetable flavonoids are simply fortuitous or the result of a beneficial co-evolution between plants and animals. At this point it is an interesting and unresolved question.

Blueberries

Dexter Blueberry Farm

Mechanisms of Flavonoid Action

The early research on blueberries and human health focused on the antioxidant properties of this fruit. The significance of antioxidants in health relates to their protective effects against oxidative stress in the body. Oxygen is vital to life – it must be constantly available for the cellular reactions that produce biochemical energy to fuel metabolism. However, oxygen is also very reactive especially when it occurs in extremely damaging forms like superoxide radicals, singlet oxygen and hydrogen peroxide. These reactive oxygen forms can readily damage cellular membranes and enzymes which disrupts cellular processes and contributes to disease development and aging. Our bodies possess extensive metabolic defence mechanisms to combat oxidative stress and damage.

The potent antioxidant power of blueberry flavonoids can be easily demonstrated in simple test tube ex-

periments where the addition of blueberry extract protects against the oxidation of various pure biomolecules after the addition of reactive forms of oxygen. Blueberries compared very favourably to other fruits and vegetable extracts, and were dubbed "Nature's #1 Antioxidant Fruit". It is important to emphasize that these simple test tube 'models' do not simulate very well what is happening in the body. Changes in structure and concentration of the flavonoids that occur during normal digestive absorption are not accounted for in these types of test tube studies.

Research on the actions of flavonoids in the body reveal that, as is often the case in biology, the story is more complex than originally thought. While new evidence from more in-depth animal and human studies demonstrated that blueberry flavonoids do indeed affect physiological functions, it was also discovered that flavonoids are not well absorbed by the body. When we eat blueberries, only very low levels (<0.1%) of the blueberry flavonoids can be found in the blood or urine. After about 12 hours they are no longer detectable in circulation. So while flavonoids are potent antioxidants, they are present at too low a level in the body to add significantly to the natural anti-oxidants (vitamin C, vitamin E, uric acid) that circulate in the blood.

Although blueberry flavonoids are only transiently present and at very low levels in the body, we know that they affect the body's physiology in a variety of ways. Blueberry flavonoid consumption can affect the expression of various genes and the concentration of gene products. It can affect very finely regulated biochemical pathways, and physiological systems can be ramped up or down in response to flavonoid consumption. Probably one of the most significant effects of flavonoids is on the mechanisms of inflammation. Chronic inflammation is a central element in the damage brought about by disease, stress and aging. In atherosclerosis, inflammation of the arteries brings about their loss of function due to their 'hardening'. In neurodegeneration, localized inflammation in brain regions is the underlying cause of cognitive loss. In diabetes, systemic inflammation is part of a spectrum of effects that contribute to the damage of this disease. As we age our levels of inflammation increases.

Inflammation is a finely tuned process, designed to ramp up or down the degree of an inflammatory response. The biochemical pathways involved with inflammation involve many intermediate steps, each of which are finely regulated at the genetic and cellular level. There is significant evidence from animal studies, and even some human studies, that flavonoids (despite their transient presence) affect these pathways with the overall effect of mitigating inflammation. The benefits noted for blueberries in disease, stress and aging are all consistent with a reduction in inflammation.

What next?

Many wish to capitalize on the health premium conferred by blueberries. Horticulturists aim to improve crop quality through breeding for a more health-beneficial phytochemical composition. Food and health product manufacturers want to develop high value products targeted for the health conscious consumer. Public health groups wish to improve the wellness of our society by raising awareness of the beneficial role of plant foods in human health.

The blueberry is unchanged - it's the same delicious berry that it always has been. However our new knowledge has transformed our appreciation for all that blueberries offer in the way of good health and nutrition. 🐾

Reference:
Kalt, W., Joseph, J.A., and Shuckett-Hale, B. 2007. Blueberries and human health: A review of current research. Journal of the American Pomological Society, 61:151-160.

Native Perennials for Your Garden
by Shirley Froehlich

Prairie dropseed (*Sporobolus heterolepsis*)

*Shirley has run **Prairie Originals** for 22 years and is based 4 km south of Selkirk, MB. She is interested in all things native and their interaction with insects. Shirley studied horticulture at University of Saskatchewan in Saskatoon.*

Over the last 20 years Prairie Originals has had a wealth of perennials offered to us from all over the world – gardeners have grown to know and love many of them. But how many gardeners are familiar with our native perennials that evolved on the Canadian prairies? We have many prairie and woodland wildflowers and prairie grasses that are excellent choices for our gardens. Native perennials are drought tolerant plants and do not require any watering once established. I invite you to get to know some of our prairie plants grown at Prairie Originals near Selkirk, Manitoba.

Tall bluebells (*Mertensia paniculata)* is a great plant for shady gardens. It likes part to full shade with medium to moist rich soil. This member of the borage or forget-me-not family has clusters of pink buds that turn blue as they open. We have seen the Hummingbird Clearwing moth coming to the blue, funnel-shaped flowers for nectar. These fascinating moths move their wings so fast they look like a hummingbird but are much smaller. The plant has attractive lanceolate leaves up to 15 cm (6 in.) long and it grows 30–60 cm tall (1–2 ft.). Tall bluebells drops large seeds so as to reseed fairly easily.

We grow tall bluebells under shade cloth since we don't have many trees and we spread about 10 cm (4 in.) of oak leaves on the beds in late fall as would happen in a natural forest setting. The mulch keeps the weeds down, helps to hold moisture, looks attractive and adds organic matter to the soil as it gradually breaks down every year. This plant is native across Canada including Northwest Territories and Yukon with the exception of the Maritime provinces. With a range that far north, this is one cold hardy plant.

Wild ginger (*Asarum canadense*) is a great groundcover for shady gardens with big, lush, velvety leaves. It tolerates deep shade, although it will be a little slower to establish. It spreads slowly by the roots to fill in an area and grows 10–15 (4–6 in.) cm tall. If planted at a 30 cm (1 ft.) spacing it takes about three years to fill in. It is generally considered a foliage plant because the unusual,

reddish brown flowers lay on the ground under the leaves. This dense groundcover is not eaten by deer.

It is not related to the culinary ginger *Zingiber officinale,* a tropical plant, but the roots have a ginger-like flavour and when cooked with sugar can be used as a substitute for ginger. Wild ginger roots have a lot of medicinal uses because of their anti-fungal, anti-inflammatory, and disinfectant properties. In the wild it grows in deciduous woods from south-east Manitoba to New Brunswick in Canada and in the eastern United States.

Smooth camas (*Zigadenus elegans*) is an excellent plant for smaller gardens. It grows only 30–60 cm tall (1–2 ft.) and has narrow, grass-like leaves. The elegant, creamy flower spikes are splashed with green and bloom in late June and July. It combines nicely with other native perennials of similar size such as our western red lily and Philadelphia fleabane. It grows in medium to moist to wet soil. Since it is a small, fairly narrow plant I suggest a spacing of 15–20 cm (6–8 in.) when doing a mass planting in flower beds. It can be mixed with other wildflowers and native grasses for an informal prairie meadow. Full sun is best for smooth camas but it will also grow in part shade. It has a small onion like bulb that is slightly poisonous. This plant is easily confused with death camas (*Zigadenus venenosus*) which is very poisonous, therefore, it should not be eaten. In the wild it is widely distribut-

Shirley Froehlich

Tall bluebells (*Mertensia paniculata***)**

ed in poplar and open woods, meadows, mountains, and stream banks. It grows all across Canada including Yukon and Northwest Territories.

Meadow blazing star (*Liatris ligulistylis*) is a plant that stands out in a crowd, just as its name suggests. It loves full sun and medium to moist soil. It has bright pink flower spikes a little different than most other flower spikes. The flowers start blooming from the top of the spike and continue on down as the season progresses. This is opposite in comparison to the blooming habit of other flower spikes. It starts blooming in late July and continues for about three weeks into August. Each plant has from one to five spikes. It is well adapted to endure dry conditions if necessary. Water and food are stored in corm-like roots and their grass-like leaves minimize water loss during the heat of the summer.

Since the plant is fairly narrow I recommend planting them 15–20 cm apart (6–8 in.) in a mass planting. Meadow blazing star can by planted in masses in flowerbeds or mixed with other wildflowers and prairie grasses for an informal prairie meadow. It is nice in combination with blackeyed Susan and Culver's root. This showy flower is very popular with gardeners for its beauty, and as cut or dried flowers. It is also a butterfly 'magnet' as it provides a lot of nectar. It is in the 'Top Ten' for nectar in the butterfly world. Its nectar is also valued by native bees and bumblebees. Goldfinches and

Shirley Froehlich

Meadow blazing star (*Liatris ligulistylus*)

other birds also love to eat the seeds. Meadow blazing star is native to the Canadian Prairies and the Midwestern United States down to Missouri.

Dotted blazing star (*Liatris punctata*) is a close relative of the meadow blazing star, however, it is much more drought tolerant and needs full sun. Dry to medium soil with good drainage works best, although it will also tolerate sandy or gravelly soil. It grows 10–30 cm tall (4-12 in.) depending on soil moisture. The drier it is, the shorter the plant will be. At our location near Selkirk, Manitoba it grows 30 cm tall (1 ft.) but I have seen it blooming at Old Man On His Back Prairie in southern Saskatchewan at only 8–10 cm tall (3-4in.). Dotted blazing star produces many flower spikes in a garden setting, giving it a somewhat bushier appearance than meadow blazing star. The roots are also different, with a carrot-like shape. The bright pink spikes are finer textured than the spikes of meadow blazing star. They also provide a lot of nectar for butterflies and seed for birds. It is native to the Canadian prairies and the Midwestern United States all the way down to Texas. It is more common in Saskatchewan and Alberta where it is drier than in much of Manitoba. Fortunately deer don't seem to bother either type of Blazing Star.

Culver's root (*Veronicastrum virginicum*). Tall, elegant and distinctive; these; these words all describe this rare and beautiful wildflower of the tall grass prairie in Manitoba. It is an excellent plant for landscaping whether it is mass planted in flower beds, mixed with other wildflowers and grasses for an informal prairie meadow, or used as a focal point or accent. With white flowers, it is very attractive against a dark coloured fence. This adaptable, long-lived plant is easy to grow and makes a good cut flower. The common name was to honour Dr. Culver who prescribed the plant as an effective laxative. The root contains powerful emetic and cathartic agents that effect gastrointestinal motility.

The bushy, robust plants grow 90–120 cm tall (3–4 ft.) with deep green, lanceolate leaves arranged in whorls up the stem. The flowers crown the top of the plant with slender, white spikes in late July and early August. They bloom for about three weeks. Culver's root prefers the full sun of the wide open prairie and medium to moist to wet soil and it tolerates partial shade fairly well. It is nice in combination with Joe Pye or meadow blazing star. It provides nectar for many pollinators such as many types of native bees, flies, butterflies and moths. Deer don't bother this plant. Culver's root is native in Manitoba and eastern Canada, the midwestern and eastern United States.

Three-flowered avens (*Geum triflorum*)

Shirley Froehlich

Three-flowered avens (*Geum triflorum*) is the spring flower of the Canadian Prairies. Some of you may know it by other names such as prairie smoke or grandpa's whiskers. This easy to grow, reliable wildflower usually begins blooming in early to mid May. The reddish-pink nodding flowers are in groups of three and are on stems 15–45 cm tall (6–18 in.). Each plant has many flower stalks so that even though the individual flowers are only 1-2 cm across (½–¾ in.), a group of them is very eye catching, particularly so early in the season. At a time when most other perennials are just starting to poke out of the ground, these vigorous prairie flowers are green and bushy and in full bloom! Later in June each flower lifts up its head as the seed forms, and attached to each seed is a long, pink, feathery style. The masses of pink feathery whiskers look just as attractive as the flowers. From a distance the seed heads look like smoke on the ground and up close they look more like whiskers. As the seed ripens, the heads turn from pink to brown and when dry, the seeds are either dispersed by the wind or eaten by birds. We saw goldfinches eating our avens seed last spring. The ferny, foliage remains as a nice ground-cover 10–20 cm tall (4–8 in.) for the remainder of the season.

As a plant of the prairie it loves full sun and dry to moist soil and is very drought tolerant. They are beautiful in combination with pussytoes, blue-eyed grass, coneflower and dotted blazing star. Its native range extends from Ontario, west to British Columbia, including the Northwest Territories and Yukon. It also grows in the northern midwest and western United States.

Prairie dropseed (*Sporobolus heterolepsis*) is one of my favourite

Shirley Froehlich

Purple Prairie Clover (*Dalea purpurea*)

prairie grasses. This elegant, ornamental grass has fine textured, green leaves that curve gracefully outward forming large, round tufts. It is a warm season bunch grass that is very well behaved in the garden. Warm season grasses wait for some heat before they green up in the spring. Seed heads are produced in July. Prairie dropseed is drought tolerant because of its very deep roots. The delicate looking flower panicles of prairie dropseed appear in midsummer above the foliage and they have a unique fragrance, similar to cilantro. The silvery seed heads in late summer provide plentiful food for birds. In September the leaves turn a wonderful pumpkin colour.

Prairie dropseed grows 30–70 cm tall (12–28 in.) in dry to moist soil and full sun. Any type of soil from sand to clay is fine. This plant is deer resistant. It grows in the wild from Saskatchewan to Quebec and from Montana to the east coast of the United States.

Purple prairie clover (*Dalea purpurea*). The glowing purple flowers of purple prairie clover and its unusual flower shape make this a favourite of many gardeners. This prairie wildflower loves full sun and dry to moist soil. It is a great plant for smaller gardens since it grows only 20–50 cm (8–20 in.) tall. The many tiny flowers are arranged on short, dense spikes 2–4 cm (¾–1½ in.) long . As the flowers begin to open from the bottom up, it gives the effect of little fur hats perched atop slender stems. The plants are quite bushy with flowers at the tip of almost every branch, resulting in up to 30 or 40 flowers on each plant. They begin to bloom in mid/late July and continue into August for two or three more weeks. It is a popular nectar plant among butterflies, native bees, bumble bees and honeybees and the cylindrical seed heads are also a good food source for birds.

Purple prairie clover is a legume with fragrant leaves. In the past the tough, resilient stems were bundled together to make brooms. The roots were also chewed for their pleasant taste – our first chewing gum! It is native from Alberta to Quebec and in most of the United States, except for the east and west coasts.

One of Jeannie's Favourite Perennials
by Jeannie Gilbert

Johnathan Gilbert

Our garden backs on to the Red River. This provides many advantages, not least of which is access to water for irrigation during dry periods in the summer. However, there are some disadvantages including ravenous deer, rabbits and raccoons, and the river itself. Several factors lead to spring flooding such as heavy fall rains and winter snowfall which once melted has to drain somewhere. In some years the garden is literally under water until mid-May. The river's sediments build up on the yard leaving a layer of thick silty deposit that suffocates all but the hardiest grasses and leaves behind what I describe as my moonscape. Needless to say, some of my favourite perennials are those that survive the frequent inundations. There are peonies and meadowsweet, swamp milkweed and lamium. There is a tall orange daylily which spreads far too freely and the hostas and ferns thrive in the heavy moist soil. However, the most cheerful is the day lily pictured here. It might be 'Stella d'oro', but I cannot be certain as it has survived from the previous home-owner's times and I do not know its name. It has a wonderful golden hue and has re-appeared faithfully for 25 odd years no matter what the weather and the river have thrown at it.

Native Plants for Problem Spots
by Chet Neufeld

Gaillardia

Chet Neufeld is a biologist, Professional Agrologist and Executive Director of the Native Plant Society of Saskatchewan. <www.npss.sk.ca>

Most of us have them—those places in our yard we can't seem to find the right purpose for or the right plant to grow. In my yard, I have three problem places I've had to deal with: extremely hot and dry, shady, and wet areas. Although I used different approaches for each area, there is one solution that they all share: native plants.

Hot and Dry Areas

My house faces southeast, so I get a lot of sun in my front yard. Also, the stucco tends to heat up and make it even hotter. Many people faced with this situation try to water more, or end up planting species that aren't adapted to these conditions. Best to accept the limitations of any area and select plants that are most likely to thrive. There are many plants that do well in this hot and sunny situation, especially plants native to the prai-

ries. Think about it—who waters the flowers growing wild on our prairie? Native prairie species are perfect because they've adapted to growing in this climate. The following are just a few of our native plants that are ideal for use in hot, sunny locations:

Trust me—almost no amount of neglect will kill these plants once established. There are also some showy grasses that survive in dry, hot soils.

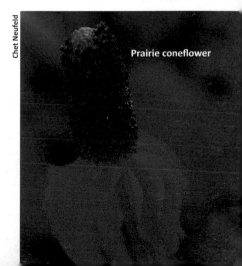

Prairie coneflower

Hot and Dry Areas

Common Name	Botanical Name	Notes
Gaillardia/ Blanket flower	*Gaillardia aristata*	Several horticultural varieties of this have been developed, but I still like the original.
Prairie cone-flower	*Ratibida columnifera*	These cheerful yellow flowers have reflexed petals.
Smooth blue beardtongue	*Penstemon nitidus*	This plant has bright blue flowers similar to a snapdragon and has waxy, bluish foliage.
Crocus	*Pulsatilla patens* ssp. *multifida*	The flowers bloom before the leaves emerge. Often overlooked once flowering is finished but forms a beautiful, soft mound of dissected leaves.
Wild rose	*Rosa acicularis*	The floral emblem of Alberta, its heavy odour will attract many bees.
White prairie clover	*Dalea candida*	This plant does especially well in sandy soil.
Golden bean	*Thermopsis rhombifolia*	This plant spreads through rhizomes and is a legume, so it will fix nitrogen.
Showy locoweed	*Oxytropis splendens*	This plant has woolly leaves, purple flowers and also fixes nitrogen.
Small-leaved pussytoes	*Antennaria parvifolia*	This forms mats of tiny greyish plants and is great as a ground cover or in rock gardens.
Sagebrush	*Artemisia cana*	Beautiful grey-green leaves and a light sage smell make this a great specimen shrub.

Shady Areas

I have shade for most of the day on either side of my house because of its east-west orientation, and the proximity of the neighbouring houses. The area is more moist than average and is kept that way with a thick layer of wood mulch. I could have planted hostas and other shade-tolerant horticultural varieties here, but opted for a more diverse (and I think more interesting) landscape. For one shady area in particular, I chose to replicate a forest floor by planting all of the species that are commonly found there. To do this, I randomly scattered a combination of grasses, sedges, flowers and small shrubs. This is in complete contradiction to my normal recommendation of grouping by colour

Giant hyssop

Chet Neufeld

Shady Areas		
Common Name	**Botanical Name**	**Notes**
Giant hyssop	*Agastache foeniculum*	Also called anise hyssop, leaves have a liquorice flavour, can be eaten or steeped to make tea.
Tall lungwort	*Mertensia paniculata*	Has clusters of drooping, bell-shaped flowers.
Northern bedstraw	*Galium boreale*	Has interesting, whorled leaves and clusters of tiny, white flowers. Is a good ground cover.
Blue columbine	*Aquilegia brevistyla*	The blue-purple flowers are native to the boreal forest.
Ostrich fern	*Matteuccia struthiopteris*	Native to prairie forested areas. Spread by rhizomes, young fronds (fiddleheads) can be eaten.
Western Canada violet	*Viola canadensis* var. *rugulosa*	Native violet tolerates moist or dry shade, flowers for months. Spreads by creeping roots, but is not aggressive.
Wild strawberry	*Fragaria virginiana*	Makes a great ground cover. Can withstand 5–10 degrees of frost. Produces tiny, delicious berries until frost.
Star-flowered Solomon's seal	*Smilacina stellata*	Tolerates moist or dry shade, has broad leaves and tiny white flowers. Spreads by rhizomes.
Jewelweed	*Impatiens biflora*	An annual with one of the most beautiful flowers in the forest. Weak stemmed, benefits from growing against other plants or objects for support.
Sticky geranium	*Geranium viscosissimum*	The leaves that are much more divided and ragged than the horticultural varieties.
Blueberry	*Vaccinium* spp.	There are a few different species of native blueberry. All do best in sandy soil and higher soil acidity.

and arranging by height, but in this scenario it works. My justification is that I've learned the rules well enough to bend them a little. The result was an interesting carpet of leaf textures and shapes punctuated by changes in height and flower colours. While you may not want to replicate what I've done, the following native plants are guaranteed to work in shady, moist areas:

A variety of grasses and sedges also grow well in shady areas, many with beautiful seed heads.

Wet Areas

Before I put topsoil over my yard, it had such heavy clay that you could have made pottery with it. Those of us who with clay soil know how long it holds water, creating almost permanently wet areas. Even with a topsoil cover, the underlying clay slows the percolation of water. One area in my yard is much wetter than the rest, but I planned it this way. My rain barrel overflow drains into this area and creates a bog garden — if life is giving me lemons, I make lemonade. I even keep a thick

Wet Areas		
Common Name	**Botanical Name**	**Notes**
Wild mint	*Mentha arvensis*	Produces tiny flowers in the leaf axils. Has a minty flavour and aroma, can be eaten raw or to make tea.
Marsh marigold	*Caltha palustris*	Yellow flowers can withstand the occasional dry period as well as standing water.
Bogbean	*Menyanthes trifoliata*	This plant has unusual, fringed, white flowers.
Bog arum	*Calla palustris*	Requires very wet areas and forms colonies via thick rhizomes, best for large, very wet areas.
Tufted loosestrife	*Lysimachia thyrsiflora*	NOT related to the noxious weed purple loosestrife. Flowers resemble yellow, fuzzy balls.
American speedwell	*Veronica americana*	This plant also likes it very moist and will live in shallow, standing water. Produces striking, little, blue flowers.
Obedient plant	*Physostegia virginiana*	Produces spikes of pink-purple flowers, grows to almost a meter. Contrary to its name, it will spread.
Closed gentian	*Gentiana andrewsii*	Native to Manitoba and a few places in Saskatchewan, it has bright blue flowers that never quite open; bees must force their way in.
Culver's root	*Veronicastrum virginicum*	Native to Manitoba, this plant has tall, white spikes of flowers.
Red-osier dogwood	*Cornus stolonifera*	Tolerates a wide range of conditions, from dry to very wet soil. Striking red stems offer colour in winter. Best for larger areas.

layer of wood mulch over this area to help prevent drying out. Even if you're not planning a bog garden, the following table of native species will thrive in moist to wet areas.

Since grasses and sedges have adapted to live in such a diversity of habitats, there are many beautiful grasses and sedges adaptable to wet areas. Many do best in standing water.

Remember these are just a few of the many fascinating native plants available for various landscaping scenarios. If you would like more suggestions, or would like to know where to buy seeds or plants of the species I've listed, please feel free to contact me at (306) 668-3940 or e-mail me at info@npss.sk.ca. Many species listed may be hard to find locally but don't get discouraged; most native plant retailers will ship your order and it will arrive in a day or two.

Support native seed and plant producers and never dig plants out of the wild—it damages the area and the plants rarely survive because their roots are damaged by the digging. 🦋

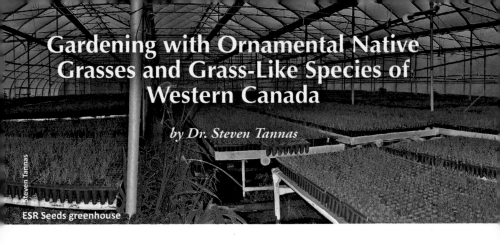

Gardening with Ornamental Native Grasses and Grass-Like Species of Western Canada

by Dr. Steven Tannas

Steven Tannas

ESR Seeds greenhouse

---

*Steven is with **Eastern Slopes Rangeland Seeds** near Calgary, AB. who are reclamation consultants and contract growers of rangeland native plants and seeds. <esrseeds.com>*

Growing up in a family of botanists gives one a unique view of the world. Most people look out the window of the car as they drive through the countryside enjoying the beautiful scenery, maybe some animals, buildings and people. But what I see are plants — thousands of species everywhere I look. My friends quickly caught on to this, bugging me about how I was always staring at the plants no matter where I went. I grew up loving plants and specifically grasses. Maybe it was because no one else took interest in them. Or maybe it was the thrill of being able to correct someone who thought all grass was grass and that was the end of it. Regardless of what sparked my interest, it steadily grew throughout my childhood. Years later I still love grasses regardless of whether they are tall or short, creeping or bunch type, scentless or aromatic. The beauty of nature would not be the same without grasses. Throughout history grasses have been critical to the human race. They have provided us with the bulk of our food (i.e. rice, barley, wheat, corn, and grass for animals). And although we seldom think about it, grasses have become a critical part of our recreation (sports fields, for example) and relaxation (parks and public green spaces).

Now fast forward to the 21st century where the environmentally friendly gardener is not just looking for functionality and beauty, but also for environmental sustainability. This poses a serious problem to a gardener as our most common garden plants have been introduced from Europe, Africa and Asia. The result has been some beautiful gardens, but also some beautiful but highly destructive weeds that are destroying natural ecosystems. This does not mean all non-native species are bad, but that as our environmental awareness increases so also do the challenges to introducing new plants into our gardens. Every year weeds prohibited by provincial governments are found for sale as ornamental species for our gardens. This is no one's fault but simply a common result of introducing new species to our environment. For example, no one knew that baby's breath left at a grave would produce a serious weed surrounding cemeteries on the Prairies. Let us consider using native plants and specifically native grasses. Native grasses will prevent the introduction of new weeds, provide host plants for wildlife, establish plant survival in our difficult Canadian climate and reduce the need for water and fertilizer.

Which native grasses and grass like species do I recommend? There are hundreds of species to choose from, but you will find an endless selection of unique and amazing species.

Tall Grass

Let's start with tall grasses. A grass standing over 2 m (6 ft.) tall in your garden is an impressive centre piece. One of my favourite species is giant wild rye (*Elymus piperii* or *Lymnus cenereus*). This large perennial bunch grass stands 2.5–3 m (8–10 ft.) tall and can easily handle zone 2–4 climates. Additionally, it is long lived (over 20 years). The environmental impact of this species includes improving duck habitat around prairie wetlands by providing shelter and improving soil moisture by acting as a snow catch during the winter. If you reside in a warmer climate (zone 3–4 and up) then there are some other large bunch grasses worth considering such as big bluestem (*Andropogon gerardii*) and switch grass (*Panicum virgatum*).

When considering your options for large grass or grass-like species around ponds there are a number of creeping species worth considering (i.e. softstem bulrush or great bulrush (*Scirpus validus*), panicled bulrush (*Scirpus microcarpus*), hardstem bullrush (*Scirpus acutus*), prairie cordgrass (*Spartina pectinata*), and bulrush or cattail (*Typha latifolia*).

Giant wild rye
(*Elymus piperii*)

Steven Tannas

These are large robust water loving plants that can be planted on a shore or planted out in the middle of the water. Managing creeping species is not for everyone, but if you are able to contain them in the right situation they are beautiful. Some of the most unique effects in a pond can include a large bulrush standing out in the middle of the water. These plants provide excellent habitat for ducks and numerous other water birds and are aesthetically pleasing.

If you are looking for a short grass-like specimen for around the edge of a small garden pond (dry regions less than 45 cm (18 in.) of annual precipitation) or anywhere within your garden (moist regions more than 45 cm (18 in.)) it is worth considering a bunch type sedge. Sedges are commonly confused with grasses, but can be easily differentiated by their triangular stems and unique seed heads. These unique features give sedges a beautiful look that is worth taking advantage of in a garden. Raynolds' sedge (*Carex raynoldsii*) is a beautiful sedge standing 30–70 cm (1–2⅓ ft.) tall with almost black seed heads that droop down. This species is well suited to growing within zones 1–3. By contrast, meadow sedge (*Carex praticola*) is a short sedge standing 20–70 cm (⅝–2⅓ ft.) tall with brown seed heads and is well adapted to growing in zones 2–4. While these two species are great examples of native sedges, there are

Steven Tannas

— Parry's oat grass (*Danthonia parryii*)

hundreds more growing in almost every environment in western Canada from which to choose.

Another species typically found in moist meadows or along the edges of wetlands is tufted hair grass (*Deschampsia caespitosa*). It has a beautiful feathery panicle (flower head) that puts on a great show in mid to late summer. In addition to the native variety, a number of tame varieties have been introduced that make an excellent show in a garden.

When considering species that are drought tolerant, you should definitely consider the spear or needle grasses. There are a number of species to choose from (i.e. western porcupine grass (*Stipa curtiseta*), needle-and-thread grass (*S. comata*), Richardson's or spreading needlegrass (*S. richardsonii*) and green needlegrass (*S. viridula*)), but any one can be very ornamental in the right situation. These species are known for their spear like seeds and can tolerant moderate to severe drought depending on the species you select. Currently my favourite needle grass is *Stipa richardsonii*. Featuring feathery seed heads, it puts on a beautiful summer show. Although this species is more adapted to zones 0–3 and prefers moderate to high soil moisture, it is likely that this species could be grown in warmer areas if watered appropriately. For dry locations, green needle grass and needle-and-thread are the best choices.

Bunch Grass

More of my favourite bunch grasses adapted to moderate to high soil moisture include foothills rough fescue (*Festuca campestris*), Parry's oat grass (*Danthonia parryii*), purple oat grass (*Schizachne purpurascens*), Idaho

Idaho fescue (*Festuca idahoensis*)

Steven Tannas

fescue (*Festuca idahoensis*) and purple reed grass (*Calamagrostis purpurascens*).

For a lush green lawn that is mowed every week, nothing can replace the decades of breeding that has gone into non-native species like Kentucky bluegrass and creeping red fescue. When considering an alternative, the best native options include bunch grasses like Idaho fescue and creeping species like blue grama grass (*Bouteolua gracilis*). Both of these species can handle moderate cutting but it is recommended that they be cut higher and less frequently than you would a traditional lawn. That said, a blue coloured lawn (*Festuca idahoensis*) is a great conversation piece.

If you like a sweet scent in your yard, then maybe sweet grass (*Hierocholoe odorata* syn. *Anthoxanthum nitens*) will provide what you are looking for. This aromatic species gives off a beautiful sweet smell every time it is cut. It is important to note that this species should be confined, as its roots are very aggressive, spreading up to 1 m (1 yd.) a year. Usually I dig a large hole in the ground, place a pot with no bottom in it, fill the pot with soil, a perfect barrier to prevent sweet grass from invading the rest of the garden.

For rock gardens I highly recommend a number of choices. Alpine bluegrass (*Poa alpina*) is one of the most unique bunch grasses in western Canada, hardly standing 10 cm (4 in.) tall and one that will not out-compete your flowers. Additionally, the use of species like Parry's oat grass (*Danthonia parryii*) and Idaho fescue (*Festuca idahoensis*) will provide beautiful features within a rock garden.

When planting native grasses remember if you select a species native to your location you do not have to amend the soil, water, or fertilize these plants. In many cases the grasses native to your location are the species that built your soils. Many of these species perform very well in poor soils. Selecting species adapted to poor fertility soils can reduce the management that is required of your garden. My best recommendation when considering native grasses is to take some time to learn about each species you plant. Make them a topic of conversation instead of just another plant in your garden.

Finally, you may think this all sounds great, but it is useless if you can't find these species. There are many native plant producers across western Canada and a simple online search will bring up growers like the Native Plant Society of Saskatchewan, the Alberta Native Plant Council or Nature Manitoba for lists of producers of native plants.

Steven Tannas

Sweet grass
(*Hierochloe odorata* or *Anthoxanthum nitens*)

When deciding where to buy plants I recommend that you find a grower with professional plant identification training. Many native plants available for purchase come from wild seed harvesting or private seed breeding programs, unlike tame species which are already classified and have gone through rigorous breeding programs. Therefore, the skill of the grower can directly impact the proper identification of the plant you are buying. ✿

Irrigation Tip

Adequate irrigation helps to prolong the bloom period of perennials, including those that are drought tolerant. Drip irrigation is an efficient, water-saving method. Place drip lines on the soil surface in the early spring where they will be concealed by plants as the season wears on. There is little or no runoff or evaporation as water is directed towards the plant's roots.

Growing Brewing Hops Commercially in Manitoba
by Sandra Gowan

*Sandra is the owner of Prairie GEM Hops of Manitoba.
The website can be found at www.prairiegemhops.com.*

I started growing hops (*Humulus lupulus*) as I wanted the challenge of growing something new. My initial goal was to find a viable niche crop for the area in which I live – I fell in love with this amazing plant! Perhaps Rebecca Kneen (hop grower from BC) planted the idea in my head when she shared her thoughts on how amazing the hops plant is. "Hops are a bit like orchids — not in the beauty of their flowers, but in the obsessions they create amongst growers."

My timing was good. In the last few years a small niche market has begun to open up for hop growers. Hops are an essential ingredient in beer, giving the beverage its aroma and bitterness, and also acts as a preservative because of its antimicrobial properties. There are more and more breweries opening across Canada. Many in the form of smaller microbreweries or craft breweries. Locally, recent changes to

Manitoban legislation make it easier to start up a microbrewery. Lastly, there is the growing desire for locally sourced ingredients.

The hops plant is described as a perennial vine, hardy down to zones 3–4. It has a chilling and dormancy requirement, so they cannot be grown too far south. It easily grows 5 m (15 ft.) or more in one season and dies completely to the ground after a hard frost. In spring the early shoots are visible as soon as the ground warms up.

There are many varieties of brewing hops – even one produced from a hops plant native to Manitoba. It has been used in breeding programs to create such varieties as 'Brewer's Gold'. Gardeners have grown the ornamental variety *Humulus lupulus* 'Aureus' or the related *Humulus japonicus* in their gardens for years.

Hops can be grown from seed, rhizomes or stem cuttings. If you want to grow hops for brewing, use only the female plants. A male plant may cross-pollinate different varieties and the fertilized flowers will produce seeds — undesirable from a brewing standpoint. The most common method of propagation is to use a rhizome or underground stem. This produces a plant genetically identical to the mother plant. Plant the rhizomes about 120 cm (4 ft.) apart as early as possible in the spring, to ensure a long growing season for the developing plant and its root system.

Hops require a long growing season. They require full sunlight, lots of moisture and nutrients, are susceptible to disease and do best if covered for winter protection. Just like any other crop they are adversely affected by weather conditions, such as wind, hail, drought or excess rain. The large surface area of the leaves, in particular, can become quite tattered.

Some varieties of hops require approximately 120 frost-free days to mature. The hops fruit (cone) is not frost tolerant so growing a late maturing variety such as 'Zeus', 'Brewer's Gold' or 'Magnum' which could encounter a frost prior to harvest, is not advised. Instead, earlier maturing varieties such as 'Fuggle', 'Hallertau', 'Sterling' or 'Willamette' might be better choices. Hops require 75 cm (30 in.) of moisture in one season. If you encounter a dry summer you will need to provide supplemental water. Moisture is best applied by a trickle or ground system. Hops are prone to fungal diseases such as mildew, so it is important to avoid wetting the foliage. Use a soaker hose that can be laid along the crowns and connected to a water source when needed.

Hops plants are heavy feeders and benefit from a fertile environment. A compost-rich soil works well to provide the proper nutrients. Hops will grow best in a well-drained soil or sandy loam with a pH of 6.5 to 7.0.

Growing hops commercially requires a lot of work! It starts in the early spring with planting new rhizomes, removing straw from existing crowns or harvesting rhizomes to sell to other growers. In early spring, select a few of the strongest shoots for training. Prune off the remaining tender shoots and try boiling or sautéing them in butter and seasoning, similar to how you would enjoy asparagus.

The hop vine needs a strong support on which to climb during the growing season. I use large wooden posts with steel cables to support their heavy growth. The 4 x 6 inch posts are sunk into the ground just over 1 m (4 ft.) below the surface. Additional beams are attached making the height of my trellis 4 m (12 ft.). Tall fence posts can also be used. A 1 cm (⅜ in.) steel cable is strung along the top of these beams. Strings are fastened to this cable for the bines to climb.

Yes, "bine" is the proper term for the hop vine. I use baler twine, but any coarse twine will do. The baler twine is biodegradable so it can be composted along with the bines after the harvest. Each plant needs a couple of strands on which to climb.

Training involves taking the strongest bines and initially wrapping them in a clockwise direction around the twine. Once they are started they will continue up this path without help. If you encounter a late spring frost and the early bines are damaged you will need to select new ones for training. Controlling the plant's undergrowth ensures the plant's energy is reserved for the bines selected for training and their subsequent flower production. Remove runners and lower foliage. If using a leaf desiccant, take care to not damage the plant. When the

bines reach the top of your trellis you can remove the bottom 90–120 cm (3–4 ft.) feet of foliage. This helps with disease control in a rainy season by promoting increased air circulation. The runners or growth from the rhizomes can also be tilled.

When the bines reach the top of the trellis they begin sending out horizontal shoots. Around midsummer, a change in day length triggers the plant to start forming burrs, the precursors to flowers or cones on these horizontal shoots.

Weed control throughout the growing season is important. Weeds steal moisture and nutrients from the hops plant. They blend like a chameleon in the heavy foliage. Weeds can also harbour diseases, which can infect the hops plant, or attract harmful insects such as aphids, thrips or spider mites.

When the cones are ready for harvest, usually late August or early September, they feel dry and papery to the touch. The characteristic hop aroma will be strong. When you pull apart a cone you will see the yellow lupulin powder, which is so important in brewing beer. There may be some brown petals on the cones but they should be picked before too much of the cone turns brown. Harvesting consists of cutting down the bines and removing the cones. The bines are be taken into a shed and manually stripped of their cones. The more hands the better when the time comes. Many an hour has been spent

Hops ready to harvest

Sandra Gowan

Hop loaded bine

with family picking cones and socializing! Bines can be manually stripped of their cones or equipment for large scale harvesting can be used to cut down the bines and remove cones. A mature hop plant can yield up to 900 grams (2 lbs.) of dried cones. Harvested hops deteriorate quickly so they must be carefully dried and packaged for storage. As soon as the cones are harvested they begin to lose important alpha acids and essential oils that are essential to beer through oxidation. Too much heat during drying can be detrimental. I use large screens above a fan, which draws ambient air for drying. When dried to about 8 –10% moisture the cones are weighed out and vacuum-sealed in packages ready for sale. Determine a cone's stage of dryness by bending it in half. If the little strig (branch) that holds the bracts breaks they are dry enough, if it bends they need more drying time.

Packaged hops are stored in a freezer and keep for several months with minimal to no deterioration. The lower the temperature the slower the rate of deterioration. Hops can also be pressed into plugs or processed into pellets. Processing involves the use of expensive equipment and the process must be done under cold conditions in order to preserve the quality of your crop. Breweries and microbreweries prefer to use processed hops.

Once the harvest is complete the hopyard must be prepared for winter and for next year's crop. The bines can be shredded and composted or they also make a good base similar to grape vines for wreath making. (Just shape them around a pail etc. and let them dry in that shape.) After the frost kills the remaining growth it can be trimmed close to ground level. Leave a few inches to help catch snow. Fall is a good time to add more compost to the crowns to provide nutrients for next year's growth. I cover the crowns with a generous amount of straw. If the crowns are not covered by straw or snow they could suffer winter-kill. In years where there is little snow this straw can make a world of difference on whether or not crowns survive a Manitoba winter.

A clean cereal straw such as wheat or barley is suitable for winter insulation. It serves a dual purpose: in the spring when it is removed from the emerging shoots it can be used as a mulch to help retain moisture and prevent weed growth. At the end of the season the straw can be worked into the soil where it provides a source of organic matter to improve soil tilth.

Hop plants can easily live 25 years. so a proper initial investment and commitment is needed.

The big question is this — if hops can be grown commercially in Manitoba, then why is it not being done? Until recently there hasn't been a demand by local breweries for local hops. With an increase in craft brewing and a trend to use locally-grown ingredients — I hope this is

about to change — although I do not envision large-scale hop production in Manitoba any time soon. That requires the creation of processing plants and an increased demand for processed hops by large local breweries. I predict an increase in hop production in Manitoba even if only on a small scale. Maybe you too would like to try growing hops if you have an acre or two available. 🐝

Note: For further reading see Page 99 of The 2002 Prairie Garden article *Growing your own Hops* by David Rudge. Also see page 71 in the 2003 issue of The Prairie Garden "Hops - An Historical Look at a Versatile Herb" by Susanne Olver.

My Favourite Perennial - the Lily
By Fran Wershler

Marilyn Latta

Counting the perennials in my flowerbed, it would appear that lilies are my most loved. I have always had some lilies, especially ones reminding me of the friends who gave them to me.

Then one summer my husband bought me a Black Jack lily in a pot and said, "You should grow more lilies." I have, and I obsessed about dark red ones, then white lilies with dark markings, then the tints and shades of red, rose and pink. The sunny beds have become larger and larger and I've lost count of the number. Brent Hunter of Neepawa once asked, "Fran when do we stop buying them?" I could not bear to think of that possibility.

The lily is most suited to growing on the Prairies. We have sunny summers, long autumns when we can divide them, or plant new bulbs, rains to settle the bulbs in, and wake them in spring, perfect lily growing conditions. Even with the advent of the red lily beetle they should survive since lily growers are out daily admiring new blooms and checking to see how their lilies are doing. Those daily checks are now a requirment to prevent lily beetle damage.

As gardens mature and shade gradually develops, we might think lily culture has to end, but 'No'. The Martagon lilies prosper in shaded and partly shaded areas. They are like orchids in dappled shade, showing a range of subtle tints and smaller blooms than the bold upfacing giants we now see in the Asiatics and newer crosses. Martagon lilies are just lovely. Yes lilies are my favourite perennial!

Designing With Perennials
The Art of Building Plant Communities
by Sue Gaviller

Groundcover: Mat forming groundcovers like this bearberry or kinnickinnick (*Arctostaphylos uva-ursi*) provide a neutral backdrop for larger shrubs and perennials. Groundcovers also provide living mulch which protects the soil from moisture loss and helps to control weed germination.

Sue teaches landscape design at the Calgary Zoo as well as running a landscape design consulting business. She blogs at <notanothergardeningblog.com>

As a design instructor and lecturer, one of the first things I tell students and workshop participants is that good design isn't so much about the use of plants as it is about the use of space. Therefore it seems unnatural for me to write about designing with perennials in a context all its own. Not that I don't love perennials and know them well – indeed, a good designer should have excellent and current knowledge of this vast group of plants. It's just that their use in landscape design actually comes at the end stage of the process, so before designing with perennials, I've first designed *for* them.

Since perennials take up space, gardeners must provide them a space that is fitting. We expect a lot from them. We insist they be show-stopping, long blooming, well behaved, and when they fail to provide what we

ask of them we blame the plant, when maybe we should look at their 'home life'. It goes without saying that their 'home' must provide all of their physical needs – light, water, air flow, good soil etc., but the actual space they occupy will visually define them, and they in turn define that space.

So I'm back to talking about space. Bear with me for a moment as I try to outline its importance. First, make sure your perennials have the space they need: room for company, more of their own kind, as well as larger neighbours (trees and shrubs), which allows them to appear in scale with their surroundings. Second, ensure the space provided allows them to fulfill their intended function; for example, if you want to look onto some planted beauty from your home office, place the beds within view. Third, the design lines you carve out can make or break your whole garden composition. Perennials can be used to accentuate good design lines (and bad ones) and good design lines will likewise highlight good perennial placement. Don't make the erroneous assumption that your garden beds must all consist of curved lines, there is a place for straight lines in garden design, too. When you use curved lines, opt for a few big bold curves, not a series of small weak ones. The eye loves to follow a long flowing line and conversely experiences discomfort when viewing too many changes in direction.

Assuming then, that your plants come from good lines (design lines that is), where do we go from there? Again, consider *space* — it can provide a starting point. For example, placing a plant that is more dominant (larger, showier, or more robust) in the space that is created by an arc or swell in a garden bed, can create an effective visual anchor. This dominant feature draws the eye and holds it, providing a visual resting place. If we consider the *function* of a given space, for example a private sitting area, we can use plants to define and enhance that space: something with a bit of height to act as a wall and maybe something that provides fragrance too. The microclimate of a particular space will also help us narrow our choice of plant material: astilbe (*Astilbe*) and Japanese painted fern (*Athyrium*), for example, will appreciate shady moist sites, while Russian sage (*Perovskia*) and beard's tongue (*Penstemon*) like it hot and dry.

As well, if we bear in mind the concept of space, it can help us utilize plants in a more purposeful fashion. A circular or semicircular space, say a patio or lawn area, could be completely bordered with a single type of perennial: a swath of daylily (*Hemerocallis*), catmint (*Nepeta*), perennial cranesbill (*Geranium*) or other similarly billowy choice repeated around the entire curve to emphasize the design lines. In fact all design lines can be emphasized in this way if so desired. Design lines

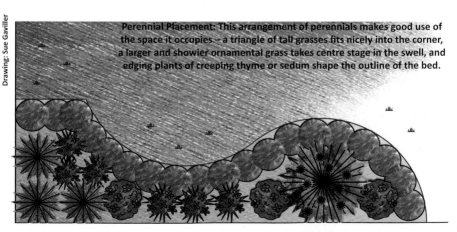

Drawing: Sue Gaviller

Perennial Placement: This arrangement of perennials makes good use of the space it occupies – a triangle of tall grasses fits nicely into the corner, a larger and showier ornamental grass takes centre stage in the swell, and edging plants of creeping thyme or sedum shape the outline of the bed.

can also be emphasized by alternating two or three different plants in a rhythmic pattern along the line.

Now that we've discussed the relationship between perennials and the space they occupy, let's talk about the visual relationship between perennials: colour, texture, and form.

Colour

Colour is what inspired many of us to start gardening in the first place and we mistakenly conclude that it is merely the colours of a garden that make it so lovely. We want season-long colour, bold colour and long-lasting colour. In time we realize that it's not all about bright colours. In fact we begin to long for more depth and substance in the garden, though we may not know exactly how to define that desire. Perhaps the essence we seek is *green* — that's right, plain old green. Green *is* a colour, one that has the power to soothe our senses as well as enrich and enliven our garden compositions. Indeed it should be the predominant colour in the garden, providing both a visual bridge between brighter colours and a most effective backdrop to stage those colours. Foliage then – dark green, mid green, light green – merits consideration when choosing perennials. Of course, there are perennials we choose specifically *for* their foliage, such as hostas, ornamental grasses, succulents and groundcovers.

Some of these foliage perennials

Pat Gaviller

Variegated Perennials: The variegated foliage of *Hosta*, *Lamiastrum* and *Euonymus*, as well as their textural contrast, create a charming picture.

aren't necessarily green, but instead, may be richly coloured red, purple, yellow, chartreuse, or even orange. Variegated foliage is also worthy of inclusion in your perennial border. Depending on the particular variegations, this foliage can be useful as a backdrop (softer, subtler variegations) or as a feature to draw the eye (brighter, bolder variegations). Whether green, variegated or brightly hued, adding foliage perennials to your garden provides consistent colour throughout the season.

A well thought out colour scheme can bring knock-out appeal to your garden composition. If you don't have a colour wheel, you can purchase one from an art supply store. It's a simple, but effective tool and will usually come with some accompanying written material on colour schemes. Give it a try and see what you come up with!

Texture

Plant texture can have a significant impact on overall garden aesthetics. Generally speaking, texture refers to the size and spacing of individual plant parts. Fine texture describes small leaves or flowers that are grouped closely together, while coarse texture describes large leaves or flowers spaced further apart. Perennials, more than any other plant group, have a vast range of textures, from very fine (*Thymus serpyllum* 'Elfin'), to very coarse (*Ligularia dentata*). Flower texture is greatly variable, from the tiny flowers of *Veronica whitleyi* to the very large blooms of *Paeonia*. Variation in texture is key: too much fine texture will end up looking busy and untidy. On the other hand, since coarse texture is visually quite dominant, too much of it will create competition for the viewer's attention. Feel free to use lots of fine and medium texture to build weightless volume, and punctuate it with coarse texture to anchor your plantings, as well as provide emphasis and contrast.

Texture also impacts colour. Fine textured flowers, *Achillea* for example, may appear to have less saturated colour, especially from a distance. This depends on how densely packed the flowers are – the more tightly packed, the more saturated the colour. For example, *Phlox douglasii* 'Crackerjack', has such a mass of flowers, jam-packed together that it appears as one block of colour. By and large, if counting on a particular flower to provide a real punch of colour, beefier flowers like *Hemerocallis* or *Iris germanica* are more effective. The smaller, finer textured flowers appear most intensely coloured when seen up close. Keep in mind each tiny flower has its own life span, and once a few of them start fading or dying off, it begins to desaturate the colour of the whole plant.

The reverse can be true as well, colour may alter perceived texture. Plants with variegations often appear to have finer texture, especially small closely spaced variegations. This effect decreases if the variegations consist of larger

Fine Texture vs. Coarse Texture: Fine textured flowers like this *Lavandula angustifolia* 'Hidcote', appear less intensely coloured than the larger *Iris germanica*, hence are best situated up close for maximum colour impact.

Pat Gaviller

blocks of colour, for example a hosta that has a green leaf edged in white or cream.

Form

Perennial plant form isn't as straight-forward as tree and shrub form because any given perennial may not always present the same form, changing as the season progresses. Nevertheless, perennials come in all shapes and sizes, and understanding the visual effects of each form can be helpful. Perennial shapes can be broken down into 4 basic groups: flat/mat, round/mound, spike/spire and fountain.

Pat Gaviller

Monochromatic planting: It is unique textures, rather than colour, that provides interest in this container planting. These three *Heuchera* 'Prince' were overwintered in the ground, allowing for them to be reused in the same container arrange-ments this year. Because the plants already had a mature root system, they doubled in size within a couple of weeks after replanting in pots.

Flat/Mat

These are low mat forming peren-nials that hug the ground. Visu-ally they act as a transition zone, connecting hardscapes or lawn to the garden and relating the scale of larger plants to the ground. Flat forms create a homogeneous backdrop for other features, making them useful for staging focal points or specimens. They can also unify a garden by interconnecting dissimilar elements – spreading groundcovers are particularly useful in this role.

- *Phlox subulata*
- *Thymus* spp.
- *Vinca minor*

Round/Mound

Rounded or mounding forms are a very common form, their soft neu-tral silhouette encouraging move-ment as the eye glides over them. They are suitable for widespread use in a garden composition, but the resultant undulating sight line, if not breached periodically with other forms, will create uncomfort-able visual movement – for me the experience can be akin to motion sickness.

- *Hosta* spp.
- *Campanula carpatica*

Spikes/Spires

This is a sizeable group with consid-erable variation, but in essence these are plants with a strong upright growth habit. Some are stiff, some supple, some are very vertical and some more vase-shaped, but all reach skyward, creating high points in the sight-line and providing con-trast to lower more neutral forms. This is the most dominant of the perennial plant shapes – the very tall varieties will actually arrest the flow of movement momentarily, saying 'stop and look at me!'

- *Calamagrostis acutiflora* 'Karl Foerster' (soft, vertical)
- *Iris germanica* (stiff, spiky)
- *Eupatorium purpureum* (upright vase)

Fountains

Plants that grow upward but then flare out and droop down are fountain shapes, a graceful form that lends elegance and style to a garden composition. They are lovely when massed, appearing as waves in the ocean, but their yielding form requires some solidity nearby to give visual support.

- *Hemerocallis* spp.
- *Sporobolis heterolepsis*

Some plants fall somewhere between one form and another; for example, some mat forming perennials are mound-like. As well, the foliage often fits into one group and blooms into another, for example *Liatris* foliage is fountain-like but the flowers are spire-like, so that when in bloom the overall effect is that of spires. *Iris* on the other hand has spiky upright foliage – even when in bloom, the overall effect is still essentially spiky. While all this presents a challenge, at any given time the key is to utilize plants of different height and form. This helps build a varied, but balanced line of sight.

For me, form and growth habit are the real determinants of a plant's continued presence in my garden – they must be handsome and well behaved season-long; no staking, tying or shearing required, or they are outta there!

Yes, we are hard on our perennials. We have high expectations of them, so let's give them a fighting chance – the right space, good company and a little time is all they need to reach their design potential. 🐾

Perennial Border: A well designed perennial border contains high points and low points, lightness and weight as well as moments of bright colour, bold texture and strong form amid an otherwise subdued composition

Planting Containers with Perennials

by Fran Wershler

Jane Reksten

Container planting is a good way to use to use a variety of plants, garden in small spaces, accent a doorway or gate, mark the edge of a patio, fill an empty corner, showcase a favourite plant, and it is less expensive than planting flowerbeds full of annuals. Greenhouse owners experiencing increasing costs pass the increase on to consumers on plant purchasing trips. For these reasons many gardeners now make planting in containers a favourite springtime event.

The 'look' for containers changes like runway fashions. Garden centres and magazines feature new looks for containers every year. Check out the ready-made containers for sale in local nurseries to choose a look you like or to see how a plant you are considering will work in your container. The 'hottest' look this year seems to include perennials.

"There was a time when dracaenas and red geraniums were very chic, but that was in the 1960's," said Lyndon Penner, an Alberta garden show commentator, at the 2012 Manitoba Horticultural Association Convention. Lyndon suggested that those 'spikes', together with the ubiquitous white alyssum, blue lobelia and yellow marigolds are now passé. Though each gardener has favourites, perhaps it is true that we choose the same ideas year after year and should try something different.

What can perennials do for your container plantings? First they offer colour, form and texture which annuals may not convey. Consider the colours in the leaves of coral bells (*Heuchera*) and use these beautiful plants in a foliage planter for colour usually provided by flowers. Supply exotic form or height to an urn planting with bold striped or dark red-green canna or elephant ear plants, (either green *Alocasia* or deep purple *Colocasia esculenta*). Iris, gladiola, calla and millet will also provide form and height. Ferns, grasses, lilies, parsley, lamium (*Lamium maculatum*), sedum, small daylilies (*Hemerocallis*), or any complimentary hosta add great texture. Many perennials offer leaf marking or variegation to complement other plants, and also the container. The gray leaved plants such as lamb's ears (*Stachys byzantine*), artemisia (*Artemisia stelleriana*) or any of the sage (*Salvia*) varieties sold in the herb section at the nursery, are very effective in containers. Hostas are attractive when a single clump is planted in a large pot.

The second reason to consider using perennials in pots and containers is to lift them out of the container and plant them in a flowerbed later in the summer or early fall. It is possible to remove one plant that does not thrive or look well after the container has been on display for a while. Replace it with another plant with the help of a small spade.

Growing plants in containers requires a careful approach to container selection, the growing medium and regular maintenance. Large containers are necessary for large plants and dry out more slowly than smaller ones. Clay or terracotta pots look attractive, drain and breathe well. Plastic pots work well for hanging plants and are light weight, but dry out quickly. Black plastic or metal trap heat and cause drying and overheating of the root systems. Newer forms of plastic and resin-blended pots are thicker so they offer more insulation. The most expensive pots are glazed pottery or ceramic that may work well in warmer zones, but on the prairies they must be emptied and preferably moved inside for the winter to avoid cracks from moisture and frost. The most important criterion in a container is drainage, and many pots do not have enough drainage holes in them. Holes about 1.25 cm (½ in.) in diameter can be drilled in all kinds of pots, though ceramic, clay or pottery may require a hole drilled with a masonry bit.

Fill a container with a good growing medium. The most successful containers are given new soil every year since many plants in a small space use most of the nutrients in the pot over one season. Garden centres sell a 'soilless mix' which they prefer for their starter plants and containers. It is sterile, contains no disease, and it is light, but contains few nutrients. It must be fertilized at planting time with a slow release fertilizer and given

A single Hosta is visually effective in a container

Jane Reksten

water-soluble fertilizer once or twice a month. Its light weight makes it useful for hanging planters, but awkward for large planters containing wind-susceptible large plants. Some people mix bagged potting soil, compost and sand or perlite in equal quantities, or fill the centre of the pot with potting soil surrounded with soilless mix. Choose a soil mix to suit your purpose and stir a slow release fertilizer into the soil.

Once the soil is mixed and the container filled try arranging your chosen plants in their pots on top of the soil. Move them around to determine the final placement and combination and then start planting using a small trowel. Tip a pot upside down in one hand with your fingers around the plant stem(s) and tap the edge of the pot on a hard surface to loosen the plant. If roots have thickened into a mat in the bottom of the pot, cut that portion away or loosen the roots on the sides before inverting the plant into position. A common approach is to crowd the plants in the container so that they look lush right from planting time and place plants closer together than you would in a flowerbed. Gently pack the soil around all the plants and water to settle the roots.

Once you have planted your containers, regular care with watering, fertilizing and cleaning begins. Initially they may not need watering every day since the need for water depends on the size of the

Fran Wershler

Hens and chickens (*Echeveria*) taken from perennial clusters to blend with less hardy purchased succulents.

container, whether it is in sun or shade, the material of which the container is made, and the weather. When you can insert a finger into the soil and feel dryness, it is time to water. Slow release fertilizer lasts a few weeks, but regular watering with a weak solution of water and water soluble fertilizer may be used with every watering or, when mixed according to directions, this fertilizer could be used every two weeks. Regular watering is necessary, but it may wash out some nutrients your plants require to grow and bloom. (note: not all nutrients are soluble in water like nitrogen which has more tendency to wash out) Dying leaves, failure to bloom, or smaller, fewer blooms attest to the need for fertilizer. Remove dead flowers, dead leaves and prune unruly stems. When you water it is also a time to inspect for insects and disease and decide upon a course of action.

Perennials in planters provide summer enjoyment, and in the fall many of them may be relocated to add interest to your perennial border for next year.

Banana plant

Sandy Venton

Bring It All Inside in the Fall - Overwintering Potted Perennials and Tropicals

by Kath Symth

Kath is a well-known Calgary-based horiculturist with over 35 years of industry experience. She has been featured on radio, TV, and as a regular speaker at both the Calgary and Edmonton Home and Garden Shows. Currently she is the Horticulturist for the Calgary Horticultural Society.

You have gone through a great deal of effort to make an exotic garden with the addition of tropical plants that you would normally only find inside a northern home, creating a soothing oasis of foliage and blooms during the growing months. As well, you may have some expensive and fussy potted perennials you wish to preserve that otherwise might not survive your plant hardiness zone. As the air cools and fall approaches, you wonder if it is possible to overwinter these for the following year. It certainly is, with a little planning and foresight.

Before owning a garden, I had a wide variety of houseplants. When I finally started tending my own patch of earth, I began growing tropicals in a variety of pots and assorted containers. The bright colours, big leaves,

and dramatic leaf shapes added a striking element to my garden. There is nothing tricky about growing tropicals in containers as long as you offer them appropriate soil, nutrients, and water. The challenge faced come the fall is to figure out how to keep them alive and prepare them to grow the following spring. It's important to plan a strategy for your fall gardening endeavour, anticipating how to bring your plants inside without inflicting too great a shock on them, or worse, bringing in unwanted hitchhikers such as insects.

Since I do not have a greenhouse, which would be ideal, I have tried, and failed, with several methods for overwintering plants. I mainly store them dormant in the basement where winter temperatures are cold but stay above freezing. Some plants stay in an unheated spare room, and some in the living room. However, I have learned that many plants can survive winter storage without light, water, and even soil. Eventually, I developed a number of methods that helped preserve my treasured tropicals and a variety of potted perennials that otherwise might not survive a winter on the prairies. Overwintering tender plants in a cool, dark area is my preferred method because it requires virtually no effort during the winter months. If you don't have a basement, you could try an unheated sun porch, attic, or garage. Many tropical plants have a natural dormant period, triggered not by the onset of winter but by the arrival of a dry season. If you can trick plants into thinking a dry season is coming, they will ease into dormancy. It is important, however, to treat bulbous plants (grown from tubers, rhizomes, or bulbs) slightly differently from plants with fleshy leaves and stems.

How cold your winters are and to what lengths you are willing to go to protect your containers are major deciding factors. One of the tricks to overwintering is to find the right place for the right plant. Some like a sunny place by a window, while others want a cool, dark place. Keep in mind that some plants are easier to overwinter than others; some are simply more trouble than they are worth. Most of all, you do not want to wait until a frost warning has you running around your garden gather-

ing plants you want to save. Here are some guidelines to successfully overwintering a variety of your valuable potted tropicals and perennials.

Borderline-hardy herbaceous perennials

Plants such as hellebores and some of the fancy foliage heucheras usually die back and are dormant in winter, while their roots sleep until it's time for new growth next spring. The goal is to maintain dormancy and provide a winter home so they will not die off. After the first frost, water plants well. Cut away any dead foliage and prune back woody perennials once the leaves drop.

At this point you can choose to leave it alone and take the risk that it will survive in your pot as is. However, even if your pot is really big and the plant is hardy within your zone, or zones lower, the likelihood of successfully overwintering the pot outdoors is not good. The reason is that although large containers hold more soil and can help insulate roots and keep soil temperatures consistent, when sunshine hits the pot (especially a dark-coloured one) alternate freezing and thawing may occur. Plants think it is spring which then triggers early growth, when it may instead be merely a brief warm period in February.

For those plants on the edge of hardiness for your zone, a more successful strategy is to dig the plants up and repot. They can be stored in a dark part of the basement, near the warmest wall of the garage, or in an unheated spare room. A root cellar is ideal. Because the plants are dormant, light isn't required, but check periodically to make sure the soil isn't bone-dry. Keep soil just moist all winter. Maintain them at 7–10° C (44–50° F) as normal room temperature is too hot and can't provide the critical rest these plants need.

When growth resumes in late winter/early spring, re-introduce your plants to normal growing conditions outdoors by gradually exposing containers to the elements for increasing periods of time.

Alternatively, for the hardier specimens you can use large Styrofoam picnic coolers. Move them into a sheltered spot, out of wind and sun. Group together the hardiest plants on the outside and the tenderest ones in the centre. For extra protection, pile leaves around the pots in the cooler, but leave the top open for air circulation.

Another method of preserving hardy perennials is to select an area such as the vegetable garden, where you can sink the pot in the ground up to its rim so that the roots will be better insulated. Cover the whole plant with about 15 cm (6 in.) of mulch, bark, or leaves. Come spring, remove the mulch and lift out your container.

Tip - Make sure you know the winter hardiness of your pots. Soil-filled containers exposed to long-term freezing and thawing may crack. Pots made of earthenware, ceramic or terracotta will not tolerate soil left in them. Concrete, wood, plastic, and metal are a little better but the last two offer little insulation for plant roots.

Tubers, corms, and bulbs

Tender summer-flowering bulbs such as dahlias, cannas, callas, gladiolus, and anemone, as well as caladiums, and elephant's ears can be preserved over the winter, with a little attention. The goal is to store the tubers so they neither rot from too much moisture or dry out completely and die.

Before the first frost in the fall trim the stems to within 15 cm (6 in.) from the base then carefully dig up summer-flowering bulbs, corms, tubers, and rhizomes. Let them dry for a day or two, then store in vermiculite in a box. Before putting roots or rhizomes in their box, prepare as follows:

- Shake off the soil—whatever falls off easily is enough.
- Trim back the foliage, brush off the soil, and lay them out in a dry, airy, warm place for two weeks.
- Turn the bulbs every couple of days in order to dry them thoroughly.
- Watch closely. If they look crinkly it can indicate excessive dryness. If needed, mist lightly with water.
- Divide if necessary and place in a cool, dark area such as the basement to overwinter. The storage container depends on the type of bulb, corm, or tuber. Gladioli and any bulbs with a papery husk

should be placed in mesh bags with plenty of air circulation.

- *Tip: Save mesh bags that oranges and grapefruit come in from the grocery store for this purpose.*
- Throw away any that show signs of rot, as rot and fungal diseases can run rampant through bulbs, rhizomes, and especially tubers if they are stored while damp.
- When preparing dahlias and canna lilies, the entire top of the plant should be cut off at the base. Dahlias, cannas, caladiums, and tuberous begonias can be stored uncovered in either trays or boxes loosely filled with vermiculite. Check every month.

Tender evergreens and tropicals

Overwintering speciality plants means big savings in your wallet and big displays for your garden next year. In the winter months, tropical and some of the common evergreen culinary plants have a slower growth rate instead of going dormant so they require lower light levels and less water. Examples include bay tree, rosemary, French tarragon, phormium, mandevilla, passion flower, brugmansia, bananas and jasmine. Your goal is to try to slow the growth of these plants so they can survive indoors during the winter in order to be put outside again once all danger of frost has passed.

Before fall frosts are expected, re-pot and put them in a shady spot about two weeks before taking indoors. Acclimatize them before moving indoors or the stress could cause leaf drop. Introduce your plants to life indoors by moving them inside for half a day, and work up to a full day over a week. Do not wait until night time temperatures are only slightly above freezing. These plants will go into shock and drop leaves.

Do a gentle pruning. Place them in the sunniest spot you have. Water regularly over the winter. High humidity helps, too. Don't fertilize until just before you reintroduce them to outdoor living.

As temperatures warm in the spring, tropical plants should go outside for three or four hours for a couple of days, gradually increasing the length of time every other day. It can take about a week before you can put them in full sun, and another week before they can stay out over night, providing temperatures are 10 degrees C above freezing.

Borderline-hardy deciduous shrubs, small trees, and vines

With plants such as miniature roses, standard roses, and Japanese maples, the stems, branches, and trunks of these plants persist over winter, but the leaves drop off in the fall. Your goal is to keep the plants dormant, within range of winter temperatures they would tolerate if grown in the garden. Woody plants have above-ground branches that hold next year's flower and leaf buds, making them more susceptible to

Boxwood and ivy

Jane Reksten

winter winds than herbaceous perennials. It's better to store them in an unheated garage, against the warmest wall. Place them in a big bucket filled with dry leaves for even more insulation – do not put a lid on it. Light may trigger growth so do not place near a window. Check soil monthly to make sure it's not bone-dry. Do not overwater, as this could cause plants to rot or break dormancy.

Broad-leafed and needle evergreens

Plants such as boxwoods, English ivy, cedars, junipers, and yews transpire (lose water) during the winter so when temperatures remain below freezing for long periods, root balls freeze solid and water is not readily available to the plant. This causes leaf damage or death. The goal is to protect them from strong winter sun

and winds. A burlap screen around them helps provide protection, but do not allow burlap to touch foliage.

Keep watering until freeze-up. Check throughout the winter to make sure the soil is moist. Water prior to freezing temperatures and again in March and April, when the root balls might thaw — a critical time.

Tender perennials - grown as annuals here

This applies to geraniums, coleus, and impatiens. First, decide if it is worth your time and effort to maintain these plants over the winter. Most are easily acquired at a reasonable cost in the spring. If you choose to continue growing these plants indoors to use again next year, trim back individually potted plants and place in a cool sunny location or under grow lights. You may also choose to take cuttings of your favourites and start new plants indoors. By the following spring, they will be large enough for containers.

Aquatics

The tender crowns, tubers, and roots of your aquatic plants need to be protected from freezing. You can move hardy water lilies to the deeper end of the pond about 60 cm (2 ft.) down. Tender specimens must be removed before the first frost. Lift the

Tip - Tightly wrapped burlap does plants more harm than good by holding ice against their branches. To protect them from wind or household dryer vent emissions, set up stake-and-burlap barriers, then fasten with large utility pins.

plants out of the pond. Cut back and discard any old, yellowing leaves then store the plants in damp sand. Keep them in a cool and dark location. A temperature down to 5° C (42° F) is ideal. To keep air flowing and plants damp, cover containers with a perforated plastic sheet. Tropical aquatics such as umbrella palm, papyrus, and arum lilies will continue to grow by a sunny window if kept moist.

Finally, here are some tips I refer to as horticultural triage:

- Water whenever the soil dries out.
- Rotate the pots to the window every few weeks so the plants don't stretch on one side toward the light.
- Provide additional humidity by grouping the plants together. Dry indoor air causes problems for tropicals. Put the plants atop trays filled with gravel and water just the gravel periodically.
- Turn the thermostat down to 16–18° C (mid-60's° F), especially at night. In early March, start using half strength fertilizer every two weeks.
- Tropicals that have summered outdoors like hibiscus or calamondin oranges should be checked for pests and treated if necessary. Use insecticidal soap for aphids and whitefly; use rubbing alcohol on a cotton swab for scale and mealy bug before bringing plants indoors. You can expect some leaf drop while they acclimatize.

- Although most plants in cool, bright settings don't grow much at all and appear in a kind of suspended animation, a few eventually drop all their leaves. If that happens, move them right into cool, dark storage to ride out the rest of the winter. This is where I often discover which plants can enter a deep dormancy akin to that experienced by plants native to my setting.

Overwintering requires a nominal investment of time and energy, but also preserves the investment you have made in your potted perennials and tropicals. With a little effort, you will have beautiful plants rebound in the spring to enjoy for another summer season and your pocket won't be the lighter for it. 🐾

Valerie Denesiuk

Aquatics in a pond ◄

Ghosts of Summer: Leave Them Standing

by Barbara Kam

Barbara Kam is owner of **Edenscapes Garden Maintenance Services** *in Calgary and the* co-author of *The Prairie Winterscape: Creative Gardening for the Forgotten Season.*

Come the first hard frost, many gardeners chop back perennials and put their gardens to bed. This gives a sense of accomplishment before going indoors for the long wait till the next growing season. We admire how "snug and ready for spring" everything looks, tucked in and put away under a blanket of snow. But here on the prairies, we don't experience the four seasons by the neat, even quarters shown on the calendar. By virtue of our northern geography our winter experience endures more than three months so that not long after the first thrill of fall clean-up the garden can look flat, boring and two-dimensional.

Consider leaving some of your perennials standing for the winter to counteract the monotonous view. The plant tops provide changes in height and texture for visual interest. Some seed heads attract birds adding the dimensions of sound and movement to the frosty scene. Even plants bent and buried under the weight of snow add contour and undulations to the landscape. Plants left standing also mark the passage of time: as certain stems begin to bend and disintegrate, you know that spring is just around the corner. The once-living plants may not provide the bright colours and glamour of the earlier seasons, but their ghosts remind us of what was and what will be.

Why do things twice? Perennials left standing will help trap snow just as well as a 10–15 cm (4–6 in.) stalk. It's a time saver for home gardeners because you only cut back a plant once in the spring rather than once in fall and again in spring. All the leaves and stems can then trap snow for insulation and provide a home for overwintering ladybugs. After the plant has weathered the winter, clean up may be as simple as raking over shorter plants or a twist-and-tug to remove the old stems without need to employ your secateurs (pruning shears).

You can leave almost every plant for spring cleanup, but if you are not sure you want to fully embrace the tousled look, you can pick your spots and decide which plants will haunt your winter garden. Choose those plants that you can see and enjoy from your window and as you navigate the walkways to your home, garage and utility area. Perennials that flower later in the season usually make the strongest winter statements. Later blooming plants are typically taller than earlier bloomers so their heads peek above the snow line. Choose strong, healthy plants from your borders that are not vigorous self-sowers for winter interest. Plants that didn't require staking in your summer garden are more likely able to support a crown of snow without breaking. (Every garden is different and those beds sheltered from the wind will have a broader range of plants that are less likely to be knocked down). Plants that really struggled with insect pests or disease should be cut back and the debris removed to minimize overwintering pathogens and insect eggs. Finally, consider how vigorously the plant self sows and the impact on your future workload. Mulch and periodic quick passes with a cultivator through the garden bed during summer can battle the progeny of most self-sowers.

Grasses are the stars of the winter perennial bed. Look to feather reed grass cultivars (*Calamagrostis acutifolia* cvs.) like 'Karl Foerster', 'Avalanche' or 'Eldorado' to stand tall through all but the harshest winds and heaviest snowfalls. Consider also purple moor grass (*Molinia* spp.) or flame grass (*Misconstrues sinensis* 'Purpurescens'). In spring, tie string around the stalks at the base and mid-height before cutting for easy clean up. Evergreen blue oat grass which does not need to be cut back in spring provides a spiky rounded contrast to the taller grasses.

Even perennials that need a bit of shade can stand tall for most of the cold season. The flower stalks of ligularia 'The Rocket' and other spiky cultivars soar to great heights. Just as gardens are a matter of taste and preference, some gardeners will leave the daisy-like ligularias' flower stalks. Depending on how the wind blows and snow drifts in your garden, you may have luck with the lacy remnants of goatsbeard or taller astilbes.

Jane Reksten

Most grasses, hardy and tender, offer good winter interest.

Spiky seed heads are great in the winter garden. Echinacea is an excellent choice to leave standing, not only for winter interest, but also as a marker for spring since it is a bit slow with its reappearance. Globe thistle is also great in the winter and birds seem to like the seed heads. While sea holly seems to fit all the requirements for winter interest, be forewarned that it is a prolific self-seeder and you will have babies to either weed or share with friends.

Taller sedums like 'Autumn Joy', can look like snow-covered mushrooms. They are one of the few broad topped plants that can support a crown of snow without snapping. Those plants with narrower, lacy or spiky flowers like liatris, goldenrod and Russian sage also stand up well. Two plants from earlier in the growing season with attractive seed heads include Siberian iris and peonies. Most people remove spent peony blossoms, but if you didn't get around to it you can leave the stalks in place until spring and enjoy the seed heads as they turn a dark, warm brown.

You can watch the garden as it ages in the non-growing season and the stalks and leaves wear down. The slow disintegration helps mark the passage of time until spring arrives. Those who find it a little too messy before spring really arrives, can put on their boots on a sunny day and do some pre-Spring clean-up. ❧

A list of perennials that look good in the winter garden:

Botanical Name	Common Name
Artemisia ludoviciana	Prairie sage
Aruncus dioicus	Goatsbeard
Astilbe spp.	Astilbe
Calamagrostis acutiflora	Feather reed grass
Cimicifuga racemosa	Bugbane
Echinacea purpurea	Purple coneflower
Echinops ritro	Globe thistle
Eupatorium spp.	Joe Pye
Helicotrichon sempervirens	Blue oat grass
Iris siberica	Siberian iris
Liatris spicata	Gayfeather
Ligularia stenocephala	Ligularia
Miscanthus sinensis 'Purpurascens'	Flame grass
Molinia caerulea	Purple moor grass
Monarda didyma	Beebalm
Paeonia	Peony
Panicum virgatum	Switch grass
Papaver orientalis	Oriental poppy
Perovskia atriplicifolia	Russian sage
Phlomis fruticosa	Jerusalem sage
Sedum x 'Autumn Joy'	'Autumn Joy' sedum
Solidago	Goldenrod
Verbascum spp.	Mullein
Yucca filamentosa	Yucca

Winter Coverage of Perennials

by Rita Campbell

Rita gardens indoors and out in Winnipeg, Manitoba.

Often the selection at garden centres will include for sale a certain number of perennials that are more suited to warmer climes and therefore, are not able to survive our prairie winters. When attracted to a plant with which you are unfamiliar, it is wise to check the plant tag first or research it in garden books or on the internet to determine if the plant is suited to growing under prairie conditions. Gardening zones in the Prairies range between zone 2–3 (http://sis.agr.gc.ca/cansis/nsdb/climate/hardiness/intro.html). If purchasing a plant that is advertised as zone 4–5, and you plan to overwinter it outdoors, identify a suitable microclimate in your yard.

A microclimate may be a planting space beside your house that has a different environment than an unprotected area in the centre of your yard. Consider a number of options for overwintering plants. Trial and error is the best way to determine which method works best for which plant. Splitting a plant, when possible, by planting it in two different areas and using different methods of cover, is a good way to determine what works best. A more tender plant placed beside a house and well covered might thrive even though it is not compatible with a prairie climate.

Sinking pots in soil: This technique works well if you want to have cedars or hostas in pots year after year rather than growing them directly in soil. In the fall, after harvesting your garden, sink the pot in soil at least to the level of the soil in the pot. Fill in any spaces around the pot with more loose soil. Leave the potted plants

Peony just coming up from a pot sunk in the soil

Rita Campbell

in the garden as long as possible in the spring, lifting them when you plant your garden. Plants can remain in pots like this for years, until they become root-bound. Remember to fertilize annually in order to replace nutrients in the soil.

Leaf cover: Using leaf cover as a protective mulch layer is a popular method of covering perennials; it is also the least work—just don't rake leaves off the perennials in the fall. There are two main drawbacks to this method. If the leaves exhibit disease or insect problems, leaving them lying on the ground can cause them to infect a new plant or increase the infection on the original host plant. It is also easier to rake dry leaves off perennials in the fall without much damage than to remove wet leaves after the winter. If the leaves are not removed early enough in the spring they can

either create a damp mat suffocating the perennial or, if the perennial has started to grow, soft new growth can be damaged by raking.

Evergreen branches: If you have a healthy evergreen that needs pruning in the fall, boughs can serve as easy cover for perennials. Gently lay them over the plants in layers thick enough to provide protection from the elements.

Burlap wraps: Taller plants such as cedars can be wrapped directly with burlap, but the plant needs to be strong enough to withstand the weight of snow. For less sturdy plants, three stakes can be placed in a triangular shape around the plant, securing the burlap to the stakes. For even more delicate plants mulch can be placed inside the wrap, but this must be removed in the spring after the weather warms before the mulch forces the plant to stay too wet and rot.

Styrofoam cones: For smaller plants Styrofoam cones can be quite convenient, but there must be enough space between plants for the base of each cone. Placing a weight on the cone will prevent it from blowing away before it has a snow cover.

Pre-formed tent covers: Available in a variety of sizes, pre-formed tent covers have pegs which hold them into the ground. For added insulation, apply mulch around the plant.

Straw covering: One of the most common forms of plant protection is to apply straw such as flax straw for winter protection. One

Pre-formed tent cover with pots sunk in the ground in front of it

Rita Campbell

of the problems with this method is that seeds left on the straw may sprout in your perennial garden.

Floating row cover with straw: This is a new method for covering relatively low growing perennials. Purchase garden fabric or floating row covers made from a synthetic fabric used to protect plants from pests. First, lay the white floating row cover on your plants when temperatures begin to drop to freezing. Once plants are dormant in the fall and the ground has frozen, lay a thick covering of straw on top of the white fabric. In the spring, this will keep the ground frozen long after the rest of the ground has thawed. After snow-melt, periodically check the soil temperature under the cover, replacing the cover if the ground is still frozen. Once you have determined that the ground is thawing, roll the floating row cover off the garden and gather up the straw. The row cover can then be replaced on the garden to equalize day and night temperatures until warmer summer days arrive. If you are industrious, the cover can be rolled off on nice days and replaced at night. The purpose of the floating row cover is to protect plants during the growing season allowing light and water to pass through and can be left on as long as you allow room for plants to grow underneath.

The main reason for winter-kill of perennials is the combination of drying winds followed by the heat of the sun which thaws the plant even though temperatures are still extremely low. Air circulation and available moisture are important to the plant's health, especially when the plant starts to re-grow in the spring. Bags of leaves can also be used to lay on plants but they too must be removed before they cause the plant underneath to rot from lack of air circulation.

If a heavy layer of snow falls before you have had time to do any of the above, don't despair. Snow is a great insulator. In the spring try to keep snow on the plants which are not protected. If a lot of the snow melts but it is not time for the plants to start growing, you can still lay some kind of cover on top of the snow which will protect the plants until the spring.

Of course, on the prairies we have learned to expect the unexpected. For example, even though the dusty miller is supposed to be an annual unless you live in zone 6–7, one winter when the snow fell fast, heavy, and early (before my gardens were prepared for the fall) dusty millers survived the winter and re-grew in the spring. Some years, hardy perennials do not survive the fluctuating temperatures of our winters, and a yearly favourite will suddenly disappear. However, in the fall when you think it might be nicer to live in a warmer climate, just remember—they can't grow peonies in Southern California. 🐦

Flowering Onions

by David Punter

Allium flower

David Punter is a Senior Scholar with the Department of Biological Sciences, University of Manitoba. His research has focused on diseases of forest trees and wild rice.

For most people the name 'onion' makes them think of tears in the kitchen rather than heads of attractive flowers in the perennial border. This is unfortunate, for many *Allium* (onion) species warrant the attention of the prairie flower gardener. These bulbous perennials, mainly natives of the Mediterranean and north temperate regions, are generally hardy on the prairies and relatively free from most pest and disease problems. They provide a good show from late spring to mid-summer and, by offering a range of colours and sizes, can blend into a variety of situations in the garden. Their bulbs, which multiply quite freely, are inexpensive and require little attention.

The majority of *Allium* species suitable for the prairies have similar preferences to tulips; namely a sunny location, rich loamy soil that offers good drainage, and plenty of water in the spring when most of their growth is taking place. They benefit from light feeding while their flower-heads are expanding. After flowering, as the leaves gradually die back and new bulbs ripen, watering is not recommended.

Several low-growing species are well suited to the rock garden or grouped toward the front of the perennial border. These include:

- *A. oreophilum* (*A. ostrowskianum*) – carmine pink, 15cm (6 in.)
- *A. moly* – golden yellow, 25cm (10 in.) and two native species,
- *A. textile* – white/pale pink, 15-20 cm (6-8 in.)
- *A. schoenoprasum* var *sibiricum* – bright rose/purple 30cm (12 in.)

This last species is chives, whose leaves are widely used as a mild onion flavouring in salads and dips. All of this group bloom early, in late May to early June. Most of the remaining candidates are of medium height and offer a succession of bloom later in the season:

- *A. aflatunense*- purple/lilac, 75 cm (30 in.), followed by,
- *A. cowanii* – white, 50 cm (20 in.), and
- *A. albo-pilosum* – pale lilac, 60 cm (24 in.).

Toward the end of June and in July:

- *A. caeruleum* – sky-blue, 60–75 cm (24-30 in.)
- *A. sphaerocephalon* – rose/purple, 90 cm (35 in.).

Finally, from July to September, two native prairie species:

- *A. stellatum* – rose pink, 30-70 cm (12-28 in.)
- *A. cernuum* – rosy white, 30-60 cm (12-24 in.).

All the native species can be obtained as seed from their natural locations. Others are available as bulbs for fall planting from local garden suppliers or Fraser's Thimble Farms <www.thimblefarms.com>. Prices range from $3.00/20 and up.

This article would not be complete without a mention of *A. giganteum*, truly the giant of the genus, with its broad leaves and large heads, up to 20 cm (8 in.) in diameter with rosy pink flowers on stems that may reach 2 m (6½ ft.) in height. Despite the assertion in some catalogues that this species is 'ruggedly hardy', I suspect that it is not well adapted to prairie conditions as I have had little success overwintering it, even in the city. The price of bulbs, $8.00 each, is also a deterrent but the adventurous may nevertheless want to give it a try. 🐦

Allium moly

Allium textile

all photos David Punter

Allium oreophilum

Spring Flowers for Naturalizing

by David Punter

D
o you have a piece of lawn or a grassy bank that needs livening up? If so, consider giving it a treatment with bulbs that naturalize well — ones that come up year after year and increase with time. For our region I would particularly recommend *Scilla sibirica* (Siberian squill) and *Chionodoxa luciliae* (glory of the snow), both of which have proven to be completely hardy in my garden, tolerate shade very well, and spread by seed quite rapidly once they are established. Their bulbs should be planted in the fall in small groups about 8–10 cm (3–4 in.) below ground. Both grow to about 10 cm (4 in.) in height and in most years have finished flowering before the grass needs cutting. If possible, the leaves should not be mown until they have turned brown.

Another good bet is the genus *Narcissus*, especially *Narcissus pseudonarcissus* (common daffodil), cultivars 'King Alfred' and 'St. Patrick's Day'. They should be planted in fall, in groups of three or four, 10 cm (4 in.) apart and with the bases of the bulbs about 18 cm (7 in.) below ground level. These varieties grow up to 40 cm (16 in.) tall and flower in mid spring. Their leaves

persist until late May so you need to mow around the clumps until they die down. Other *Narcissus* species, such as *N. poeticus* (pheasant's-eye) and *N. cyclamineus* (dwarf daffodil) also naturalize well.

Because of their early maturity, all these species do well under trees. The bulbs are usually available in bulk from local garden centres or home improvement stores. They range in price from $4 for 20 to $40 a hundred.

I have also tried *Leucojum aestivum* (snowflake), *Galanthus nivalis* (snowdrop), *Muscari botryoides* (grape hyacinth), *Fritillaria meleagris* (snake's-head lily), *Ixiolirion tataricum* (Siberian lily) and *Crocus* species. but with less success. They appear to be less hardy and do not persist well in our area.

There are other spring-flowering native plants that provide ground cover and interest in deep shade. These include *Sanguinaria canadensis* (bloodroot), whose orange juice has been used to treat skin problems such as ringworm and eczema; *Asarum canadense* (wild ginger), useful as a substitute for true ginger, a mild stimulant and an appetizing salad; and *Trillium cernuum* (nodding trillium). All of these naturalize well. ❧

Un-named lily #2

Wendy Daley

A Quest to Find the Ultimate Garden Lily
by Wendy Daley

Wendy is an instructional assistant with the School of Environment at Olds College at Olds, AB

Olds College has been working with the Alberta Regional Lily Society for a number of years, so when the suggestion came to trial a lily for the College's 2013 centennial, it seemed like a perfect fit.

The journey began in the fall of 2008 when four hybridizers, all members of the Alberta Lily Society, donated Asiatic lily seedlings that they thought had potential. The total donation was a minimum of three bulbs each of 13 different unregistered Asiatic lily cultivars.

To not lose track of this precious gift, the bulbs were planted in rows, 30 cm (12 in.) between bulbs and 1 m (3 ft) between rows. A metal underground name tag was placed beside each bulb. For extra measure we labelled wooden stakes at the end

of each row as well as a wooden stake at each bulb and put the planting plan on an computer spread sheet.

For the next three years each lily would be evaluated in the hopes of finding the next most stunning introduction. But what would the ultimate selection for the centennial lily look like? If we wanted a "good" garden lily what traits did we need to look for?

A few of us sat down and discussed the traits we thought made a good garden lily. Our 'must-have list' included hardy to zone 2b, sturdy stems, long blooming time, high bud count and low susceptibility to disease. What about colour? It seems as if, like cars and clothing, flower colour trends changes year to year. One year everyone will want yellow. The next year people are sick of yellow and pink seems to be the colour of choice. Could we possibly guess what the flavour of the year would be in 2013? The height of an Asiatic lily can range from 25 cm to 1.2–1.5 m (10 in. to 4–5 ft.). We discussed whether one height was more desirable than another and decided all had a place in the garden. Flower orientation on Asiatic lilies can be either up, out, or downfacing but again we agreed that all were of equal value.

Data sheets were put together for each of the lilies and each summer we meticulously recorded heights, counted buds and blooms and watched for any sign of disease or insect pest. We looked forward to the trek out to the plots three times a week to see how many new buds had emerged or new flowers had opened. Thanks to the great air circulation caused by our wide open area, we had no signs of the fungus *Botrytis*.

One bump in the road occurred in 2011 when the lilies had to be moved due to future expansion of Olds College. Construction was to start in June and I regretted trying to move the bulbs at that time of year. We watched for any sign of progress and I procrastinated on the move as long as I could. Fortunately, for the first time in my life, procrastination paid off. Construction was delayed and we were able to move the lilies in the fall of that year.

Choosing one lily of the 13 donated was an extremely difficult decision. Each one had many desirable traits but all were very different. In the end we chose to name a series of four lilies. Our first selection averages around 30 cm (12 in.) high and has golden yellow upright flowers with a red brushmark in the centre of each

Un-named lily #1

Un-named lily #3

Un-named lily #4

All photos Wendy Daley

petal. This lily blooms from about mid-July to mid-August. The second stands 60 cm (24 in.) and is a clean upright flower the colour of an orange pumpkin. Standing a little higher (60 cm/24 in.) and blooming a little bit later than the first (late-July to the beginning of September) this lily makes a good companion to the first one. Lily #3 has an average height of 75 cm (30 in.). This lily blooms from the end of July to the end of August in a splash of dark and light pink. Lily #4 is a very floriferous upfacing red that stands to 90 cm (35 in.) tall. It blooms from the third week in July until the middle of August.

I'm thrilled with the decision we made to create a series rather than choose just an individual lily. The diversity of the lilies chosen allows a gardener to have lilies in bloom from mid July until the beginning of September in an analogous colour scheme of vivid red, soft pink, pure orange and bold yellow. The range in height allows for planting in the front, middle and back of the garden.

Following selection, the lilies were sent to be tissue cultured. There is nothing wrong with growing lilies in the field, but increasing their numbers by tissue culture provides greater numbers of bulbs in less time.

Subsequently, we can grow them in the field or force them into two growth cycles in one year by subjecting them to cold storage for 12–15 weeks. Afterwards, they will be grown in ideal conditions in the greenhouse for 12–15 weeks followed by another cycle of cold and then planting outside.

Our next step was to name and register the lilies. When we received the forms from the International Lily Registrar, I realized how much information was required for each of the lilies. Not only did they want to know flower colour both top and bottom, but also the colour of the throat, nectary, pollen and stigma as well as the diameter of the flower and the length of the tepals. We had stem height and number of stems but I didn't think to measure the length of the leaves or look at how glossy they were. What an eye-opening experience it was for me. There is much more detail to a lily flower than one first sees. I will always look at this plant with more respect than I ever have before.

Suggested names for the lilies were brought forward at the last Annual General Meeting of the Alberta Regional Lily Society and a group of lily enthusiasts at Olds College are working on naming the lilies, but to date, none of the lilies have been formally named. I've discovered finding a name not already been registered, and one that portrays the college and it's centennial, is a challenge.

Our goal is to introduce the lilies in the spring of 2013 and have them ready for distribution in the fall of that year. They will be available through the Alberta Regional Lily Society <arls-lilies.org>.

Plate 2. Clump of irises showing symptoms of *Heterosporium* leaf spot.

Diseases and Pests of Rhizomatous Iris
by Ron Jackson

Ron Jackson was chair and professor of Botany at Brandon University for many years. On retirement, he became a Fellow in the Cool Climate Oenology and Viticulture Institute, Brock University. He is the author of several technical texts and articles on wine and related subjects.

Rhizomatous irises are tough plants, withstanding more abuse than most perennials. Nonetheless, they are not totally immune from problems. There are two main diseases and a potentially lethal pest, destroying the rhizomes. The most common, and most visually disfiguring, is possibly the least damaging. Others occur, but are so insignificant, or nonexistent in our neck-of-the-woods, as to be academic. Thus, there is no reason to discuss them here.

Leaf Spot
Most growers of garden irises will probably be more familiar with leaf spot than they would care to admit. The blight is caused by a fungus most familiarly known as *Heterosporium*

iridis. Its spore-bearing structures (conidiophores) are the source of the dark specks or streaks that develop on older leaf lesions (see photo above). The spores they produce are the major means by which the fungus spreads. They are regrettably long-lived and can survive over winter on the ground. The fungus also probably survives within infected plant remains. Although thorough removal of all leaf remains in the fall (preferable), or early spring, is beneficial, it is rarely, if ever, effectual in eliminating the disease once established. Having battled this disease for much of my life (it is definitely a worthy, but despicable, adversary), the only apparent benefit of sanitation, relative to this disease, is in delaying the onset of infection (the leaves look better longer).

If the early part of the growing season is rainy, even a few weeks delay will not protect the leaves from becoming unsightly by midsummer. Removing infected leaf sections, as soon as the earliest signs of infection appear, only slows the inevitable onslaught. The fungus produces spores prodigiously; they are readily dispersed by wind and rain; rhizomatous irises are highly susceptible; and you are but one against the many. Try spacing each clump such that they are well exposed to the drying action of sun and wind.

Keeping the plants looking well kept seems possible only with spraying fungicides. Regrettably, the government's fear of consumers, and their use of pesticides, plus the lobbying by environmentalists, has severely restricted legitimate access to fungicides. If you can find folpet (e.g Later's Folpet), this is currently the only fungicide registered for domestic use on iris. It may have to be used frequently to be effective. Sulphur is also reported to be of value, something that from my personal experience seems unsupported by the facts. For commercial use, chlorothalonil (Daconil) is also registered. Since all these agents work only by physical contact with the fungus, they are only protective, not curative. A corollary is that the fungicide must also adhere to the surface of the leaf. This is a major problem with irises, due to their upright status and waxy coating, both resulting too often in much of the spray running off the leaf. To limit this action, one ideally needs a mixture with an adhesive property which helps to ensure that the fungicide sticks to the leaf surface where it can be of value. Where a spreader-sticker is not commercially available, adding a few drops of liquid detergent per litre to your fungicide is better than nothing. The sprayer nozzle should also be adjusted to supply a fine spray. Small droplets have a better chance of providing an effective cover and avoiding wasteful runoff. Repeat application is necessary, usually every seven to ten days, because the fungicide is only effective on contact with the fungus. The fungicide will remain effective until washed off by rain or new leaf growth has occurred. This is especially important early in the season when the disease is reestablishing itself on your irises. Application is best begun as soon as leaves begin to grow in the spring, and before symptoms become obvious. Distinct lesions tend to appear about or just after the flowers bloom.

The first sign of infection is the presence of small, light-beige to pale-yellow specks. At the earliest stage, lesions are difficult to observe

Georgy Pesstov

Plate 1. Closeup of a lesion of *Heterosporium* leaf spot showing formation of spores

unless detected from behind, viewed by strong transmitted light. Lesions typically appear first on the tips of the vegetative leaves or those on flower stalks. As the lesions enlarge, becoming lens-shaped, the centre turns a pale brown, being surrounded by a yellow (chlorotic) halo or a water-soaked zone. The focal point of the lesion may appear almost pale grey. As more lesions develop, the water-soaked edges disappear and the spots turn almost colourless in the centre with darker brown-red edges. Eventually surrounding tissue dies and the whole leaf may turn brown, usually starting from the tip and progressing downward. The tips and upper part of the leaves curl, twist, and may bend downward as they dry. Under humid conditions, sporulation (formation of spores) may begin generating dark streaks, or a dispersed, slightly sooty appearance when fully developed.

Sporulation is most easily visualized with the aid of a 10X hand lens. A hand lens is an indispensable tool for any gardener. Not only does it make identification of fungal disease agents much easier, but it facilitates the sighting of minute but destructive pests such as mites and thrips.

Although making the plants unsightly, and an embarrassment, leaf spot does not kill the plant. Other than the sickly appearance, the major damage is restricting the degree of flowering the subsequent year. For a new cultivar this is serious. It severely limits the joy one anticipated when selecting and purchasing the specimen(s). For established clumps, a few less blooms are unlikely to be noticed.

Predominantly Rhizome Infections

Bacterial Soft Rot

Bacterial soft rot is a serious rhizome disease caused by *Erwinia carotovora*. Despite its destructive potential, all that is known about it has been derived from casual observations, not experimentation. It can appear in new or established plantings. It is easily distinguished from other

Plate 3. Bacterial rhizome rot of iris. Plate 4. Winter kill of iris. Plate 5. Iris rhizome partially destroyed by *Botrytis convoluta*. Plate 6. Decayed rhizome showing the just apparent, black, erumpent sclerotia of *Botrytis convoluta* along the edge of the diseased tissue. (all photos by R. S. Jackson)

infections via its odour. It causes a foul-smelling rot that is very soft and wet (Plate 3). This is very different from the whitish, somewhat stringy texture of rhizomes showing winter-kill (Plate 4). Winter-killed rhizomes have no distinctive odour when examined in early spring.

Soft rot is observed mainly during the growing season, often in association with infection by the iris borer. The bacterium is thought to gain access to plant tissues via iris borer wounds in the leaf. Once in leaf tissues, infection spreads down to the base of the plant and subsequently into the rhizome. Early symptoms are water soaked regions associated with a slimy ooze, first evident by pulling the overlapping leaves outward. The affected leaves begin to turn yellow and wither – the whole leaf fan frequently falls over.

Control of soft rot is primarily directed at preventing iris borer attack. Infected sections should be cut out with a knife and destroyed. After each cut, the knife should be disinfected with 70% rubbing alcohol or 10% household bleach. Healthy sections of rhizome are best coated with sulphur or bulb dust, and allowed to dry for several days to heal, before covering with soil.

Botrytis Rhizome Rot

Botrytis rhizome rot, caused by the fungus *Botrytis convoluta,* is probably the most destructive of bearded iris diseases. Thankfully, it also seems to be one of the rarest. It is not known to affect other irises.

It was first observed on imported irises that were dead on arrival in Canada in the 1930s. The association with transport appears to be a common feature. My own experience with this disease fits this pattern. The irises I imported appeared fine on arrival. To my horror, half of my plants were dead the following spring. They showed the telltale signs of infection. The leaf spikes were brown and covered at the base by a grey-brown velvety covering, appearing superficially as if they were covered with splattered mud. This, I discovered later, was due to the densely packed sporulation of *B. convoluta*, compressed by rain (right side of Plate 5). Because the dead leaf fans are easily detached from the rhizome, they can surreptitiously be lost with other dead plant remains during spring cleaning of the garden. Thus, their presence may be missed in established iris clumps. Even more distinctive is the appearance of grey to black, erumpent, tough, gelatinous-like structures, technically called sclerotia (Plate 6). They tend to develop on the surface, or just under the outer 'skin' (periderm), of the rhizome and roots in the mid to later part of the spring. These become visible to most people only on **careful** inspection, when these dead rhizomes are dug up and adherent soil shaken off. The diseased tissue is brown and pulpy in texture (Plates 5 and 6), with only a mild, not unpleasant, mushroomy odour.

Although the fungus is very destructive, it appears unable to attack the rhizome when the iris is able to grow and defend itself against attack. Thus, we have the seemingly odd situation where infections are predominantly associated with iris rhizomes in transport for extended periods, or appearing on newly arrived rhizome stock the subsequent spring. Rhizomes stored dry for a long period are rendered defenceless against at-tack, as are infected rhizomes during the winter months. Experiments have shown that the fungus can grow in rhizomes stored in a refrigerator or slightly below freezing. If the rhizome has not fully succumbed during the winter, it seals off the diseased tissue and tends to outgrow the infection.

Occasionally, the fungus can initiate infection on leaves during the growing season (Plate 7). This appears uncommon. Infection of

Comparison of Different Sources of Rhizome Death

Comparison of Botrytis Rhizome Rot with Bacterial Soft Rot, "Winter-kill" and Rhizome Senescence. (from R. S. Jackson (1972). Botrytis rhizome rot. A review. Bull. Am. Iris Soc.204, 35–40.)

Botrytis Rhizome Rot	Bacterial Soft Rot	Winter Kill	Rhizome Senescence
Rhizome			
dry	wet	wet	dry
spongy	mushy	solid	tough
light-medium brown	brown-yellowish	whitish	brown
no distinctive odor	foul odor	no distinctive odor	no distinctive odor
easily torn apart	easily torn apart	splits along length	torn only with difficulty
Leaf fans			
dry	wet	wet	not present or shriveled
brown	brown	pale brown/purplish at base	brown if present
Signs of disease			
grey/brown mat of spores	not present	not present	not present
sclerotia	not present	not present	not present
Where primarily observed			
young offsets	young or established offsets	affects rhizomes regardless of age	affects only old rhizomes
When primarily observed			
spring	mid- to late-season	spring	any time of year

senescent or dead leaf tissue in the fall is thought to be the site of infection, invading the rhizome during the winter months.

If the disease is found, the infected tissue, and surrounding soil and roots, should be removed (to include the sclerotia) and destroyed as soon as possible. In most situations, this will usually eliminate the disease, if not immediately, within a few years. The only fungicide that was known to be effective against the disease (Benomyl) is no longer available.

Iris Borer

Irises are affected by few serious insect pests, but what they lack in number, they make up for in the severity of the one they do have. I refer to the infamous iris borer (*Macronoctua onusta*). Its adult stage is a small brownish, nondescript moth. Because of its night-flying habit, it is rarely seen. In contrast, its larva stage is clearly and repulsively evident when fully formed. They are light reddish brown with a dark head. At this stage they are found burrowing out the centre of a rhizome. Initially, they are minute, pale larvae (hairless caterpillars) that begin their feeding on leaves. They can be found in the folds of leaves on which they are feeding in late spring/early summer.

Eggs are laid on foliage or other debris close to, or overlying, iris rhizomes in the fall. The insect overwinters as clusters of eggs. This is another reason to remove and destroy all old foliage after a killing frost in the late fall. The eggs hatch shortly after iris growth begins in the spring, (when the leaves are about 10 cm (4 in.) long). The miniature larvae migrate to and up the leaves. Here, they burrow into the tissue and begin to feed. At this stage their action is evident only by pulling the leaves of a fan apart (Plate 8). With careful and delicate investigation, the minute larvae can be observed. From a control perspective, this is the best time for insecticidal application (the larvae are small, highly susceptible, and only minimal amounts are required to be lethal). Regrettably, it is also the time when need is least apparent. In addition, for any insecticide to be effective, it must be systemic (e.g., dimethoate or Cygon). Contact insecticides that remain on the surface of the enfolding foliage are only effective shortly after egg hatching and before the young larvae enter the leaf. This window of opportunity is so short as to be essentially useless. A systemic insecticide (Cygon is registered for commercial use on iris) should be applied shortly after leaf growth. As the insects grow, they

Dr. Clifford Sadof Purdue University

Iris borer and frass

soon become much more resistant. By the time they have descended and are established in the rhizome, insecticides are basically ineffective. At this stage, the larvae grow especially rapidly, reaching almost 5 cm (2 in.) in length and about 6 mm(1/4 in.) thick. At this point, the rhizome and its occupant should be removed and destroyed. If not, the larvae tunnel out of the evacuated rhizome into the soil, where they pupate. In late summer, they emerge as adults, mate, and the females lay their eggs for the next season.

Early stage infection tends to be noticed only on close observation. They appear as small, pale, brown lesions, often accompanied with water soaked regions above, but mainly below the lesion. Sawn edges of inner leaves may be revealed when enclosing leaves are pulled aside (Plate 8). This is also likely to reveal a slimy exudate and insect frass, resembling wet sawdust. If such signs are seen, the whole spike of leaves should be removed and destroyed, or the infested area crushed to kill the young larvae. Subsequently, as their damage increases, the leaves turn yellow and eventually brown, typically falling over. If your irises are known to be infested with iris borer, inspection of the young leaf spikes should take place on a weekly basis until midsummer. By this time, any infested sites should have revealed themselves.

If feeding does not kill the rhizome, the often associated bacterial soft rot does. If rot sets in earlier, it produces early stage soft rot at the base of the plant, as described above.

Unlike sanitation with leaf spot, hygiene is often very effective in eliminating iris borer. All dead plant parts should be removed and destroyed after a hard frost (when all egg-laying females will be dead). Effective elimination is also dependent on there being no close neighbour, whose irises are already infested, and who is unaware or unconcerned. In this case, there will be an annual supply of egg-laying females attracted to your irises. Thus, the task of removing all dead leaf remains and stalks around your irises will be a perpetual requirement, plus vigilance in the early part of the season checking for signs of infestation. Currently, iris borer is not widespread on the prairies, but has been found in Manitoba. 🪶

Plate 7. Infection of leaves by *Botrytis convoluta*.
Plate 8. Early stage leaf damage caused by iris borer.)

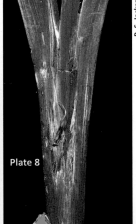

R. S. Jackson

Plate 7   Plate 8

The Lively Garden
Perennials for Wildlife
by Nora Bryan

Bumble bee in tulip

---

*Nora is an accomplished gardener and certified arborist. She is a frequent speaker, columnist for the Calgary Herald, and co-author of **The Prairie Gardener's Book of Bugs**, and **The Prairie Winterscape**.*

Perennials make our gardens a delight for wildlife – big and small, invited or uninvited! This article is about the joys of hosting wildlife through perennial planting, so it's mostly about the birds and the bees –and the wasps, and flies, and beetles and other small critters that benefit our gardens.

Although always present in our gardens, each perennial has its season to shine. Spring ephemerals such as crocus/pasqueflower (*Anemone patens*) own the show in April and the first part of May while the threat of freezing temperatures and snow remains very real. These will be long tucked back in the ground for their summer sleep before later blooming perennials even begin to rub the sleepiness from their buds.

Indeed, it is the 'passing of the torch' from early bloomers to later bloomers that makes perennials so important to sustaining valuable wildlife. Purposefully planting a variety of perennials designed to bloom from as early in the season to as late as possible is a wildlife gardening strategy. Hosting wildlife, in particular insects, helps build populations of beneficial predators. These are the 'good' bugs that eat the 'bad' bugs. Does planning a garden like this seem like the same thing as succession planning of bloom periods for aesthetic reasons? Well, it is! Succession planting as a pest control strategy – who'd a-thought it!

Let's take a wander through the seasons and see what treats could be in store for us and the critters with whom we could share our gardens.

Stirrings of Spring

Insects and flowering plants have danced an evolutionary tango for about 130 million years. When hibernating adult insects emerge in spring, they need nourishment right away. The first lady beetles you see when you gently rake off the leaf mulch to see what's poking out of the ground need protein. By now, everyone knows that lady beetles are major vanquishers of the unlovely aphid. But in April, these aphids are nowhere to be found. So what's a hungry beetle to do? In my garden lady beetles are found inside the crocus and other small early blooms. They may be warming their tiny bodies in the shelter and reflected sunlight of the cupped petals, but they are also feeding on the pollen from the crocus anthers. Pollen happens to be protein-rich. Plants produce more pollen than they need. The beetle eats a little and more pollen sticks to the beetle, which might be helpfully transferred when the foraging beetle alights in a different flower.

You know spring is truly underway when bumble bees and yellowjacket wasps are on the wing. Fertilized new queens have survived the drama of fall mating and have successfully hibernated in a protected spot. When the accumulated warmth of spring is sufficient these young queens emerge and begin to look for flowers to satisfy their empty bellies. Bumble bees collect both pollen and nectar. Wasp queens bring nectar to their developing broods. When my garden fills with striped squill (*Puschkinia*) and Siberian squill (*Scilla sibirica*), the bees and wasps are soon amongst them.

If you get down on your knees and take a good look at those foraging insects, you might see some 'bees' that look not quite like bees. Perhaps you will have discovered syrphid flies. Syrphid flies are also called hover flies. Some are tiny and dark and rather obscure except for the darting, hovering flight that may catch your eye.

These hovering flies are your garden allies. Syrphid flies cruise around drinking nectar but their main purpose is to mate and lay eggs. The eggs are laid on plants with aphids, because aphids are what the larval syrphids need! Having a garden abuzz with insects is a healthy garden infused with natural pest control.

Syrphid fly on thistle

Nora Bryan

Darlene Stack

Nashville warbler on echinacea bloom

Strolling Through Summer

As summer unfolds our gardens become places of rampant bloom. Not only are there more types of plants in bloom, they are taller. Delphiniums, rudbeckias, lilies and summer phlox compete for our attentions. This is Nature's design. In spring, before grasses have grown tall to meet the wind and before trees leaf out, there is an opportunity to grab sun and warmth without having to grow very tall. As the earth warms and resources become more abundant, plants compete for summer's gifts. There are more butterflies, bees and other insects on the wing exploiting the pollen and nectar that Nature has intended for them.

Along with the re-greening of the garden, come summer's birds from their winter quarters. Why do tiny chickadees remain to endure the bitterness of a Prairie winter while warblers and robins wing south? Birds have amazing little metabolic furnaces. If a bird can find enough to eat, it can stay warm. Chickadees are masters of foraging and storing seeds and other delectable morsels. These tiny birds eat seeds and fruit as well as insects, so they thrive all year. Warblers and robins eat mostly insects, and so must follow the food, which is why they migrate.

A Northern summer is a very lively place, compressed into a very small number of weeks. There is so much blooming all at one time. Northern gardens are deservedly renowned for their summer colour. Where there are flowers, so are their evolutionary partners, the insects. Insects are very high in protein, which is just what mama and papa bird need to feed their brood. Even seed-eating birds like chickadees switch to a 'meat' diet when they are raising their family.

Of course, we know from childhood that flowers do more for birds than just act as decoys for insects. Hummingbirds take nectar from deep-throated flowers just as bees and butterflies do. When flowers set seed, birds eat those too. Although plant-munching insects do what they can to hide from birds, birds have good eyesight. Sparrows might find the delphinium worm that bothers your monkshoods before you notice. Caterpillars may be gleaned from leaves, especially in gardens where pesticides are not sprayed indiscriminately.

Birds also use bits of perennial plants for nesting. Goldfinches delay nesting until July or August, which is late compared to other migrating birds. There is a motive to their apparent procrastination. These familiar yellow birds not only eat thistle seed, but they line their nests with the fluff. Would you leave thistle in your garden? Most would not, but not being too quick to deadhead spent blooms is one more way to make your garden wildlife-friendly.

Following Into Fall

As foliage fades and plant stalks bend against the wind, our first impulse may be to tidy up for winter's inevitable return. But we should not be too hasty with the shears. If we learn from the lesson of the goldfinch, we would better serve our winter birds by leaving perennial plant stalks up, especially the late-blooming monarda, false sunflower (*Heliopsis helianthoides*), globe thistles (*Echinops ritro*) and other tall, late blooming plants. Nature, in her genius, has planned it this way. The tall plants of late summer

provide sustenance for fall migrating birds. Even snows won't soon cover these stout-stalked plants. Consider removing and composting the spent remains in spring instead of fall.

Plant stalks also trap snow and fallen leaves, helping to hold a valuable winter mulch layer on vulnerable plant crowns. So, even in death, your perennials are making your garden a better environment for themselves and the creatures, big and small. This 'death' is not a real death of course, just an escape underground for a brief sleep until spring brings our faithful perennial back into the light once again.

The key to creating a flower garden that is also a wildlife haven, is to include flowering plants that bloom throughout the growing season, from early spring to the onset of winter. Let plants live out their cycles. Don't be hasty with the tidying up, and of course don't use pesticides.

I hope you are not disappointed that I have not provided lists of 'wildlife-attracting' perennials. Lists of bee and butterfly flowers are easy to find on the internet.

Most of the plants we grow in our garden have tremendous wildlife value, especially native or near-native and natural species. Highly hybridized double flowers have lesser value for wildlife, but interactions between the myriad lives being lived in our gardens is so complex, and often unseen, who knows for sure? 🦋

Monarda

Nora Bryan

Gasplant
Perennial
On Fire
by Sheryl Normandeau

Marilyn Latta

eryl has been a resident of Calgary, AB for seventeen years. She is a gardener, writer, blogger, and a volunteer for the Calgary Horticultural Society. She holds a Prairie Horticultural Certificate and Bachelor of Arts, and previously managed a retail garden centre.

I first saw a gasplant specimen a few years ago, during a visit to the George Pegg Botanic Garden, located near the hamlet of Glenevis in Alberta. George Pegg (1910-1988) was a botanist and ornithologist whose extraordinary passion for nature, gardening, and plant preservation can still be felt as you walk through the original site of his garden and homestead. If you are in the area, touring the garden and arboretum is highly recommended.

I was captivated by the size of the plant, the exceptional beauty of its creamy white flowers, and, of course, its common name, inspiring me to research the plant so that I could learn more about it.

Perennial gasplant (*Dictamnus albus*, syn. *Dictamnus fraxinella*, *Dictamnus caucasicus*) is also commonly known as dittany, or burning bush, although it is not to be confused with the shrub *Euonymus alatus*. Gasplant may also be referred to as fraxinella, a common name derived from the Latin "fraxinus," due to the resemblance of the foliage to that of ash trees. Despite some variation in nomenclature, there is only one species of the genus *Dictamnus* in the entire world.

Gasplant is a longtime favourite in English gardens and was likely introduced to North America in the 19th century from Europe and Asia. Show-stopping, five-petaled, spiked blooms occur in shades of white, pink, and purple, and are borne on multiple stalks. The stems, leaves, and blooms all possess a fresh citrus scent, making it a powerful attractant for bees, butterflies, and hummingbirds. Here is the fascinating part: the lemony oils produced by the plants are actually flammable, and given the right conditions, can be set alight with a match, giving off an audible popping noise in the process. Unfortunately the same oils are also a major skin irritant and, like poison ivy, can cause severe phytophotodermatitis. **Be sure to wear gloves and long sleeves while tending gasplant.** It is listed on the Government of Canada's poisonous plants information system <www.cbif.gc.ca/pls/pp/poison>. Due to its toxic nature, it is advisable to locate gasplant in an area where it will not prove harmful to children or pets.

One benefit of the plant's irritating oils, however, is that deer and rabbits generally avoid *Dictamnus*, and it is largely unaffected by the insects and diseases that may attack other plants. Slugs are an exception; the slimy pests may ravage the young tender shoots of gasplant, in which case the use of baits and traps as a control measure will be helpful.

Gasplant is more than simply a horticultural oddity! A beautiful and lasting addition to any garden, gasplant is very hardy and may even grow in a protected zone 2 spot. Gasplant prefers full sun, but will perform well in a part-shade location. Regular watering is a must, as the plant is not particularly drought-tolerant. Gasplant will not thrive in water-logged conditions, so well-drained soil is necessary. Amend clay-like soils with organic matter if required. Most prairie soils are suitable for gasplant. Side dressing with a balanced compost at the start of each growing season may contribute a potential source of nutrition.

At its mature height, it will easily reach 90–120 cm (3–4 ft.), with a spread of 90 cm (3 ft.), the size of a small shrub. Due to the woody nature of its mature stems, it rarely requires staking, and needs little in the way of maintenance once established. Gasplant, however, is notoriously slow-growing and it can take years for it to even get going and it may not grow at all in the first few summers after

Gasplant

Bernd Haynold

planting. Don't give up on it! Gasplant is extremely long-lived; 20–50 years in one location is not unusual, so your patience will be duly rewarded. Careful consideration must be taken when deciding upon a location to plant it, not just due to its eventual size, but because it should not be moved once planted. It possesses a long taproot and will suffer greatly or even die if an attempt at a transplant is made. For this same reason, successful division is nearly impossible. It is not recommended to attempt to propagate gasplant from seed, as plants take up to four years to flower once established in the garden. If time is not an issue, seeds can be collected in late autumn from the pods that develop on the plants and later sown. (If the seed isn't harvested, these decorative, bronzy seed pods may be left on the plants to provide winter interest). Start the seed indoors after a chilling period of 4–6 weeks in the refrigerator. Germination will take a whopping 30–40 days.

Transplants are the best option, if you can find them in the garden centre – the white flowering *Dictamnus albus* 'Albiflorus' may not be readily available, but a good retailer can locate plants for you. Harder to obtain is *Dictamnus albus* 'Purpurea,' a purple-pink variety that possesses less fragrant flowers than 'Albiflorus'. A red-pink type, 'Rubra,' is only marginally hardy on the prairies and is a gamble to grow in unsheltered locations.

Try positioning gasplant at the back of borders, to allow for its

Shirley Normandeau

Gasplant

eventual height, and give it sufficient spacing. It can also be used in mixed beds, and looks fantastic when paired with plants such as beebalm and campanula. Gasplant blooms only for approximately two weeks, in mid-summer, and planting it near late bloomers such as daylilies, yarrow, or cranesbill ensures colour further into the season. Gasplant's attractive glossy deep green foliage looks pleasing against the striking leaves of peonies, even after both plants have bloomed. If care is taken when handling gasplant, flowers may be cut for fragrant bouquets. Despite the need for patience and a good pair of gloves, this unusual plant is well worth the effort. 🌿

(Excerpts from this article previously appeared in "Plant Portrait: Gasplant" in the December/January 2011 issue of the Calgary Horticultural Society's newsletter *Calgary Gardening*).

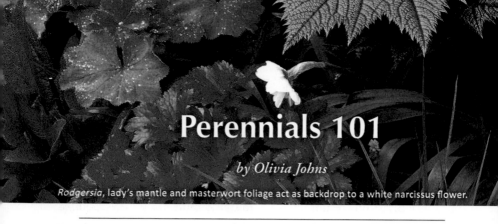

Perennials 101

by Olivia Johns

Olivia Johns has over twenty years of experience gardening in Calgary and central Alberta, and spent many years in a variety of positions at the Calgary Zoo and Botanical Gardens, most recently as Senior Manager, Horticulture and Grounds.

Perennials by definition are plants that live for years, unlike annuals or biennials that generally live and die in one or two seasons. Many gardeners have developed a passion for these garden plants, seeking out new options each year, while also welcoming back those that were planted in previous summers. Like many gardeners, I consider plants to be a bit of a vice — especially perennials — a habit that I have no interest in kicking. In my Calgary garden I look forward to seeing my perennials each spring, hoping they return better than ever and I haven't suffered too many winter losses, although this does create space for new plants.

Nestled among my trees and shrubs, perennials make up the bulk of my garden, and often are enhanced by a few colourful annuals. Perennials provide a wide array of options that include colours and sizes for all types of garden, including containers. There

is a perennial to suit every nook and cranny in your yard, whether it is small or large, and any colour preference or style. Creating continuous blooms throughout the season is easy with a little research. Once you start looking, you will find no limit to what you can grow in your garden, keeping in mind your available space, exposure, soil type, and, of course, the hardiness zone of your particular region.

Perennials, ranging in sizes from seedlings to mature plants, can be purchased at garden centres, nurseries, plant sales hosted by local horticultural societies and all types of growers. Perennials are great to share with fellow gardeners, friends and neighbours as they can be divided when mature or overgrown. Perennials can also be grown from seed, but be prepared for a season or two before you see blooms. A few things to consider when choosing perennials are:

1. What actually overwinters in your climate (ie. hardiness zone)? Most

local garden centres only sell perennials that are hardy, but not always, and often they are sold right next to annuals.

2. Know what corners of your yard are full sun, part shade and full shade, and choose plants that will flourish in these areas. Growing a shade plant in full sun, for example, can produce disastrous results.

3. Know what type of soil you have and consider a soil test to determine nutrient deficiencies. Amendments may be required to provide optimum growing conditions. Emulate where ever possible the natural growing environment of plants. For example, most shade plants thrive in moist, woodland areas; add organic material to your soil to increase its moisture holding capacity. Plants from alpine regions generally prefer a well drained and sandy or rocky soil, so by adding sand or grit you can provide conditions preferable to these sun loving plants.

4. Consider how much space you have. Perennials come in a variety of heights and widths, from ground covering woolly thyme to six foot tall delphiniums and all sizes in between. Some perennials will stay happily in their little growing space and others can be very aggressive and take over an entire flower bed, so be aware of their growth parameters.

Now that you're well on your way to deciding what perennials are right for you, and you've chosen the right plant for the right place in your garden, it's planting time. Dig a hole,

drop in plant, cover roots, and water. It can be that simple but making sure that your perennial is planted properly will help to ensure its healthy survival. Before digging the plant hole, make sure that your space is weed free. Loosen up the soil on the sides of the planting hole to enable roots to spread more easily. Tools required may include a pair of gloves, a trowel, a shovel and a watering can. Ensure that the hole you dig is big enough and deep enough to accommodate the size of the root ball, but not too deep. The top of the plant's root ball should be level with the surface of the soil. Cover well with soil and make sure that you have good soil to root contact by adding a little pressure to the soil around the plant. This also helps to remove any air pockets. Water well and fertilize throughout its first growing season to get it established. Mulching the surface of the soil and adding compost will also benefit your newly planted perennial.

Perennials often are thought of as requiring less maintenance than annuals, but they still do require some

Reflexed pink petals of echinacea mix with the yellow flowers of *Rudbeckia* (brown eyed Susan).

Teresa Lopata

looking after to keep them performing well and looking great in your garden. Watering, fertilizing and weeding are necessary chores to keep your plant healthy. Deadheading, staking, dividing and cutting back are also common activities associated with growing perennials.

Deadheading is the removal of spent blooms. By removing dead and dying flowers from your perennials you can encourage more blooms later in the season and maintain a tidier shape. Regular deadheading also allows your perennial to direct its energy to growing stronger roots and more flowers (make sure you leave a few flowers to mature if you want your plant to produce seeds).

Provide support to taller perennials with stakes or plant rings. This prevents them from falling over or collapsing under the weight of heavy blooms and branches. Stakes for all sizes and types of plants are available at most garden centres, but can also be fashioned from bamboo canes or branches and a roll of twine. Anything that supports the plant will work, depending on your preference for colour, size and visibility.

Perennials should periodically be divided in order to maintain healthy plants, prevent overcrowding, rejuvenate older perennials and to establish more plants. It might seem like a daunting task, but with the right tools and plan, plant division can be very rewarding. This is a task, however, that requires some familiarity of the plant's growth habits, root structure, and blooming period. Generally, spring blooming perennials should be divided in the fall, and mid- to late-summer flowering perennials can be divided in the spring. Perennials with fibrous roots, such as daylily, can be cut down through the middle of the clump, ensuring that each new division retains sufficient roots and stems.

Cutting back perennials allows for end-of-season clean-up, deters overwintering pests and prepares your plant for the following spring. Any perennial that provides winter interest can be left untouched and is often encouraged in our short growing season. A pair of gloves and a sharp pair of pruners or garden scissors are the only tools required. In my garden, I leave about 15–20 cm (6–8 in.) of stems to catch snow for added winter protection and to make it easier to locate the plant in the spring. Asiatic lily stems left standing provide a good marker to prevent mistakenly digging up lily bulbs in the spring. A bit of leftover plant debris may make for extra cleanup in the spring, but also provides additional cover in the event of a late spring frost.

Perennials are like family and friends. We enjoy seeing them each spring, and are a little sad to see them go in the fall. We tend to them throughout the summer, can get a little frustrated when they don't behave as they should and are disappointed when they don't make a return. Enjoy your gardens, and delight in the new, but don't forget the tried and true! ❧

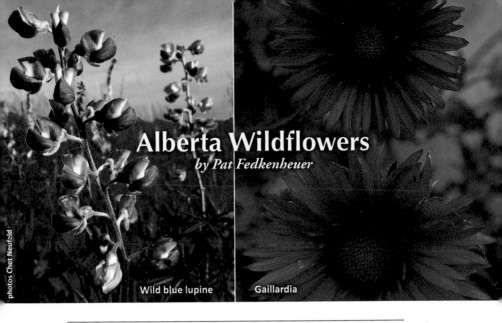

Wild blue lupine   Gaillardia

photos Chet Neufeld

Alberta Wildflowers
by Pat Fedkenheuer

Pat is a well-known Calgary native plant expert offering advice and plants. You'll find her sharing her passion for wildflowers with schools, garden clubs, greenroof projects or at one of the local farmers markets.

There are many excellent perennial choices for gardeners hoping to bring a touch of the natural areas of Alberta into their garden. The plants profiled below will all perform well in a garden setting.

Wild blue lupine
(*Lupinus argenteus, L. sericeus*)
The Alberta lupines are good forage and their silky rich green leaves and sky blue colour enhances the beauty of Alberta's rangeland. This nitrogen fixing legume is a perennial that is easily recognized and is common in the prairie and foothill regions throughout Southern Alberta. Lupines flower from the end of June into August, are mainly blue, but can be white or pink growing from 30–60 cm (1–2 ft). tall with six to nine palmate leaves that are alternate and silvery-haired on the bottom. Lupines add a rich beauty along our roadsides and into the hill country.

Cut-leaved anemone
(*Anemone multifida*)
This hardy perennial herb blooms in colours of pink, white, yellow or reddish tinge in May, June and July throughout prairie grasslands, woods and high mountain slopes of Alberta. The five petal, dainty flower head atop the hairy stems and the whorled, deeply-cut leaves are the distinguishing features for the common name of this anemone. The seed is a round or thimble shaped head of white, woolly one-seeded achenes where insects or larvae may seek protection.

Gaillardia, blanket-flower
(*Gaillardia aristata*)

This perennial brown-eyed Susan is a favourite wildflower from early settlers to current wildflower enthusiasts. From 30–60 cm (1–2 ft.) tall, yellow wedge shaped ray-florets, around an orange-brown, domed cluster of florets. This showy wildflower's habitat includes grasslands, open coniferous forests and foothills to montane throughout Alberta. Leaves are basal, alternate and hairy grayish-green with daisy-like flowering blooms from June to August. Gaillardia provides a home to insects, nectar for bees and food for birds. I call it Alberta's "Happy Flower" — it brings a smile to everyone's face.

Smooth aster (*Symphyotrichum laeve, syn. Aster laevis*)

This perennial herb grows throughout Alberta with its blue or lavender daisy flowers around yellow centres

Smooth aster

from July through September. This common wildflower can be seen along the roadsides, fields and open woods growing from 60–90 cm (2–3 ft.) tall with alternate, lance shaped, smooth, blue-green thick leaves. There are many native asters in Alberta (20 plus) and all are important to our eco-system providing forage, food and homes to many insects, butterflies, bees, birds and critters. A garden would not be a garden without an aster.

Bluebell or harebell
(*Campanula rotundifolia*)

This easily recognized native wildflower grows in shade or sun, good soil or gravel, sand or rocky crevice, in the mountains, foothill and prairie grasslands of Alberta blooming from June – September. The blue-purplish bell-shaped, nodding blooms on a narrow stem grow from 15–45 cm (6–18 in.) in height. These beautiful bells add a graceful note to our prairies with the slightest of breezes. Bluebells get grazed with forage, bees can be seen pushing into the bells and children delight in one of the first flowers they come to know. Get down and take a closer look…you may find the "heart" near the root.

Be sure to purchase native plants from reputable suppliers and to refrain from bringing plants home from your hikes. Leave them for everyone else to enjoy!

Gardening for the Five Senses
by Lynn Collicut

"The greatest gift of the garden is the restoration of the five senses"
Hanna Rion

Lynn is retired from Agriculture and Agri-Food Canada's Morden Research Station in Manitoba where she developed hardy ornamental plants for prairie gardeners. She is a former member of The Prairie Garden committee.

Sensory gardens are often designed for children or as therapeutic gardens, but we can use our senses in our own gardens. Our experience and feelings of engaging and enjoyment in our gardens expands and deepens as we use more of our senses. Using our senses really helps us to be in the moment. Many of the current anti-stress and anti-anxiety methods focus on slowing down and really being present; this is often called "mindfulness". The more we use our senses of sight, hearing, touch, taste and smell, the more we are in the present moment in our gardens.

Sight

Sight is, of course, the major sense employed in the garden. The creation and enjoyment of visual beauty is very fulfilling. Visual aspects include: landscape design (the pleasing combinations of trees, shrubs, flowers), as well as decks, patios, paths, furniture and lighting. Herbaceous perennials can visually add texture and colour. The large bold leaves of plants such as bergenia (*Beregenia cordifolia*) and ligularia (*Ligularia* spp.), add interest and contrast with the finer foliage of Japanese ferns, sweet cicely (*Myrrhis odorata*) or European pasqueflower (*Pulsatilla vulgaris*). Contrast the bold shape of lily blooms with the finer flowers of baby's-breath (*Gypsophila paniculata*). Leaf texture is a bit more subtle, but engages our visual senses – shiny leaves versus fuzzy leaves, the deeply veined leaves of some hostas, or the waxy texture of succulents. Drops of rain on lady's mantle (*Alchemilla mollis*) are a visual treat for our eyes. Leaves can also be grown for colour, for example the many shades of coral-bells (*Heuchera*), 'Palace Purple' being the most common; variegated or blue hostas; and the grey of lambs-ears (*Stachys byzantina*).

Colour is a topic on its own, but major principles include warm versus cool; complementary, analogous or monochromatic schemes; the use of white; and remembering that green is always present in the garden as a colour. The warm colours, being red, orange and yellow, give an upbeat, energetic feeling. They seem to advance visually in the yard and hold up in the strong prairie sunlight. Cool colours include blues, violet/purples and greens. These seem to recede in a landscape and generally give a more restful tranquil feeling. Pastels and muted variations versus a full expression of the colour also influence our response.

Adding white always changes the mixture and can brighten, refresh or tie strong colours together.

Colour combinations can have a strong effect on our visual sense. Much depends on personal preference and choice. Strong contrasts and drama result from complementary colours such as blue-orange, purple-yellow and red-green. Visualize 'Blue Clips' bellflower with 'Orange Pixie' lilies as a backdrop; or purple salvia with yellow sundrops. Another eye popper combination is tall orange lilies in front of Jackmanii clematis. Analogous combinations are usually easy on the eyes and easy to create: red, orange and yellow; red, orange-red and yellow; blue, purple and green; blue, blue-violet and violet/purple. Finally, monochromatic combinations use shades and tones of one colour such as the white blooms of a 'moon garden'. Of course this is always in addition to the green colour of the leaves. Also pleasing are groupings of reds and pinks or deep blues through to pastel sky blues.

Sound

Although it would be nice to have a harpist, jazz quartet or guitarist in the garden, there are other sounds to stimulate hearing. Granted, water features are easily used to create sound, but if we are more creative and observant, we can 'hear' our plants as well. A good place to start is the use of annual or perennial grasses. With their long linear leaves and tall seed heads, wind rustles through them all summer and into the

Fran Wershler

Lady's-mantle with stone, wood and an artistic pot

fall and winter. Other grass-like plants like daylilies and iris, also move in the breeze and create sound. By leaving seed heads on plants, fall and winter breezes create a different kind of sound, more of a subtle rattle and shaking. If you have room, trees like trembling aspen (*Populus tremuloides* Michx.) create fluttering sounds in the wind. Bird baths, houses and feeders entice wonderful spring songs and chatter of birds in the yard. Larger yards can accommodate frogs in ponds and thus spring croaking. Wind chimes add ephemeral tones to the sound garden.

Touch

Like sound, touch is a lesser used sense in the garden, but once you cultivate the habit of touching plants around your yard, it becomes second nature, and really adds to your garden experience. Include plants with fuzzy leaves such as lambs-ears or lady's-mantle. Position a pot of rosemary so you run your hand over it as you pass by. You will enjoy both the texture and smell of the leaves. Mosses are nice to grow for that 'touch aspect'. You may not have thought of water, smooth stones, and the bark of trees such as birch or Amur chokecherry (*Prunus maackii*) or pieces of driftwood to stimulate the sense of touch in the garden.

Taste

Of course our sense of taste is fully engaged in vegetable and fruit gardens. Add in all the herbs we grow and we have a very full experience of this sense. Try some of the edible flowers to expand your appreciation – for example, peppery nasturtiums add zip to a salad. Use grape leaves for wrapping dolmades, or stuff daylily and squash flowers for an edible treat.

Smell

Fragrance is probably the other main attribute we associate with the flower garden. Typically we look to the rose for scent, but dianthus or pinks have an interesting clove fragrance, and leaves of lemon balm and lemon thyme give a refreshing lemon scent. Other familiar scented flowering plants include lilacs and lily-of-the-valley. Leaves of lavender, mint, monarda, and hyssop provide wonderful smells when their leaves are rubbed between your fingers. Oriental lilies have a very strong perfume as do angels trumpet flowers. We usually don't attribute fragrance to iris or hostas but the cultivars of *Hosta plantaginea* have pleasing, fragrant, white flowers late in the season. As well, some of the irises have surprisingly pleasant scents, for example Six Hills Giant is a tall bearded, purple variety that smells like grape Kool-Aid.

Try using some new senses in the garden - your overall experience is sure to be heightened.

Neighbours' grass clippings ⸢
over leaves and woodchips ⸢
the first layers in the 'lasagna
method of soil creation for n
new front yard forest garden

A Pioneer Edible Forest Garden in Urban Winnipeg
by Darlene Belton Cullimore

Darlene Belton Cullimore is a Master Gardener and permaculture practitioner.

Permaculture is a branch of ecological design and ecological engineering which develops sustainable human settlements and self-maintained agricultural systems modeled from natural ecosystems.

Having been captivated by permaculture principles and practice for several years, I resolved, when I moved to my new Winnipeg home in the fall of 2009, to develop edible forest gardens in the front and back yards. This circa 1950s city neighbourhood has many mature trees – though none in my yard – and is slowly 'transitioning' to a new generation of young families.

My neighbours' front yards feature a few shrubs and trees, small ornamental gardens and large expanses of lawn, typical of Canadian residential landscapes. An edible forest garden in my front yard and my non-traditional permaculture-based gardening methods could be a startling and negatively viewed change to this pattern unless I proceed cautiously.

Passionate as I am about permaculture, I want to stimulate curiosity, interest and perhaps new adherents among my neighbours in this friendly urban nook, so I am taking special care when developing the front forest garden, intending to do so in gradual steps. I plan to feature edible plants that are also ornamental and to retain some lawn for passageways, but over time will convert the existing Kentucky bluegrass to a more drought-tolerant, low-maintenance mix of fescue grasses.

Edible forest gardening lies at the heart of what I feel permaculture is all about: the facilitation of richly diverse, healthy ecosystems that meet human needs for food, beauty and community. Our blueprint is the natural forest. But, we get to select the specific plants that will work for us in our home landscapes, as well as for the ecosystem. The more I learn about how forests 'work' (who rototills a forest?), the more insight I gain to support me in this ambitious task.

I've found inspiration for my forest gardens by visiting the edge of nearby forests, where I linger and observe carefully. I watch how the grasses and wildflowers of the meadow transition to low shrubs, then taller ones, then to small trees and finally to the majesty of the 'climax' canopy. These are the 'successions' that nature follows to create a forest from disturbed land, revealed to us in metres of space rather than in decades of time.

Then I walk into the woods a short way, and look down, even poke around a little. Between the trees and understory plants lies a thick bedding of fall leaves from years past in various stages of break down to humus, home to a myriad of organisms, members of the living soil food web, the core of a healthy self-sustaining forest ecosystem. Such experiences bring to life what I read and have learned in workshops. These basics, which anyone can observe within a few kilometres of their home – soil and succession – are the watchwords for starting an edible forest garden.

A forest garden should mimic a young woodland, which features more diversity than a mature forest, and my attention is focused on the edges of my cultivated woodlands where edible annuals and perennials

-lies-bleeding or *Amaranthus caudatus* (a ical ancient grain, with gorgeous cascades f wine-coloured flowers that ripen into), plus red millet - which is actually a glos deep maroon, butternut squash, ground rries, eggplant, okra, and sweet peppers, is zinnias, all of which I grew from seed.

flourish. Building up the type of soil that sustains a forest is the first step. Sheet-mulching, sometimes called 'lasagna gardening', disturbs the existing impoverished ecosystem of the typical lawn and begins a process of turning it to a healthy carbon-based, fungal-dominated soil that can support the new edge-of-woodland plants as well as berry shrubs, and fruit and nut trees.

I am also careful to include some nitrogen-fixing perennials, shrubs or trees, plus 'dynamic accumulators', that is, plants with long tap roots that draw essential minerals from the sub-soil and, as their roots and leaves die back and break down, release these nutrients for other plants. A thick mulch of shredded leaves protects the soil from compaction caused by driving rain, conserves moisture, reduces weed germination and continues soil-building by nurturing the soil food web. My overall goal is to facilitate a resilient, self-sustaining and therefore low-maintenance forest system.

Each fall since 2009 and directly over the existing lawns, I have sheet-mulched by hand a few new forest garden beds a year. First, I begin with a carbon layer – often newspaper or cardboard, then leaves, followed by grass clippings from neighbours; next, I add imported manure and soil. My first front-yard 'lasagna' bed engendered much skeptical comment, but the result, now flourishing as a mixed ornamental shrub and perennial garden,

has won acceptance, even interest, along the street.

I formerly gardened in a zone 5b region of Ontario, and have certainly seen that sheet-mulching/lasagna gardening is much more challenging in my zone 2b area with heavy clay soil; for one thing, it takes longer for the layers to break down and the grass beneath to die back – up to two years versus three to four months, and this has slowed the implementation of my plans considerably. I prefer that the beds are mostly 'finished' before planting perennials and shrubs, though I am happy to plant annual vegetables and flowers in unfinished beds.

Last fall I approached a company hired to do branch trimming in the neighbourhood, and received a free truckload of woodchips! Rather than using newspaper as the first layer of my front yard lasagna garden, I used the woodchips. Now my challenge is to ensure that nitrogen in the soil is not exhausted as the woodchips break down, so I am exploring options such as fresh grass clippings from neighbours, alfalfa pellets, used coffee grounds and plantings of nitrogen-fixing legumes in the lasagna beds. I may yet regret my spur-of-the-moment request!

Forests contain up to seven 'stories' or layers, from the rhizosphere to the climax canopy, including a vertical vine 'story', and these layers should be part of an edible forest garden too. With no mature trees for vines to scramble up, I installed an obelisk in the back yard, a lattice trellis, and have also used sunflowers as living ladders. For space reasons, I am choosing not to plant a large tree and will rely on my neighbours for my forest garden's climax canopy, though I am thinking of installing a couple of mid-size hazelnut trees in the front – nuts being an excellent food source.

In fall 2010, I planted two native highbush cranberries and a hardy Techny cedar (*Thuja occidentalis* 'Techny') in my first forest garden in an existing wet area in the back of the yard. Saskatoons, three of my favorite ninebark cultivars, honeyberries, and a chokeberry for the birds were also included. A Nanking cherry joined existing rose bushes in the drier part of the same bed, nestled against an existing line of grapevines covering the property's fence. In keeping with the permaculture rule of multiple functions for each garden element, my goals for these tall-to-medium shrub 'layers' were: to create a windbreak and microclimate; block an unappealing back lane view; generate a substantial yield of berries; and to maximize aesthetics using a diverse mix of native species and site-appropriate shrub cultivars.

In front of the shrubs, at my new edible forest garden's edge, there are insectary and medicinal flowering annuals and perennials, and prairie grasses, interwoven with a mix of my favourite annual and perennial vegetables chosen for beauty as well as culinary appeal. I am researching and developing appropriate companion plantings or 'guilds', which consist of many-species plant groupings that work harmoniously to build soil and ward off predators and disease, a technique well understood by indigenous farmers in pre-Columbus North America.

The result last summer, two years into a long transformation process, was a burst of colour and movement, with bees and butterflies, plus predatory insects and birds controlling insect pests. The new humus-rich mulch-covered topsoil is never tilled, which minimizes weed germination and promotes mycorrhizal fungi and other soil organisms to support strong, disease-resistant plants. This may not be everyone's idea of the perfect garden, but I glory in its exuberant diversity and productivity. The early success of this first forest garden encourages me in the slow process of developing the others.

In Manitoba, the growing permaculture community is supported through The Harvest Moon Society (www.harvestmoonsociety.org) which offers workshops and courses at its permaculture demonstration site in the town of Clearwater, two hours southwest of Winnipeg. Many internet resources are available to aid your journey into this exciting and productive form of gardening. ❧

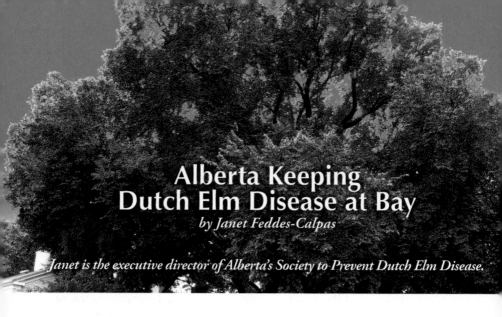

Alberta Keeping
Dutch Elm Disease at Bay
by Janet Feddes-Calpas

Janet is the executive director of Alberta's Society to Prevent Dutch Elm Disease.

The province of Alberta is constantly aware of the threat of Dutch Elm Disease (DED) pressing its borders from two sides, Saskatchewan and Montana. DED has killed millions of elms throughout North America since 1930, when it was first introduced by infected wood from Europe.

Alberta is one of the last geographic areas in North America to be free of DED. The province does not have native elms, however, hundreds of thousands of elm trees have been planted. Through the shelterbelt distribution to farmers, there were a half million elms, American and Siberian, distributed before 1976. The elm has been the preferred tree to plant, not only for its stately beauty, but also for its impressive list of useful attributes. It grows fast on a wide variety of soils and is easily transplanted. Elm trees live longer than other ornamental

species in Alberta and are more disease resistant (with the exception of DED). The elm tree is one of few species that can survive the extreme Alberta climatic conditions.

DED is a deadly disease caused by the fungus *Ophiostoma ulmi* that can affect all species of elm trees. Once the fungus is in the tree it clogs the elm's water conducting system, causing its leaves to wilt and the tree to die, usually within one or two seasons. The fungus is spread from one tree to another by two species of insect vectors, the smaller European elm bark beetle (SEEBB) *Scolytus multistriatus* and the native elm bark beetle (NEBB) *Hylurgopnus rifipes*. The two beetles breed in dead and dying elm trees. Once pupated, adult beetles leave their brood gallery and fly to healthy elms to feed, thus transporting the fungus on their bodies from one tree to the next. Another possible vector of

DED is the banded elm bark beetle (*Scolytus schevyrewi*) (BEBB). This beetle can kill elms through its feeding activity and gallery construction.

In 1975, when DED was first identified in Manitoba, plant pathologists and entomologists in Alberta formed the DED Action Committee. Dr. Ieuan Evans, provincial plant pathologist with Alberta Agriculture at that time, cited the threat of a possible outbreak of this disease as the reason for Alberta Agriculture's amendment to the Alberta Agricultural Pests Act to include the fungal pathogen and the beetle vectors. With this provincial act, provincial municipalities, counties and municipal districts have the responsibility and authority to prevent and control DED.

The Plant Protection Act of Canada regulates the movement of the DED pathogen. This federal act restricts importation of elm trees into the province from DED infested provinces.

By observing the Manitoba situation it was felt that early detection of the vectors would enable the identification, containment and elimination of any infection before DED could get permanently established in Alberta. There was also an emphasis placed on increasing public awareness on both the care of elms and signs of disease. Through the efforts of Alberta Agriculture, a provincial prevention program was started, that included monitoring for the beetles along the Alberta-Saskatchewan and United States ports of entry and enhancing public awareness. The firewood confiscation program at the Alberta/US ports of entry was also implemented at that time.

In 1993 the Society to Prevent Dutch Elm Disease (STOPDED), a nonprofit organization, was formed and worked very closely with Alberta Agriculture. Their mandate is to foster and promote the survival of the American elm (*Ulmus americana*) in Alberta and to protect Alberta's landscape trees threatened by pests, with emphasis on invasive alien species. Members include federal, provincial and municipal representatives, nurserymen, landscapers, commercial and municipal arborists, research scientists and other interested Albertans.

A provincial elm inventory was completed by the STOPDED in 1999. Alberta has some 750,000 mature elms, while mostly concentrated in urban areas, they are also found in rural communities as shelterbelts and on homesteads. The elm inventory also indicated that 10-50% of the trees planted in municipalities are elm trees.

In 2005, the Provincial DED Prevention Program was dropped by the Alberta Government. As a result of lobbying, STOPDED now receives government funding to operate and administrate the program. The primary components of the program are vector monitoring in municipalities, provincial parks, nurseries, and ports of entry, surveying trees for the disease, maintaining the elm inventory, advocating proper tree pruning and proper elm wood disposal, public awareness, and firewood confiscation at the port of entry.

Since 2004, the SEEBB has been found in low numbers throughout Alberta. As a result of these captures and the elm inventory, additional traps to monitor for beetles have been set up in communities having over 500 elms. A total of 117 municipalities, 30 provincial parks and all Alberta/Montana border crossings are monitored for the beetles.

STOPDED works closely with all the US ports of entry with the firewood confiscation component of the program. Bins have been placed at all the entry points and firewood carried by travellers are confiscated and placed in the bins. Such wood is properly disposed of by burning. Brochures explaining the risk of firewood are handed out to travellers.

With a coordinated province-wide effort, Alberta has been successful in keeping Alberta DED free. STOPDED members across the province take an active role in the prevention of DED, setting up traps and identifying and reporting suspect trees to the hotline. All suspicious elms are tested by Dr. Stephen Strelkov at the University of Alberta. To increase public awareness, Dutch Elm Disease Awareness Week is held every year from June 22-28 throughout the province. Enforcement is made possible through both the provincial and federal acts. If elm trees are pruned during the pruning ban period, beetles which are active at this time can be attracted to the scent of fresh wounds and possibly infect otherwise healthy elms with DED. For this reason Alberta has an elm pruning ban from April 1 to September 30th.

Despite the tragic effects of DED, elm enthusiasts in Alberta currently have reason to be optimistic about the tree's future. We now have a thorough understanding of the nature of DED and its mode of transmission, so that its destructive effects can be kept to a minimum. Research continues on more resistant elm trees and disease prevention. It is understood by all that a prevention/management program is essential to keep elm losses to a minimum.

For more information on Alberta's Provincial DED prevention program, or how to become a STOPDED member, call the toll free Provincial DED hotline at 1-877-837-ELMS or check out the web site at www.stopded.org. 🦌

Editors note: See the **2012 Prairie Garden - Trees**, page 10 for news of Asian cultivars such as 'Discovery Elm' proven to be resistant to DED.

From Coneflower To Cactus: Climate Change And The Prairie Garden

by Marilyn Maki

Marilyn Maki is a host and weather specialist with CBC Radio Winnipeg and an avid prairie gardener.

On March 16th, 2012, I stood in my Winnipeg garden and scattered a handful of cosmos seeds. It was a beautiful 20 degree Celsius day, one of several that we had already enjoyed that month. It was two full months before we normally plant on the prairies but I reasoned that if the seeds didn't take, I would try again later in the spring.

We had already experienced several months over the winter where records had been threatened. March set a record as the warmest March in Winnipeg since we began recording temperatures in 1872 - a whopping 8.3 degrees Celsius above normal. And while it may have been an anomaly, climate scientists say this could be the new norm.

University of Winnipeg climatologist, Danny Blair, studies global warming and its impact on our growing season on the southern prairies. His research indicates that Winnipeg's climate has warmed almost two degrees in the last 40 years and at this rate we will warm another three degrees by the end of the century. Of the four seasons, warming is most noticeable in the winter.

By the year 2100, we could have a climate similar to Nebraska or Wyoming, says Blair. Spring will arrive earlier and the first frost will arrive later. Our climate will be dryer. We will see more extreme precipitation and less snow in the winter. Our plant hardiness zone will change too, propelling us from a cool 2b to a balmy zone 5.

Karen Tanino is a plant specialist at the University of Saskatchewan who is researching the effects of a warming climate on plants. She says there are obvious benefits of a longer season. We can grow more varieties of herbaceous perennials, trees and shrubs. We can also grow more annuals and a longer season is great for ripening crops like tomatoes.

While a back yard filled with luscious rhododendrons or a thick yew hedge may seem like Nirvana, Tanino warns that a changing climate can create drawbacks as well. Extended autumns may not allow plants enough time to prepare for winter. Less snow cover means less insulation for plants, and even with milder winters we would still have the risk of those -40° days. Earlier springs mean earlier blooms, still vulnerable to the damage of a subsequent frost or a late season snow.

Pests and diseases often killed or controlled by our cold winters, could survive and even thrive. A perfect example is the mountain pine beetle in western Canada. The spread of the beetle has been linked to climate change and they are expected to wipe out 80 per cent of British Columbia's pine forest by 2013.

There could also be effects on our native prairie plants. In Iceland, research shows that native plants in Alpine areas that rely on snow are dying off because of less snow cover. Shallow rooted trees and shrubs are also affected.

So, what will our prairie gardens look like by the year 2100? Will our well-tilled plots be filled with hybrid hellebore and heirloom roses? Or will the native coneflower move north and make way for the cactus? It's something I think about as I stand in my garden with another handful of cosmos seeds. 🦌

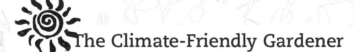

The Climate-Friendly Gardener

A Guide to Combating Global Warming from the Ground Up

For some interesting reading, have a look at *The Climate Friendly Gardener, A Guide to Combating Global Warming from the Ground Up* by the Union of Concerned Scientists, a U.S. based think-tank. It is a resource link provided to students enrolled in the University of Guelph's "Theory and Principles of Sustainable Urban Agriculture and Horticulture". It contains practical tips and information geared toward everyday gardeners.

www.ucsusa.org/food_and_agriculture/what_you_can_do/
the-climate-friendly-gardener.html

Facts About Peat Moss, Composts And Manures

by Ieuan Evans

Dr Evans is a well known plant pathologist with agronomic expertise who lives in Spruce Grove, AB

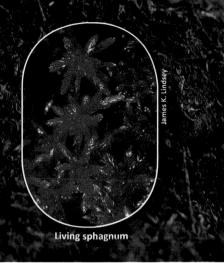

James K. Lindsey

Living sphagnum

Peat moss in North America is a horticultural mainstay for home gardens, greenhouses, horticultural potted plant sales and landscaping. In Canada, peat is found in many forms such as sphagnum, reed, sedge and sapric categories. All of these peats occur in natural but varied stages of organic decomposition from coast to coast. Sphagnum peat moss is by far the most commonly used form. This light to dark brown dead peat moss should not be confused with the sphagnum moss imported primarily from New Zealand. The latter is from a living sphagnum moss that is dried and used to line hanging baskets or as a potting mix for orchids.

Peatlands are found around the world but almost 80% are located in Canada, Russia and the United States. In Europe, twice as much of the harvested peat is used for energy production (some 60 million cubic metres) than for horticultural uses.

European reserves of peat are being depleted significantly and various measures are in place in Europe to conserve peat usage. This is particularly true in the United Kingdom, where peat reserves are critically low.

Canada, with approximately 270 million acres or more than 25% of the world's supply of peat moss, harvests only 40,000 acres annually.

Standard sphagnum peat moss has roughly the same nutrient value of nitrogen, phosphate and potasium as most cow, sheep or horse manure. The darker or black peat mosses have nitrogen levels comparable to poultry manure, though the nitrogen in the peat is less available over a single season than that of animal manure. These nutrient rich peats are the black peat soils of Ontario, Manitoba and Alberta.

Sphagnum peat generally has a pH of around 3 to 4, whereas some of the more decomposed nutrient rich black peats have a pH range of

5 to 7.5. Sphagnum peat moss is a natural, organic soil conditioner that helps acidify some of our more alkaline prairie soils. It is Nature's natural compost.

Peat moss will hold up to 20 times its weight in water, especially important in sandy soils. It is also beneficial to heavy clay soils, as it aerates these, reduces leaching, absorbs soil nutrients and protects soil from hardening.

Peat allows for excellent water and air exchange capacity and is a renewable (albeit very slowly) resource that is sold in very convenient compressed packaging.

Composts vary much more than peat mosses in weight, moisture content and nutrient capability. Many composts, manures and peats have high to very high carbon (C) to nitrogen (N) ratios. The approximate C:N ratio of carbon in vegetable trimmings is 25:1; grass clippings 19:1; straw 80:1; farm (cattle, sheep) manure 80:1; sawdust 142:1; and sphagnum peat moss 50 - 60:1.

The ideal C:N ratio is around 10:1, the same ratio as that of soil humus (organic matter). The higher the C:N ratio of material added to your garden soil, i.e. sawdust or pine needles (100:1), the more that nitrogen and other nutrients are tied up by the soil bacteria and fungi that feed on this organic source. If, for example, you add 50 lb.. (22 kg) of peat moss or cow or sheep manure to your garden soil, you should also add up to 10 lb.s (4.5 kg) of ammonium sulphate, 16-20-0-13 (N - nitrogen, P - phosphate, K - potash and S - sulphur) to compensate for the nutrient tie-up. If you are using pine needles or sawdust you could double the amount of added fertilizer. The soil amendments least likely to tie-up soil nutrients are alfalfa pellets (18:1), grass clippings (19:1) and well rotted garden compost (20:1).

Composts, while typically low to very low in nutrients much like peat moss, can greatly help in moisture holding in sandy soils, increase air exchange and porosity in clays, and help retain soil moisture and nutrients. Composts made from food scraps, grass clippings, oak leaves and vegetable trimmings have more available nutrients than those made from pine needles, sawdust and various leaves. Compost is an

Commercial baled peat

excellent soil conditioner, especially in low fertility soils. Regardless, it rarely supplies all of the nutrients needed to grow good crops of potatoes, carrots, beets and corn. Supplement with an application of organic or synthetic fertilizer.

Poultry manure — compared to cattle, sheep or horse manure — is very much higher in plant nutrients. In cattle and sheep manures, much of the available nutrients are lost in the animal's urine. This doesn't happen with poultry since all of the excreted nutrients are in the manure. The C:N ratio of poultry manure is much less than 20:1, often ranging from 3–5:1, therefore macronutrients such as nitrogen, phosphate, potassium as well as micronutrients, are readily released into the garden soil. Even so, to provide the equivalent of 100 lb.. (50 kg) of nitrogen per acre (hectare) to garden soil,

something around 400 - 800 lb.. (200–400 kg) of dried manure needs to be applied to the typical one sixth acre garden. Poultry manure ranges from 1.5 to 3.5% nitrogen, phosphate and potash, i.e. 400 lb. (200 kg) of manure at 3.5% nitrogen will give a rate of around 17 lb. (8 kg) of nitrogen to the one sixth acre garden for optimum non-legume vegetable crop production.

In summary, peats, manures and composts are excellent soil amendments, but it must be remembered that they are all generally low to very low in the essential macronutrients (N, P, K and S) that are necessary to grow bountiful garden crops of vegetables. On the other hand, in certain situations, peat, manure, and compost may be the only amendments needed to grow and maintain a vibrant and productive landscape. 🌱

Perennial Plant Personalities

Vita Sackville-West (1892-1962) Today, Sackville-West may be best known for her white garden at Sissinghurst which primarily uses a monochromatic colour scheme and remains the most widely visited garden in England. Her influence can be seen today in the interest in creating garden rooms. An author and poet, she gardened for escape from disappointments in her life. A famous phrase, "If a plant does not please, 'hoick it' " lives on, in one form or another.

Gertrude Jekyll (1843-1932), a prolific British author, horticulturist and garden designer, inspired a generation of gardeners through her creation of a new style of English garden. Jekyl favoured less formal garden design and had a passion for woodland gardens and cottage style herbaceous borders. Jekyll's influence on the use of colour, mixed planting, and gardens organized for seasonal interest has continued through the generations.

Daniel J. Hinkley - A modern-day plantsman, horticulturist, author, plant collector and lecturer in the mould of some of history's greatest plant explorers. Hinkley, whose favorite pastime is to dig in the soil, has travelled the world in search of rare and unusual plants, returning from his journeys to add them to his famous nursery, Heronswood Nursery, located near Kingston, Washington. Today his nursery holds more than 10,000 species.

Red Lily Leaf Beetle

by John Rempel

John is a lifetime member of the Charleswood Garden Club and has been active in the Manitoba Regional Lily Society (MRLS) for the past 15 years. He has been growing and hybridizing lilies for many years, and for the past 6 years has tracked the spread of the lily beetle in Manitoba.

Lily growers in Manitoba have faced a new adversary in the last few years. This is the red lily beetle (*Lilioceris lilii*). This beetle is native to parts of Europe and Asia, but had been confined to Ontario and Quebec. In 2001, the beetle was first reported in Manitoba in the Portage la Prairie area and then made its way to Winnipeg in 2006. No one can say exactly how the beetle made its way west to Manitoba, but the most likely explanation is that the beetles came in from eastern Canada via a commercial shipment of plants that were widely distributed in western Canada.

The adult beetle is actually quite beautiful in its outward appearance. It is only 6–9 mm (¼–⅜ in.) in length. It has shiny bright red wing covers with black antenna, head, legs and underside. The larvae are a light brown and look similar to potato bug larvae. The larvae cover themselves with their own excrement and look like black blobs on the lily leaves. This is to discourage predators.

The beetle feeds on the *Liliaceae*, *Nolinoideae*, *Solanaceae* and *Smilaceae* families, but breeds only on true lilies (*Lilium* species). It does not attack daylilies (*Hemerocallis*). Adults may be found nibbling on companion plantings, but major damage occurs mostly on lilies. The most damage occurs in spring from the egg-emerging larvae, and later in the season by the newly-emerging adult beetles. The larvae and adult beetles feed on the leaves and will strip the stems in short order if not controlled.

The lily beetle has no natural predators in North America. Research is being done at The University of Rhode Island using parasitic wasps (a natural predator) imported from Europe. The wasps lay their eggs in the beetle larvae and the wasp larvae then kill the host beetle larvae. This project has shown some good results. Permission has been received to conduct trials in Canada and is occurring through Carleton University.

Life Cycle of the Lily Beetle

It is important to understand the life cycle of the beetle to effectively control it. The adult beetles overwinter in the top several inches of soil or under plant debris in the surrounding area. They may be some distance away from your lilies. Care should be taken when sharing or trading lily plants in an area with a known infestation to ensure that the pest is not accidentally spread in this fashion.

The adult beetles emerge in early spring, several weeks after snow melt, in anticipation of newly emerging lilies. On average the beetles emerge from the ground about April 15th. In 2012, beetle sightings were already reported in late March because of the record warm temperatures in Manitoba. The adults mate during this time and the female subsequently prepares to lay eggs in irregular rows on the bottom leaves of the emerging plants. The eggs are reddish orange or light brown in colour. Each female can lay up to 450 eggs in each season.

The best control tactic at this time of year is to handpick the adults before they get a chance to lay their eggs. Caution is needed as the adults will drop from the plant if they are disturbed. You can place a white paper collar or cloth around the base of the plant to catch any that escape your grasp.

The eggs hatch in about 7–10 days and the emerging larvae will feed on the lily leaves for 16–24 days. They can strip a plant of leaves in a matter of days if no action is taken—which seriously weakens the bulbs for the next year's growth. As they go through several instars (moults), they continue to cover themselves with their own feces to discourage predators (including squeamish humans). Adult beetles are strong fliers, so it is possible for reinfestation to occur due to an infestation in a neighbouring garden. It is therefore prudent for neighbouring gardeners to participate in a joint control program.

After the larvae finish feeding, they will drop to the soil and encase themselves in a small cocoon and pupate for 16–22 days. Disturbing the soil around the plants may help control the emerging adults who, as part of their feeding cycle, will climb the surrounding lilies and feed until fall. It would seem that in Manitoba that these adults do not mate or

John Rempel

Larva of beetle

lay eggs until the following spring. Some beetles may survive two seasons. Anecdotal evidence also seems to imply the new adults swarm and fly to new locations in August or September before they bury themselves to overwinter. Gardeners who have had no beetles all summer may wake up to find a late-season infestation of beetles in their lily patch.

Control

As it is considered to be a minor pest, no specific products have been approved by government agencies for the control of the lily beetle. Many anecdotal reports exist of various methods that growers have devised, from home remedies to commercially available pesticides, that are not designed to specifically target the lily beetle. As always use your own discretion when trying some of these controls. In a field trial, I used a 0.5% pyrethrum based contact spray with adults and larvae with good results. Direct spray only the lily beetle adults and larvae so as to protect beneficial predators such as lady bugs and green lacewings. A one litre spray bottle is sufficient for controlling small infestations. The best and safest method is to handpick and destroy the emerging adults in spring, just as many of us do with the Colorado potato beetle (*Leptinotarsa decemlineata*). Besides being vigilant, educate your neighbours regarding this pest. With the work done by The Manitoba Regional Lily Society (MRLS) in educating gardeners and retail bulb sellers, many gardeners know how to identify and control these beetles. The media have been very helpful the last few years informing the gardening public of the situation.

Serious gardeners need not have a paranoid fear of this new pest. Weekend gardeners beware. Check your plants regularly for these pests. 🐚

Damage inflicted by beetle

Ed Czarnecki

The Canadian Prairie Lily Society based in Saskatoon, SK reports the lily beetle hasn't showed up in their region. The lily beetle has been reported in several places around Alberta including Calgary and Edmonton. For more information see the Alberta Regional Lily Society's website <arls-lilies.org>. Gardeners are asked to report lily beetle sightings to Adam Yakabuskie with the Alberta Regional Lily Society at lilybeetle@arls-lilies.org or Dr. Ken Fry, entomology instructor at Olds College at kfry@oldscollege.ca.

Book Review
Perfect Perennials
for the Prairie Gardener
By Dawn Vaessen, Published by Fifth House, 2011

Reviewed by Jeannette Adams

Perfect Perennials for the Prairie Gardener written by Calgary based author, Dawn Vaessen, provides a well organized, colourful resource guide for both the novice and experienced gardener.

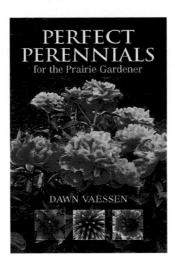

The main focus of the book is the author's featured list of hardy perennials for the prairie garden. These are listed alphabetically by their common name along with the botanical name. A descriptive paragraph about each plant offers reasons why it is a good choice for a prairie garden, as well as its specific characteristics. The "Quick Notes" on each plant offer more detailed facts as to size, colour, site location, and top choice varieties, as well as interesting bits of information regarding the name, origin and history of the plant. A full page coloured photograph accompanies each plant.

The first five chapters are where the novice gardener will find the most valuable information. Ms. Vaessen, a master gardener, discusses the realities of the prairie climate, soil conditions, and provides lists of suggested plants for specific growing conditions, including a short list of perennials that are hail-resistant. Helpful hints for choosing gardening tools are included in the chapter on preparing your flower bed and caring for your perennials. One chapter deals with possible threats such as weeds and diseases, and also points out the differences between harmful and beneficial insects.

I recommend this book to any prairie gardener beginning a perennial garden as well as the experienced gardener looking for an easy to follow reference guide. 🦗

You can bury a lot of troubles digging in the dirt.

Author Unknown

Why an Interest in Insects?

by Dr. Robert E. Wrigley

*Dr. Robert Wrigley has served as Curator of Birds and Mammals and
the Museum Director at the Manitoba Museum as well as Curator of the
Assiniboine Park Zoo in Winnipeg. He has published 18 books and numerous
popular and technical papers on a variety of natural-history subjects.*

I don't know how many times I have been asked about my interest in insects. I must admit, insects never held any particular fascination for me in the past, in spite of being an animal ecologist. I was so focussed on another group — mammals — I hardly noticed all but the most eye-catching species such as butterflies. Then a friend showed me some amazing tropical beetles with strange shapes, big horns, elongated mandibles, and spectacular colours. I was so intrigued that I had to learn additional information about them. The more species I acquired through my field trips and exchanges, the more fascinated I became, to the point that I now spend all my spare time researching and curating these remarkable creatures. I am not alone, for a number of famous people such as Charles Darwin also enjoyed collecting beetles. Each specimen is a little gem representative of an exotic environment from some distant place in the world, which I will never have an opportunity to visit.

In Southeast Asia, raising beetles and other insects as a hobby, or devouring them as delicacies, is a passion. While the thought of eating insects in our culture is generally repugnant, we do savour their close relatives — shrimp, crab and lobster (we eat what we are taught to!). Insects were an important and reliable source of food for our ancestors, and no doubt have saved countless lives from starvation when other foods were unavailable. Insects have also played prominent roles in human mythology — appearing on cave-wall paintings in Europe as long as 32,000 years ago, while the sacred scarab dung beetle (*Scarabaeus sacer*) was held in great esteem in Egyptian religions over 4,000 years ago, associated with the Sun God Khepri.

As a founding member of the board of the Friends of the Assiniboine Park Conservatory in Winnipeg, MB, I once proposed an exhibit of pinned butterflies and bees for one of the plant halls, but was surprised to hear a few other members say that displaying "dead bugs" had no place in a conservatory of plants. I then realized that many people have little idea of the intricate roles insects play in horticulture.

Surprisingly, insects and flowering plants have been co-evolving intimately for over 100 million years, ever since the extraordinary radiation of these angiosperms during the Cretaceous Period — plenty of time for complex interactions to develop, such as specialized herbivory, pollination, camouflage, and chemical 'warfare.' There are numerous examples of insects (e.g., praying mantids) and spiders evolving body shapes and colours that make them almost invisible while resting on branches, leaves and flowers; certain insect larvae even resemble bird droppings on a leaf! Plants produce

a variety of complex chemicals that deter browsing by insects, while others give off scents that attract predators of the insects that are attacking their leaves. Insects generally manufacture their own defensive chemicals, while others, the monarch butterfly for example, incorporate toxic plant substances into their own bodies, which help prevent predation by birds. Plant galls of various shapes are frequently seen in the garden and in nature — the plant's response to the feeding activities of tiny wasps, beetles, moths and flies. The amazing interactions of plants and insects will keep scientists occupied for centuries.

I recall being astounded when I learned that insects are so important in ecosystem functioning that the natural world would collapse and

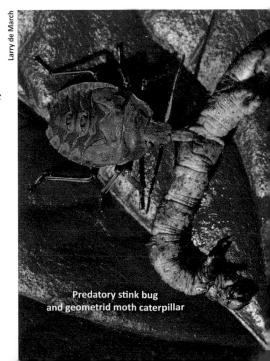

Larry de March

Predatory stink bug and geometrid moth caterpillar

turn toxic in short order if insects suddenly vanished. We rely on a number of free services provided by insects. Without insects, all plants dependent on insect pollination would become extinct in short order, the consequences of which would be that our economies and civilization would descend rapidly into chaos. Bees pollinate the majority of our food crops, so imagine the phenomenal loss of human life from starvation, social unrest, and outbreak of wars if many types of food were unattainable due to crop failures. Insects also assist in the decomposition of human and other animal wastes and dead plant material, thereby recycling nutrients for new life.

One fact that may strike fear into the hearts of gardeners is that half of all insect species chew, suck, gall or mine plant tissues. In fact, every species of plant has one or more insects that feed on it. Insects make up three-quarters of all named living species (excluding bacteria

and viruses), and hence dominate in all ecosystems except marine ones. Over 55,000 species of insects have been documented in Canada, and continuing investigations will increase this to at least 100,000. Each prairie province is host to around 20,000 species. No one has any idea how many species of insects are alive today, and estimates range wildly from 2-50 millions, with 15 millions perhaps being a reasonable number (Most are not even discovered and named yet.). What is truly amazing, this estimate is less than 10% of the extinct species that either died out or evolved into new forms in the past. While we now live in the so-called "Age of Mammals," it would be far more accurate to say that we live in the long-running "Age of Insects."

There are more than 60,000 species of leaf-devouring leaf beetles (family Chrysomelidae) alone (only 38,000 of which are described to date). This family has many local representatives, including the dreaded red lily beetle (*Lilioceris lilii*), which recently invaded Manitoba gardens. I picked four-dozen specimens off my wife's lilies last summer and prepared them for the Wallis-Roughley Museum of Entomology (University of Manitoba). Long-horned beetles (Cerambycidae) number over 35,000 named species, and weevils win top billing for being the largest family of any animals or plants, with 50,000 named species,

Snowberry clearwing moth

Larry de March

and hundreds of new ones are discovered each year. In other words, insects are extraordinarily successful and abundant almost everywhere, so it should not be surprising to see them show up in your garden.

Meadowhawk dragonfly

Insects evolved from marine arthropods (jointed-legged animals such as crustaceans) as early as the Silurian Period, 420 million years ago. The first definitive insect fossils date from 400 million years ago, during the Devonian Period, and even these early forms were thought to have developed sets of wings — the first animals capable of flight.

Insects range in size from 0.3 mm (1/100 in) feather-winged beetles (Family Ptiliidae) to giant Goliath scarab beetles (*Goliathus*, Scarabaeidae) the size of one's fist. Stick insects (e.g., *Pharnacia kirbyi*, Phasmatodea) can reach a length of 55.5 cm (22 in), and an extinct griffenfly (*Meganeuropsis permiana*), related to dragonflies, which lived in the early Permian (280 million years ago) of Kansas, had a body length of 43 cm (17 in) and a wingspan of 71 cm (28 in) — the largest insect ever recorded.

Insects owe their phenomenal success to a number of features such as small size (which increases niche and habitat opportunities), ability to evolve quickly, and wings to escape from predators or when local living conditions become unsuitable, to new locales. Larval and adult stages of certain insects exploit different habitats (e.g., aquatic versus terrestrial),

thereby avoiding competition for food resources within the same species. The group shows an astonishing ability to exploit nutrients from any organic source — leaves, stems, roots, live and dead wood, sap, spores, pollen, nectar, fruit, seeds, fungus, plant and animal organic matter, and living as parasites both on and inside plant and animal bodies. Another fascinating feature of insects and other arthropods is that the skeleton is on the exterior rather than the interior of the body, as in humans and other vertebrate animals.

Many of the 32 orders of insects are present in the prairie provinces, with over 80% of species consisting of beetles (Coleoptera), flies (Diptera), wasps and ants (Hymenoptera), and butterflies, skippers and moths (Lepidoptera). When I was the Zoological Editor of "The Encyclopedia of Manitoba," I asked colleagues for estimates of types of insects in the province (with similar estimates applying to Saskatchewan and Alberta), and here are a few: Flies 6000, Wasps 5000, Beetles 2500, Bugs 1400, Moths 600, Aphids 400, Bees 250, Butterflies and Skippers 144, Dragonflies and Damselflies 100, Ants 81, Mosquitoes 50. Many of these species are residents or visitors to our gardens, although we may not be aware of their presence.

Humans have mixed reactions to insects, when we think of them at all. Insects may scare, annoy, bite and infect us with dangerous pathogens, even live in our homes (carpet beetles and bed bugs). True, they may attack our garden plants, but then we would not even know colourful and scented flowers were it not for insects, because plants evolved flowers, nectar and pollen for the sole purpose of attracting pollinating insects. Predatory and parasitic insects help control the numbers of other kinds of insects, including many we call plant pests.

Gardeners often plant milkweeds (*Asclepias*) and other species to attract butterflies, and are pleased to see ladybugs and dragonflies, since these two types are known for eating prodigious numbers of insect pests such as aphids and mosquitoes. However, the discovery of plant-devouring and sucking insects, or stinging species such as wasps in the garden may be alarming, causing some individuals to rush to the garden store for toxic chemical sprays and powders. Having an insect-free garden is an unattainable goal, so one may as well take a realistic and broader view of insect pests. Insects have been living on your special plot of land for millions of years, in a succession of habitats, and it is really humans that are the intrusive exotic species in the insects' traditional homes. Some accommodation and disappointments regarding insect depredations should not ruin the ultimate experience of raising beautiful plants in the garden.

To give an example of the herbivourous powers of insects, 3-17% of total leaf area in deciduous forests is lost annually due to leaf-eating insects. The major loss of coniferous trees due to spruce budworm moth species (*Choristoneura*) and bark beetles (*Ips*), especially during years of major outbreaks, is well known across North America. The rather sudden death of billions of trees greatly alters ecosystems and results in the release of massive amounts of carbon to the atmosphere.

Invasion by exotic species is an ongoing problem, as plants and insects are transported (accidentally or purposefully) around the world. The cabbage white butterfly (*Pieris rapae*) is an example of a foreign species that appears in everyone's garden, often damaging vegetables and decorative plants in the mustard

Monarch butterfly

Larry de March

family (e.g., cabbage and broccoli). In an effort to use biological control of crop-eating pests, both native and exotic, lady beetles (family Coccinellidae) have been introduced and released in great numbers. The native convergent lady beetle (*Hippodamia convergens*) is commonly found in gardens, as is the introduced multicoloured Asian lady beetle (*Harmonia axyridis*). Unexpectedly, the latter has caused the loss of populations of native lady beetle species.

Biologically speaking, it is questionable to release any foreign organism into a new region, for the consequences are often unforeseen and damaging to natural ecosystems. The majority of garden plants are not native to Canada, but at least most of them stay put in people's yards. However, there are exceptions such as purple loosestrife (*Lythrum salicaria*), which has caused major problems to wetland ecology. Two species of exotic leaf beetles (*Galerucella*) have been imported in an attempt to control the loosestrife. As garden plants are shipped to new areas, soil organisms and insect pests hitch along for the ride. Most gardeners are unaware that each spade full of soil contains insect eggs, larvae, pupae and adults, plus microscopic animals such as mites, springtails, protozoans; roundworms, earthworms, mites, centipedes and millipedes, numbering in the hundreds of thousands of individuals. Various kinds of bacteria are also present in uncountable numbers. Soil is a precious living ecosystem, with each creature playing its role in the food web as herbivore, predator, shredder, decomposer, or parasite. Their activities help maintain the structure of soil required for healthy plant growth.

Ironically, insects were partly responsible for my giving up on my succulent-plant collection. I had accumulated several hundred plants (mainly native to Africa) in my home greenhouse, but became discouraged at having to resort occasionally to insecticides to control insect pests (those infamous mealybugs, spider mites, scale insects and whiteflies). I eventually donated my collection of plants and library to the Assiniboine Park Conservatory and took up entomology — I realize this sounds a lot like, 'If you can't beat them, join them!' I now have over 20,000 specimens of 9,000 species of beetles in my personal collection, and I donate about 2,000 specimens annually to the Wallis-Roughley Museum of Entomology and the Manitoba Museum. These specimens display every colour of the rainbow and are every bit as beautiful as, for example, hummingbirds and coral-reef fish. Insects in the garden can provide great pleasure to those with an open and enquiring mind. I hope this article encourages gardeners to take a closer look at their insect visitors, for they are real marvels of nature. 🐝

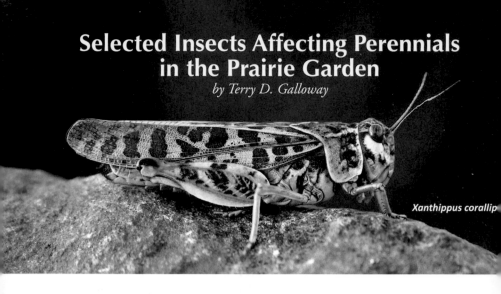

Selected Insects Affecting Perennials in the Prairie Garden
by Terry D. Galloway

Xanthippus corallip

Terry has been an entomologist since the age of six. He is with the University of Manitoba's Department of Entomology. Terry has worked on biting flies, fleas, lice, bugs, ticks and mites.

Prairie gardeners are turning more and more to our native plant species to enrich their efforts, especially to native perennials. It makes good sense when you consider how beautiful and hardy they are, perfectly suited to the local environment, and often requiring little supplemental water and special care. However, adopting this strategy for the garden opens the door to a wonderful spectrum of insects that also are well adapted to their environment, and some of which are specialists which feed on many of the native perennials we choose to enhance our space. I have chosen to write about a few of these particularly interesting specialists, as well as our traditional enemy of prairie gardens and crops—the grasshoppers.

Grasshoppers

Paul Riegert (1980) provided fascinating accounts of the difficulties early European settlers encountered in their efforts to cultivate the prairies. One such account is that of Walter Traill in 1867, who was then in charge of Fort Qu'Appelle:

"One afternoon I set out in the hope of getting an antelope. It was a bright summer day and as I rode past a field of some twelve acres of barley near the Fort I noticed that the crop was looking splendid and almost ready to harvest. Suddenly I was aware of a heavy black cloud on the western horizon which looked like an approaching storm, but the sky around me remained clear and thinking it was a prairie fire in the distance I rode on until dusk. On the way home I again passed the barley field and it was not too dark to see that it was now a blackened ruin.

'Did you have a fire?' I asked the watchman who opened the gates for me. 'The barley for our saddle horses is all burned.'

'We had no fire,' he said, 'did you not see the grasshoppers?'

Then I looked around and saw them three inches deep inside the Fort. They had devoured everything in the garden except roots, stripped the trees, and fallen into the lake until the outlet was blocked, and they were piled up on the shores in wind-rows…They came in clouds like smoke and for twelve days the air was alive with them as high as one could see. They darkened the sun and lay an inch deep on the ground… Farming here is all a delusion."

We haven't seen grasshoppers in such numbers on the prairies for a long time, but that doesn't mean they can't be present in numbers great enough to cause havoc in the garden. Grasshoppers are a diverse lot, with more than 80 species of true grass-hoppers (Acrididae) recorded in the prairie provinces (Vickery and Kevan 1983), including the now extinct Rocky Mountain grasshopper, *Melanoplus spretis*. Most species overwinter in the egg stage, laid in pods in the soil. There are notable exceptions such as *Chortophaga* and *Arphia*. Although their eggs are laid in the soil, they overwinter as late nymphs and moult to adults in the very early spring. They are the grasshoppers we see in May, with yellow or red wings crackling as they fly. Most of our grasshoppers complete their life cycle in one year, though the robust giant, *Xanthippus coarllipes*, with its yellow-ish wings and red hind tibiae, takes two years. Out of all these species of grasshoppers, there are only a few that ever confront prairie gardeners as a serious threat.

The two-striped grasshopper, *Melanoplus bivittatus*, is a generalist feeder with a slight preference for broad-leafed plants. The migratory grasshopper, *Melanoplus sanguinipes*, and the clear-winged grasshopper, *Camnula pellucida*, also feed on a wide range of host plants, but they have a preference for grasses. These species all do best and reach their greatest numbers following hot, dry summers, conditions where longevity and survival are favoured. Urban gardeners are unlikely to see many of the immature stages of these species hatching from the eggs and feeding as nymphs on their perennials, since there may not be suitable substrate available to adult females. Most people see these insects invade their gardens from elsewhere once the winged adults develop. These insects are notable for their ability to fly considerable distances and for their destructive feeding habits. They have powerful, chewing mouthparts and a voracious appetite. Grasshoppers may consume the leaves, buds, fruits and flowers in the garden, and they may even clip the heads from many of our favourite plants. Despite the damage we suffer today, we should be thankful we don't have the prairie plagues faced by the early settlers.

Aphids

Every gardener sooner or later discovers aphids on their plants, and in Manitoba we are blessed with a diversity of them. When Grant Robinson and Bob Lamb compiled a list of the species recorded in the province in 1991, they recorded 324 species on 175 species of host plants. Most of these infest native species of plants, and most of them are small and inconspicuous, sometimes difficult to detect until their colony balloons in size or as we see their honeydew dripping from the leaves. However, there is an interesting group of aphids that feeds mostly on native Asteraceae, and they are anything but inconspicuous.

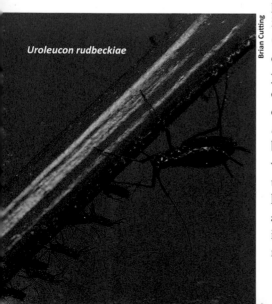

Uroleucon rudbeckiae

Brian Cutting

Aphids in the genus *Uroleucon* are very large for an aphid, long-legged, and the species I'll describe here are a brilliant red. Specifically, I want to describe *Uroleucon rudbeckiae*, a species which is found on tall coneflower, *Rudbeckia laciniata*, a popular native perennial. As is characteristic of aphids, populations of *U. rudbeckiae* are found throughout most of the growing season and the populations are made up of only females. In fact, only females hatch in May from the eggs which were laid the previous fall in leaf litter around the host plants. These females make their way onto the newly developing coneflower plants and once they reach the adult stage, extraordinarily begin to give birth to live young (vivipary) without ever having mated (parthenogenesis). Throughout the season as their host plants mature and begin to flower, these bright red aphids maintain parthenogenetic vivipary, producing wingless (apterae) and winged (alatae) offspring. The apterae stay close to home and produce many young, while the alates are free to fly off to colonize distance patches of coneflowers. Colonies of *U. rudbeckiae* can reach substantial numbers, depending on the degree to which their natural enemies attack them. There are fly larvae, lacewings, lady beetles, and parasitic wasps that all take their toll on these seemingly defenseless aphids. The aphids maintain an upper hand only by their impressive reproductive output and their remarkable mobility. As the days shorten in late summer, the female *U. rudbeckiae* respond by producing males, for the first time in the season, and a specialized type of female, the ovipara. These oviparae mate with the males and lay eggs, which ultimately pass the winter in the leaf litter.

Coneflower isn't the only species of native perennial infested by these strikingly beautiful red aphids. There are many species of Uroleucon that infest false sunflower (Heliopsis), prairie sunflowers (Helianthus) and goldenrods (Solidago), all popular species with prairie gardeners. Next time you find your plants infested with these fascinating insects, rather than reach for the spray can, enjoy observing them and note what they are doing.

Goldenrod gall fly

Speaking of goldenrod, one of our most cold hardy species of insects is associated with this genus of plants, especially Canada goldenrod, *Solidago canadensis*. This insect is a beautiful brown and white striped fly, the goldenrod gall fly, *Eurosta solidaginis*. Its biology was thoroughly investigated some time ago by Uhler (1951) and it since has become the focus of many investigations on everything from cold hardiness to insect/plant coevolutionary relationships. Adult flies typically

Terry Galloway

Goldenrod galls made by the goldenrod gall fly (*Eurosta solidaginis*)

emerge in late May to June in the prairies, as the current year's plants begin to reach upwards. The males assemble on the tips of the leaves and display with twisting wings and dances to attract a mate. The mated female explores the stem of the plant looking for just the right leaf bud. When a suitable site is found, the female inserts an egg into the tissue. The legless larva hatches in just a few days, and in response to its presence, the plant develops a spherical gall, sometimes growing to more than two cm (¾ in.) in diameter. It is inside the gall that the maggot develops, feeding in the very centre. By the time the goldenrod senesces in the fall, the maggot has completed its development and enters a state of diapause in the centre of the gall, but not before it has excavated a tunnel to just beneath the surface of the gall. In this state, the larva is able to withstand the lowest temperatures the Canadian prairies can throw at it. I have cut open these galls in

Patrick Coin

Goldenrod gall fly

mid-winter, and at -20°C (-4°F), the maggots are still soft and can even move, albeit very slowly. What an incredible adaptation to our climate! I have also observed that these maggots are a tasty, fat-laden morsel for woodpeckers and small rodents. As spring temperatures rise, the maggot begins to develop and pupates inside the gall. When the adult fly emerges, it travels out through the tunnel previously created by the maggot, and it pushes its way through the thin membrane to escape the gall. Almost every patch of goldenrod around the country has stems with these typical ball galls. An interesting exercise is to collect galls in spring, after diapause has been broken, and allow the flies to emerge in a small container in your home where you can observe them more closely. Of course, you may not always get a gall fly. There are many parasitoids that attack these flies, and even para-

sitoids that attack other parasitoids; there are also inquilines (organisms that live in the 'homes' of other species) that feed on gall tissue, such as the tumbling flower beetle, *Mordellistena*. These galls represent an amazing community of insects, and are a wonderful opportunity to observe some of the complexities of the natural world.

Milkweed

Butterfly gardens have become a popular goal and many prairie gardeners habitually plant milkweed species with the primary aim of attracting monarch butterflies, as Jeff Marcus described in the 2012 Prairie Garden. However, milkweeds are also host to a variety of interesting specialist herbivores beyond the monarch. For example, you might find your milkweed infested with colonies of tiny aphids (*Myzocallis*). Or, if you're lucky, you might even discover milkweed longhorn beetles, *Tetraopes* spp. The adults may be up to 17 mm (⅝ in.) in length, they are bright red with black spots, and as their common name implies, they have long black antennae with white rings, a truly handsome group of species. Milkweed beetles have one generation a year, and adults begin to appear on their host plants in midsummer. They feed on the leaves and flowers, sometimes aggregating in considerable numbers on certain preferred plants and living quite happily alongside other species of

Milkweed longhorn beetles

Joe Willis

milkweed specialists. At a casual glance, these beetles seem docile and slow-moving. However, if you take the time to watch them carefully, you will see that all is not so settled in the life of a red milkweed beetle. The males are quite aggressive towards one another and will compete actively for the largest females. In fact, don't be surprised if they produce a high-pitched squeaking sound when you pick them up between your fingers, the result of a file and scraper mechanism on the thorax (Lawson 1977). Both males and females mate with wild abandon, many times throughout their lives, and indeed, many times throughout the day. As a result, each batch of eggs laid by a female is likely to have mixed paternity (McCauley and Reilly 1984). However, it's this critical point in the life cycle that determines whether you will have beetles only dispersing into your garden or whether they may become established. Females lay their eggs in the stems of the previous year's milkweed plants, or even in nearby grass stems with a sufficient diameter. The female chews a small hole in the hollow stems and deposits several eggs inside. The larvae hatch from the eggs, fall to the ground and burrow into the soil to feed on milkweed roots. They mature by summer's end and then spend the winter in the soil, where they pupate the following year. As you can see, your expectations in planting milkweed can be much greater than simply attracting monarch butterflies.

Indeed, by planting a variety of native perennials, you open up the opportunity to invite many species of native insects into your garden. It's a great chance to develop an interesting landscape as well as to increase the biodiversity of your garden. This always stimulates learning more about the insects you find and understanding better how species interact. 🐝

References:

Lawson, F.A. Stridulatory structures in two milkweed borers (Coleoptera: Cerambycidae: *Tetraopes* spp.). Journal of the Kansas Entomological Society 50: 172-178.

Marcus, J. 2012. The prairie butterfly garden. The 2012 Prairie Garden. pp. 150-155.

McCauley, D.E. and L.M. Reilly. 1984. Sperm storage and sperm precedence in the milkweed beetle *Tetraopes tetrophthalmus* (Forster) (Coleoptera: Cerambycidae). Annals of the Entomological Society of America 77: 526-530.

Robinson, A.G. and R.J. Lamb. 1991. Aphids of Manitoba. Research Branch, Agriculture Canada, Technical Bulletin 1991-7E.

Reigert, P.W. 1980. From Arsenic to DDT: A History of Entomology in Western Canada. University of Toronto Press. xii + 357 pp.

Uhler, L.D. 1951. Biology and ecology of the goldenrod gall fly, *Eurosta solidaginis* (Fitch). Memoirs of the Cornell University Agricultural Experiment Station 300: 3-51.

Vickery, V.R. and D.K.McE. Kevan. 1983. A monograph of the orthopteroid insects of Canada and adjacent regions. Vol. II. Lyman Entomological Museum and Research Laboratory, Memoir No. 13.

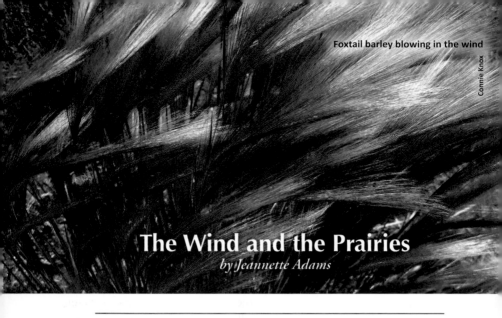

Foxtail barley blowing in the wind

Connie Knox

The Wind and the Prairies
by Jeannette Adams

Jeannette is a Master Gardener and involved with the Millennium Gardens project and the West Kildonan Horticultural Society in Winnipeg, MB.

Prairie writers often characterize the wind in their novels or short stories. The wind on the prairies is a constant companion that displays many moods and has a great influence on the lives of prairie inhabitants. We are reminded of the dramatic powers of the wind when intense storms flatten buildings and uproot trees, but what about the subtle damage caused by wind throughout the seasons? Icy blasts of north wind can kill tender emerging perennials and damage flowering shrubs in late spring. Hot southerly winds in summer can scorch leaves and dehydrate plants, and sudden storms can leave the blooms of peonies, delphiniums and hydrangeas twisted and broken. In winter, wind desiccates conifers leaving them with browning branches. How can prairie gardeners deal with this moody companion?

First, assess your location and decide if long or short term protection is needed. People often choose to plant a shelter belt. Poplar and willow trees are fast growing; however, they are usually short-lived, become messy and even dangerous after a few years and are definitely not meant for smaller properties. Smaller trees or hedging shrubs are a better choice. Fences and buildings such as sheds provide shelter if situated to cut the prevailing winds. You can also create screening by planting vines such as Virginia creeper or native grapes on a trellis or chain link fence.

When choosing what to plant, take into consideration the plant's hardiness. Plants are classified according to hardiness zones and one determining criterion for assessing hardiness is wind velocity. When choosing perennials, look for ones described as having sturdy stems such as 'Becky' shasta daisies and the new Millennium series of delphiniums. Clumping perennials with flowering spikes such as Siberian iris, salvias or veronicas can withstand rain and wind better than ones with heavy clustered blooms. Planting in layers with tall plants inter-planted with medium and short plants allows plants to support one another.

How you nurture your garden also influences how much damage wind can cause. Be sure to locate plants in the environment best suited to their needs. Shade loving plants will dry out quickly, becoming scorched by too much sun or hot drying winds. Keep them in the shade and well watered. To prevent winter burn of evergreens, be sure to give them a good soaking in late fall. Newly planted conifers may need some form of "tented" protection. Go easy on the fertilizer, especially high nitrogen. This encourages rapid, tender growth that is more susceptible to wind damage. Mulches are useful in a number of ways. In summer, organic mulch around your trees, shrubs, perennials and vegetables helps to maintain more even soil temperature as well as conserving moisture. Winter mulch can be applied to provide protection against cold and wind. Be sure to water your plants well in late fall and wait until frost has set in, then apply a dry, loose mulch such as flax straw or oak leaves. Hopefully, the snow

will cover this mulch and keep it in place over the winter. Leaving some tall grasses or late blooming perennials helps capture snow and provides added protection. In spring do not be too anxious to remove the covers as perennials that survived the winter can be killed by a chilling wind.

A lot of heavy bloomers benefit from some type of support system. Peonies should be surrounded with a sturdy peony ring. Put the ring in place when the peony starts to emerge, this trains the tender young stalks rather than trying to bundle leaves and budded stems through the ring. Iris and lilies can be supported with individual stakes, but be careful when pushing these into the ground so as not to pierce the rhizome or bulb. Tall clumping perennials such as echinacea, rudbeckia, summer phlox and daisies can be provided with support by using cut down tomato cages or appropriately sized stakes and

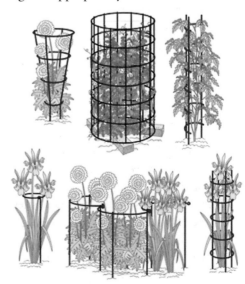

garden twine. The tall, heavy spikes of delphiniums require sturdy stakes and flexible ties such as strips of panty hose. Again, it is best to position these support rings or stakes in the ground early in the season. When choosing a trellis to support climbing plants such as clematis, be sure to acquire one that is strong enough to support the mature weight and height. It is heartbreaking to find a beautifully blooming clematis face down on the ground because the trellis couldn't support it during a windy night.

In spite of the damaging effects, wind also has its benefits. In spring we appreciate its warm gusts to dry up excess moisture and remove winter debris. Some plants require

wind to aid with pollination while other plants, such as monarda, require good air circulation to prevent mildew from developing. In fall the wind hastens leaf drop, making for a quicker fall clean-up.

On the prairies, wind is a constant companion whether in the form of a refreshing summer breeze or part of a fierce winter blizzard. It influences how we live so we need to understand its many moods. In David Bouchard's illustrated book *If You're Not From the Prairie*, he writes, "If you're not from the prairie, You don't know the wind."

If you're a gardener anywhere, you need to know about wind. 🐝

Hostas, My Favourite Perennial *by Sandy Venton*

Valerie Denesiuk

Hostas are truly one of my favourite perennials. There are about 200 in my garden and I plan to order more. It doesn't matter if they are giants or micro-minis – they all have a place in my garden. Hostas come in a huge range of sizes and colours - green, blue, gold, or variations. Leaf shapes include rounded, cupped, oval, and lance. Most varieties prefer shade to semi-shade, but there are a few which can withstand full sun. They are almost foolproof and unless you actually stand on them, or totally neglect them during a drought, they will simply soldier on until conditions improve.

Several years ago, in order to make room for a new garage, I had to lift numerous hostas from one of my shade beds. The hostas were dug, stuffed into pots, dragged down to the bottom of the garden, and left there. In fall they were dragged back, holes were dug, and the hostas were stuffed in yet again. There was no careful digging, putting soil around the roots, or anything even remotely resembling "gardening". They stayed there over the winter. They were then dug up in the spring, shoved back into pots, dragged back to the bottom of the garden, ignored, and then finally replanted into the new bed later that summer.

I have to say that all of those poor mistreated hostas made it through that harrowing time, and the shade garden looks as though it had never been moved. I couldn't possibly list my favourite hostas, but if you are at all interested in hostas, go to www.hostalibrary.org for pictures and descriptions. You'll be amazed!

In Memoriam:
Pete Peters

*by Colleen Zacharias
and Linda Pearn*

*Information excerpted from
Winnipeg Free Press Passages and
Manitoba Agricultural Hall of Fame website*

The Prairie Garden Committee said goodbye this year to a past committee member, Peter Jacob Peters, who passed away in Winnipeg on June 6, 2012 at the age of 98 years following a brief illness.

Born in Krasnovka, Russian Ukraine, Pete's family emigrated to Canada in 1925, settling first near the town of Morris, Manitoba and then moving to Gretna, MB. Pete had careers as teacher, wireless mechanic in R.C.A.F., and interpreter with War Crimes Commission.

Following this Pete enrolled in the Faculty of Agriculture. In 1954, he was awarded the University of Manitoba Gold Medal in Agriculture.

In 1955, Pete joined the Extension Service of Manitoba Department of Agriculture as the potato specialist. His early work in potato marketing and variety evaluation, improved tubers, storage and grading paved the way for the commercial potato industry in Manitoba. He was a driving force in the establishment of Gardner Sales Co-operative, the Manitoba Potato Commission, the Manitoba Potato Marketing Board and ultimately Peak of the Market.

He soon became affectionately known as 'Potato Pete'. A letter from England, addressed only to 'Potato Pete, Canada' actually found its way to him!

During this career, Pete was also involved in the strawberry industry which resulted in the formation of the Strawberry Growers Association of Manitoba which is the present day Prairie Fruit Growers Association.

By 1979, the year he retired from the Manitoba Department of Agriculture, Pete had been awarded honorary life memberships in the Manitoba Horticultural Association, Vegetable Growers' Association of Manitoba, Western Canadian Society of Horticulture, Manitoba Institute of Agrologists, and the Strawberry

Growers Association. He received the Outstanding Individual Award from the Canadian Society for Horticultural Science, as well as merit awards from the Canadian Horticulture Council, Manitoba Agriculture and the City of Winnipeg. In 2009, Pete was inducted into the Manitoba Agricultural Hall of Fame.

In addition to publishing three volumes of poetry, Pete wrote and published "A Century of Horticulture in Manitoba - 1880 to 1980", including historical information compiled by the late J. Petrum "Pete" de Wet.

Pete served as Secretary-treasurer of the Manitoba Horticultural Association and President of the Western Canadian Society for Horticulture.

From 1969 to1980, Pete was Chairman of The Prairie Garden Committee. Susanne Olver, who has served on The Prairie Garden Committee for more than 35 years, recalls his dedication and commitment to producing a quality horticultural publication. "He ran a tight ship and was a highly intelligent man". Susanne adds, "One of my fondest memories is a trip that he arranged to northern communities on behalf of Manitoba's horticultural societies. I was proud to accompany Pete and his wife Bertha to Thompson, Leaf Rapids, Swan River, The Pas, and Flin Flon for a series of presentations. It was a wonderful trip that included a visit to Phyllis Pierrepont at Bowsman who hosted a barbeque for us." 🐝

Match the Flower Pictures
from page viii

H   1 Gentian

I   2 Primula

E   3 Canada violet

F   4 Pasqueflower

B   5 Masterwort

G   6 Sundrops

D   7 Swamp milkweed

C   8 Bloodroot

A   9 Astilbe

The 2012 Prairie Garden
Award for Excellence

was awarded to
Renata Klassen
(Saskatoon, SK) at a luncheon at
the TraveLodge in Winnipeg on
Wednesday, September 5th, 2012.

*by Colleen Zacharias and
Ed Czarnecki*

Renata Klassen

Sandy Venton

The Prairie Garden Award for Excellence is awarded annually to an individual or group making a significant contribution to the advancement and/or promotion of horticulture on the Northern Great Plains. This is the thirteenth year that The Prairie Garden committee has presented this award.

Renata, a dynamic and energetic woman, is a retired school teacher who has lived in Saskatoon all of her life and whose first experiences with gardening began at the age of five when her parents gave her a small garden plot to tend on their family farm located in the Eastview area of Saskatoon.

In 2008, when she and her husband, Allen, sold their farm, Renata became interested in the idea of creating a community garden in Eastview. With the help and support of her husband, Allen, a retired University professor, Renata began by assessing the needs of the community and how they could best be met. This included meeting with representatives from Childhood Hunger and Education Programs (CHEP). Dana Krushel, former community gardening coordinator with CHEP, recalls that, "Renata was the ideal person to work with on a community project as she has a lot of energy and vision. She was a great bridge with resources that CHEP had to offer."

Renata enlisted the support of the Eastview Community Association to assist in organizing and managing the garden. Together they began negotiations with the City of Saskatoon and have enjoyed a productive working relationship with Karen Farmer, Community Consultant, Community Development Branch. Renata successfully negotiated with the City for available land and resources and then she, together with her team of determined volunteers, set to work on preparing the soil for a community garden as well as ensuring an adequate water supply. Sherry Buller, a member of the Eastview Community Association's Board of Directors, applauds Renata's efforts in negotiating an arrangement for water with a neighbouring apartment complex.

By Spring of 2009, Eastview's first community garden on city owned property opened on Louise Street, located on the East side of the South Saskatchewan River.

Inspired by the great success of this initial garden, Renata worked closely with the Saskatoon Public School Board, spearheading the landmark opening of a garden on school-owned property behind John Dolan School, a school for children with disabilities and special needs. Today Renata continues as the registrar in charge of assigning plots and together with the volunteer gardening committee, engages the school children in growing food and flowers.

Renata's leadership skills combined with her caring, generous spirit, persistence and creativity has earned the respect and admiration of many, inspiring them to lend their assistance.

Two community gardens soon became three and currently three local schools - Alvin Buckwold, John Dolan and Pope John Paul II - have plots which are available for use by neighbourhood residents, including the many residents of senior complexes and apartments in the area. Immi-

grant families from Africa, Asia and South America enjoy the opportunity to grow fresh vegetables and together with their neighbours, participate in building their community.

The gardens have contributed to a unique educational experience for many members of the community. Novice gardeners wishing to become involved must first learn gardening basics and Renata has shared her expertise through workshops, writing articles and working alongside families in the gardens. Renata and Allen have also created raised beds to enable gardeners with physical disabilities to participate, creatively salvaging old garbage bins discarded by the City and filling them with soil.

Community gardens have the power to transform a neighbourhood and on behalf of the residents of Eastview, the Eastview Community Association proudly awarded Renata with "A Citizen of the Year" Award in recognition of her contribution to building community through establishing the gardens. Karen Farmer adds, "The community gardens that Renata has helped create and sustain have been tremendously positive places for dozens of families, adults and children, and for her community as a whole".

Congratulations, Renata, on winning The Prairie Garden Award for Excellence for 2012. 🦫

More information about the award and previous winners can be seen at:
www.theprairiegarden.ca/award.html

The Prairie Garden
Award for Excellence

has been presented annually since 2000 by The Prairie Garden in order to recognize horticultural achievements.

Eligibility

The Prairie Garden Award for Excellence shall be awarded to an individual or group making a significant contribution to the advancement and/or promotion of horticulture on the Northern Great Plains. Areas of involvement may include community activity, plant introduction or breeding, preservation of horticultural sites, teaching, research, extension and photography.

The Award

The award shall be cash in the amount of one thousand dollars ($1000.00) and a suitably inscribed gift.

Nomination Process

Letters of nomination should include in-depth details with appropriate documentation of the candidate's achievements in horticulture. This will be the only source of information used to compare to other nominations.
All nominations must be received by May 31, 2013.

Nominations should be submitted to:
The Prairie Garden Awards Board
P.O. Box 517
Winnipeg, Manitoba   R3C 2J3

Announcement & Presentation

The recipient will be announced by September 1, 2013 with a presentation ceremony to follow as soon as practical thereafter. The winner will be featured in The 2014 Prairie Garden.

The Prairie Garden *is an annual horticultural publication published by a group of volunteers for the furtherance of prairie horticulture.*

The Prairie Garden Conversions

Centigrade to Fahrenheit Temperature Conversion

Degrees Celsius	Degrees Fahrenheit
35°C	95°F
30°C	86°F
25°C	77°F
20°C	68°F
15°C	59°F
10°C	50°F
5°C	41°F
0°C	32°F
-5°C	23°F
-10°C	14°F
-15°C	5°F
-20°C	-4°F
-25°C	-13°F
-30°C	-22°F
-40°C	-40°F

Approximate Metric to Imperial Measurements

Centimetres	Inches
1 cm	.4 in
3 cm	1.2 in
5 cm	2 in
10 cm	4 in
15 cm	6 in
20 cm	8 in
25 cm	10 in
30 cm	12 in
40 cm	16 in
50 cm	19 in
60 cm	24 in
70 cm	27 in
80 cm	31 in
90 cm	36 in
100 cm	39 in

Exact Conversions

Metric to Imperial
1 millimetre [mm] = 0.03937 in
1 centimetre [cm] = 10 mm = 0.3937 in
1 metre [m] = 100 cm = 1.0936 yd
1 kilometre [km] =1000 m = 0.6214 mile

Imperial to Metric
1 inch [in] = 2.54 cm
1 foot [ft] = 12 in = 0.3048 m
1 yard [yd] = 3 ft = 0.9144 m
1 mile = 1760 yd = 1.6093 km

Themes for The Prairie Garden Back Issues

We have back issues in varying quantities. Please use the form on the next page to order any of the following to complete your reference library.

2012 – Trees
2011 – Healthy Gardening
2010 – Annuals & Biennials
2009 – Deciduous Shrubs *
2008 – Roses
2007 – The Edible Landscape
2006 – Myth, Magic & Meditation
2005 – Lilies
2004 – Pleasing Prairie Places *
2003 – Themes & Extremes
2002 – Landscape Design
2001 – Container Gardening   *Limited Stock*
2000 – Herbs
1999 – Perennials *
1998 – Trees for The Prairies
1997 – Propagation
1996 – New Themes in Prairie Landscape
1995 – Accessible Gardening
1994 – ~~Xeriscaping Garden in Dry Conditions~~ * *Sold Out*
1993 – ~~Garden Herbs~~ *Sold Out*
1992 – Garden Oddities
1991 – Sustainable Landscaping
1990 – Bulbs and Perennials   *Limited Stock*
1989 – ~~50 Years of Prairie Garden~~ * *Sold Out*
1988 – Gardening Indoors
1987 – ~~Perennials on The Prairies~~ *Sold Out*
1986 – New Ideas
1985 – Large Area Gardening *
1984 – ~~Small Gardens~~ *Sold Out*
1983 – Better Living Through Gardening
1982 – New Concepts, Gardening in Winter
1981 – ~~Native Heritage~~ *Sold Out*
1980 – Mostly Trees and Shrubs *
1979 – Mostly Annuals   *Limited Stock*

* Contains a content index for the previous five years.

The Prairie Garden
PO Box 517, Winnipeg, Manitoba R3C 2J3
Phone: (204) 489-3466; Fax: (204) 489-1644
Email: sales@theprairiegarden.ca   Website: theprairiegarden.ca

---

❑ The 2013 Prairie Garden $13.95
Special quantity prices to horticulture societies and garden clubs:
10 – 49 copies $8.75; 50 – 149 copies $8.25
150 or more copies $7.75
Volume discounts to commercial outlets on request.

❑ Please add my name to the STANDING ORDER LIST in order that I
may receive a copy of *The Prairie Garden* every year starting with the
2014 issue. I will send my remittance upon receipt of each issue.
Standing Orders are charged at a discount rate.
(Do not check this box if your name is already on the Standing Order List)

BACK ISSUES (while quantities last) 2012:Trees – $6.00
Previous issues (listed on the previous page) prior to 2012
will be sold at $4.50 each while stock remains

POSTAGE AND HANDLING CHARGES APPLY ON ALL ORDERS
1 book – $3.50; 2-4 books – $12.75; 5-10 books – $22.95
11 books or more – Canada Post Weight Charges to apply
Postage will be charged at cost on all orders received from outside Canada.
All prices in Canadian dollars.
These prices supercede all previous price lists and are subject to change without notice.

✂ — ✂

Name			
Address			
City	Prov/State	P.C./Zip	
Qty	Year / Issue	Price Ea	Price

	Subtotal
Please enclose cheque payable to:	Postage & Handling
"The Prairie Garden"	TOTAL